MW00623437

CINCINNATI
IN THE
CIVIL WAR

6/13/21

Dear Jim,

    Thank you for your deep interest in the Civil War. Thank you for all that you do to preserve our history!. You do so much good!!

All the best,

David J. Mooney

CINCINNATI
IN THE
CIVIL WAR

The Union's Queen City

DAVID L. MOWERY

THE
History
PRESS

Published by The History Press
Charleston, SC
www.historypress.com

Copyright © 2021 by David L. Mowery
All rights reserved

Front cover (clockwise from top left): Lieutenant General Ulysses S. Grant. *Courtesy of the Library of Congress*; Sergeant Powhatan Beaty. *Courtesy of the Library of Congress*; Major General Joseph Hooker. *Courtesy of the Library of Congress*; First Ohio Cavalry departs for war on steamboats anchored at Cincinnati's public landing. *From* Pictorial War Record *(1861), p. 330.*

Back cover (from top): Price's Hill Battery, overlooking Cincinnati and the Ohio River. *From* Frank Leslie's Illustrated Magazine, *November 16, 1861*; Twenty-First Wisconsin Infantry crossing the Ohio River pontoon bridge from Cincinnati, September 13, 1862. *Courtesy of the Library of Congress.*

First published 2021

Manufactured in the United States

ISBN 9781467139960

Library of Congress Control Number: 2020951678

Notice: The information in this book is true and complete to the best of our knowledge. It is offered without guarantee on the part of the author or The History Press. The author and The History Press disclaim all liability in connection with the use of this book.

All rights reserved. No part of this book may be reproduced or transmitted in any form whatsoever without prior written permission from the publisher except in the case of brief quotations embodied in critical articles and reviews.

For my family, friends and fellow Cincinnatians

CONTENTS

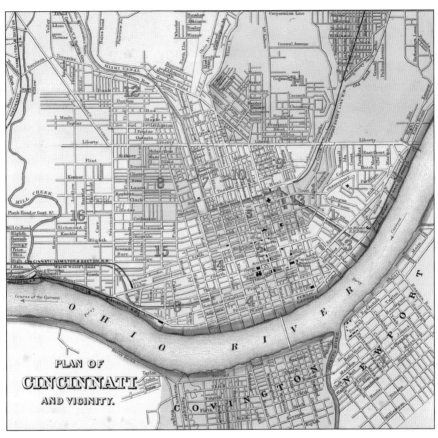

Map of Cincinnati, Covington and Newport in 1860. *From* Mitchell's New General Atlas *(1860).*

PREFACE

When one tries to measure the impact that Cincinnatians made on the American Civil War, the task seems daunting. At that time in America's history, Cincinnati, the "Queen City of the West," was the largest metropolis in the Northern states west of the Appalachian Mountains. Not only was the city massive enough to contribute large numbers of soldiers to the Union armies, but its manufacturing capacity was the most productive in the West as well. In addition, Cincinnati boasted significant political clout in the U.S. government, which kept President Abraham Lincoln always concerned about Ohio's welfare and that of its southern neighbor Kentucky. Throughout the war, for his most important decisions, Lincoln took into consideration their consequences for the border states of Kentucky, Missouri, West Virginia, Maryland and Delaware, which acted as geographical buffers between the Union and the Confederacy. If Kentucky seceded, the center of conflict would most assuredly move northward onto Ohio's soil, and Cincinnati would become an embattled city. The Union could not afford for that to happen. Its war machine desperately counted on the continual flow of manpower and supplies that Cincinnati provided to suppress the rebellion.

When one defines the geographical term "Greater Cincinnati," residents generally understand it to mean the areas positioned inside the Interstate 275 loop expressway and within a few miles outside of it. Being a native of Cincinnati, I stay true to this definition. My history of Cincinnati in the Civil War, therefore, includes some of the history of Covington and Newport in

Kentucky. Even during the war, these two Bluegrass cities were inextricably linked to Cincinnati, as if they were suburbs of the great metropolis. It is difficult for a historian to separate Covington and Newport from Cincinnati when it comes to telling the Queen City's whole story.

My study attempts to summarize the key events, people and places of Cincinnati during the five years of the Civil War. My work also highlights some new facts that have been uncovered through more recent research. Over the last 150 years, hundreds of publications have been written on many of the subjects covered in this book. Their detail is to a level that I could not possibly match in just a single book. One work that I consider the most complete history of Cincinnati during the Civil War period is Robert Wimberg's five-volume set titled *Cincinnati and the Civil War*. Wimberg extracted details from the Cincinnati newspapers and from other sources, such as diaries, reminiscences, the Official Records of the War of the Rebellion and secondary studies, and he arranged those facts into a day-by-day history of the city. It's an incredible resource for anyone undertaking research on Cincinnati or on the history of the Civil War in the western theater. My book focuses more on introducing the reader to Cincinnati's role in the Civil War and on providing a reference for certain special topics.

One special topic that makes my book unique is the long list of Civil War and Underground Railroad sites found in the modern Greater Cincinnati area. I have incorporated Global Positioning System (GPS) decimal coordinates with the sites because many are now gone. Nonetheless, the Greater Cincinnati region offers many museums, buildings and parks that revisit the time of America's greatest internal struggle. Other special topics in which I dive deep include a list of the commissioned U.S. Navy gunboats that the Cincinnati boatyards contributed during the war and a section on the city's Spring Grove Cemetery, which hosts the United States' fourth-largest number of interments of Union generals of brevet brigadier general or higher rank.

Perhaps the most important focus topic that my study produced is a table of all the Union regiments and artillery batteries known to contain residents of Cincinnati or of Hamilton County (the county in which Cincinnati is located). No other publication has done this as completely. I was inspired by the efforts of Henry and Kate Ford, whose *History of Hamilton County, Ohio* (1881) created the first compilation of Civil War units having soldiers who were Hamilton County or Cincinnati residents at the time they enlisted. Unfortunately, the Fords worked with limited primary source material, and so, as they admitted, their list is quite incomplete. Also, it concentrated only on the men who joined Ohio units. However, I followed the Fords' same search criteria, but I expanded my research to embrace all the states and territories of the United States as of 1865. My research assistants and I scoured all the available Federal state rosters and enlistment tables, both published and unpublished, to build a list of Union units with soldiers who joined as residents of Cincinnati or Hamilton County. More than any other portion of this book, the resulting table clearly shows Cincinnati's importance to the Union war effort. Cincinnatians fought in every major battle of the Civil War except for those that occurred west of Texas.

Some acknowledgements are definitely in order. First, I would like to thank Cincinnati historians Dave Glib and Ann Senefeld for their assistance in narrowing down the locations of the Civil War fortifications in the Mount Adams neighborhood of Cincinnati. I learned much from Dave and Ann, and they motivated me to write more about the forgotten Civil War batteries located on the Buckeye side of the Ohio River; my book holds the result. Second, I would like to thank Hal Jespersen for his outstanding maps, for which he goes beyond the call of duty. Next, I cannot begin to express my deepest appreciation for my two research assistants, who happen to be my mother and brother, JoAnn Mowery and Daniel Mowery. They worked tirelessly with me over a six-month period to inspect, line by line, hundreds of available roster books and enlistment register documents from all the states. We often went to the level of recording the soldier's or officer's name to verify residency. I could not have constructed the Union units table without their efforts. Also, Daniel found the Hamilton County Civil War veterans' discharge records, and he discovered the definitive primary source that verified the position of the Butcher's Hill battery site in Mount Adams. His skills as a researcher are unmatched. Lastly, I'd like to thank my loving wife, Dawn, for her support through the countless hours of my absence in researching and writing this book. She is the rock I stand on; she reminds me often of the wives of Civil War soldiers who waited patiently for their men to come home from the front.

THE STORM OF WAR

Cincinnati attributes its sobriquet, "The Queen City," to the poet Henry Wadsworth Longfellow. His poem "Catawba Wine" pays tribute to millionaire Cincinnatian Nicholas Longworth's alcoholic wonder that originated in the vineyards of Mount Adams in the 1820s:

And this song of the Vine
This greeting of mine,
The winds and the birds shall deliver
To the Queen of the West
In her garlands dressed
On the banks of the Beautiful River.[1]

The "Beautiful River" and Cincinnati were forever joined on December 28, 1788. On that day, a group of eleven families and twenty-four men led by Colonel Robert Patterson landed their flatboats on the north bank of the Ohio River opposite the mouth of the Licking River. These pioneers soon cleared the area of vegetation and built cabins for themselves. They named their new settlement Losantiville, a Native American term. The name did not last long. General Arthur St. Clair, the first governor of the Northwest Territory, came to the fledgling community on January 2, 1790, to inspect the newly constructed Fort Washington. He disliked the name Losantiville, and so, with the stroke of a pen, he renamed the town Cincinnati after the Society of the Cincinnati, a veterans' group of Revolutionary War officers, to

An 1866 panoramic photograph of western Cincinnati taken by J.W. Winder from the south tower of the Roebling Suspension Bridge. The view spans from Price Hill (*far left*) to the foot of Vine Street (*far right*). The tall spire on the right is St. Peter in Chains Catholic Cathedral, and the tallest steeple in the center belongs to Holy Trinity Church. The steamboat *Gen'l Lytle* (*center right*) transported Union troops during the war. *Courtesy of the Library of Congress.*

which St. Clair belonged. Fort Washington quickly became a critical military installation on the Ohio River. The U.S. Army used it as a base of operations for campaigns against the Native Americans in the territory. Naturally, with Cincinnati positioned in a war zone, the military's presence allowed the town to grow into a river city. Over the next fifty years, Cincinnati thrived as thousands of settlers and tradesmen used the Ohio River as a transportation highway to distant places such as New Orleans and Pittsburgh.[2]

The Northwest Ordinance of 1787 formed the Northwest Territory. The ordinance not only opened for settlement the vast lands encapsulated by the Mississippi River, Ohio River, Great Lakes and Pennsylvania but also prohibited slavery within its boundaries. The Constitution of the young United States failed to resolve the question of slavery. Slavery, a key to the success of agrarian economics in the country, had existed in the original thirteen British colonies since the early seventeenth century. Despite this fact, the U.S. government's first major act abolished the expansion of slavery

into one of its territories. Thus, Cincinnati was born with the ideal that all men were free—but only on paper.[3]

Reality told a different story. White Cincinnatians, many of whom were transplants from Virginia and Maryland, had grown up in a society where Black people were subservient. These persons of mostly English and Scottish descent harbored the mindset that Black people should never be allowed the same rights and opportunities as White. When the newly formed State of Ohio passed the Black Laws in 1804 and 1807, severely restricting the equal-opportunity rights of African Americans, Ohioans made it clear they did not want Black residents to stay. Cincinnati's African Americans, who represented Ohio's largest Black population, reacted predictably. Between 1829 and the late 1840s, four major race riots occurred in Cincinnati, so many that the national media nicknamed it the "Queen City of Mobs." The violence greatly curbed the growth of the African American population in Cincinnati. The Black population dropped from 9.4 percent in 1829 to 2.3 percent in 1860.[4]

In addition, the neighboring state of Kentucky, separated by only four hundred yards of water from Cincinnati, permitted the institution of slavery within its borders. For Cincinnatians trying to make a living, Kentuckians were major customers, and tolerating their ideals was

The eastern half of J. W. Winder's 1866 panoramic photograph of Cincinnati. This view spans from the incomplete Roebling Suspension Bridge *(far left)* to the Fulton boatyards *(far right, in distance)*. The large steeple to the right of the bridge is the First Presbyterian Church, and the tallest hill in right center is Mount Adams, crowned by the Church of the Immaculata. *Courtesy of the Library of Congress.*

important for successful trade. Also, African Americans were thought of as prime competitors for the low-income jobs in the city. Most White citizens feared that the Queen City had become a "dumping ground" for former slaves, who would naturally seek the city's unskilled labor positions that poor Whites demanded. Therefore, even though African Americans lived in Cincinnati as free men, they truly were not equals. John Malvin, a freedman who had moved in 1827 to Cincinnati from the slave state of Virginia, experienced firsthand the prevailing prejudice of those living in the Queen City of the West at that time. "I thought upon coming to a free State like Ohio, that I would find every door thrown open to receive me," Malvin wrote. "But from the treatment I received by the people generally, I found it little better than in Virginia."[5]

Cincinnati's economic boom during the steamboat era of the 1830s–50s brought a change in attitude toward the less populous ethnic groups. As the city became more refined, distinguished New Englanders moved into the

region, and thousands of immigrants from Europe traveled to the Queen City to find their fortunes in a new land of opportunity. Particularly large in numbers were the German, Irish and Jewish immigrants who settled in the Cincinnati area. White American nativists, called the Know-Nothings, violently opposed the minority immigration of the 1850s, and Cincinnati witnessed its fair share of rioting. Immigrants of many races and creeds felt unwelcomed by earlier generations of Cincinnatians. These oppressed people identified with the plight of the enslaved African Americans. Yet these same White minorities continued to regard free Black residents as economic rivals who should be suppressed. Historian Nikki M. Taylor, in her book *Frontiers of Freedom*, described antebellum Cincinnati as having "three intersecting identities: northern in its geography, southern in its economics and politics, and western in its commercial aspirations."[6]

The influx of immigrants to Cincinnati was greatest among German and Jewish Americans. A widespread economic depression struck Europe in 1845, and many blamed their misfortunes on the Jewish people. The rise of anti-Semitism in the Prussian states sent thousands of German Jews to the United States. Hundreds of them traveled over the mountains and on the rivers to settle in Cincinnati, where they hoped for a better life of equality.

The number of Jewish Americans in America tripled during the period of 1850–60. Meanwhile, the Revolution of 1848 in the German states forced the evacuation of many thousands of Germans who came to live in America. Cincinnati offered numerous business opportunities to allow a new start for hardworking, family-oriented, skilled workers. The German American population of Cincinnati flourished. By 1860, citizens of German descent accounted for 27 percent of Cincinnati's population, the largest of any minority group. Many of them settled in the predominately German "Over-the-Rhine" district of the city to separate themselves from the Cincinnati Protestants who disliked their culture and religion.[7]

The Irish immigrants who arrived in Cincinnati in the late 1840s represented 12 percent of the city's population in 1860, making them the second-largest minority. The Irish Americans resided primarily in the city's Third Ward. They generally accepted the dangerous or unskilled jobs, for which the African Americans also competed. Irish Americans and African Americans often clashed because of economic reasons, while Protestant Cincinnatians showed prejudice toward Irish Americans over their religious practices. However, the Irish Americans of the city were deeply Unionist, like their leader, John Baptist Purcell, the Irish Catholic bishop of Cincinnati from 1833 to 1883. The Irish Americans would fight to preserve their adopted country.[8]

In the 1830s, a brave few Cincinnatians began a movement to abolish slavery from all the states. Known as abolitionists, they would make the city a hotbed of antislavery activity in America. One of them was James G. Birney, who published his national abolitionist newspaper, *The Philanthropist*, in Cincinnati beginning in 1836. Mobs twice destroyed his newspaper's printing press, and Birney moved to another city to find safety. By the end of the decade, a branch of William Lloyd Garrison's Anti-Slavery Society had formed in Cincinnati, and the movement took root. One of those Cincinnatians filled with antislavery sentiment was a youthful upstart attorney from New England named Salmon Portland Chase. He employed his energies to defend the liberty of runaway slaves and those persons who had assisted them. Chase used the law to show the discrepancies and weaknesses in the arguments defending the institution of slavery, and by doing so, he earned national recognition as the "Attorney General of Runaway Negroes." Chase helped form the antislavery political parties of America, including the Liberty, Free Soil and Republican Parties.[9]

Cincinnati's participation in the Underground Railroad expanded greatly during the 1830s and 1840s. The Underground Railroad was a community of dedicated persons, both Black and White, who worked together to secret

Salmon Portland Chase served as President Abraham Lincoln's secretary of the treasury. In 1864, Chase was appointed chief justice of the U.S. Supreme Court. *Courtesy of the Library of Congress.*

enslaved persons to Canada. Local conductors like Levi and Catherine Coffin, John Van Zandt, Samuel and Sally Wilson and Zebulon Strong risked their reputations, freedoms and lives to hide and move runaway slaves to safety. Many thousands escaped slavery and reached the security of Canada through the tireless work of these individuals.[10]

Educational institutions in Cincinnati also pursued the ideal of abolitionism. The most famous of them was the Lane Theological Seminary, located in the Walnut Hills suburb of the city. Dr. Lyman Beecher brought his family, including daughter Harriet, to Cincinnati in 1832, when he assumed the first presidency of the seminary. Two years later, Theodore D. Weld and the student body hosted the Lane Seminary Debates. The eighteen-night event changed the thinking of intellectuals across the country. These individuals no longer advocated for colonization of African Americans; instead, they sought complete dissolution of slavery everywhere. Harriet immersed herself in the excitement of the antislavery movement during this period of her life, and after she married antislavery professor Calvin Stowe, she became an ardent abolitionist. Harriet Beecher Stowe drew on the experiences of her life in Cincinnati when she wrote her famous novel *Uncle Tom's Cabin*, which she published in 1852 to worldwide acclaim.[11]

The rise of the Republican Party in the late 1850s enjoyed favor among a large percentage of Cincinnati voters, especially the minorities. Cincinnati's German Americans, Irish Americans and Jewish Americans agreed on two issues: loyalty to the Union and the condemnation of slavery. The editorials from the city's two German-language newspapers, the *Cincinnati Volksblatt* and the *Cincinnati Volksfreund*, consistently promoted the retention of the Union and opposed the extension of slavery into the territories. The editors considered slavery an evil with which the South would need to contend. However, these same newspapers resisted the abolitionist movement. Abolitionism was cause for disunion, and preservation of the Union supplanted the need to remove slavery from the existing states. Because the Democratic Party leaned toward keeping slavery alive in new states, Cincinnatians looked to the Republican Party to remove slavery from U.S. soil while keeping the country together.[12]

Lawyer and former U.S. congressman from Illinois Abraham Lincoln appeared in Cincinnati on the night of September 17, 1859. Lincoln stood on a second-floor balcony overlooking the Fifth Street Marketplace and delivered a two-and-a-half-hour speech to a large throng of onlookers who had made the trip from Cincinnati, Newport and Covington. Much to the crowd's satisfaction, particularly the Kentuckians, Lincoln assured the people that he intended to neither remove slavery from where it existed nor repeal the Fugitive Slave Act; rather, he wished to prevent slavery's expansion. Lincoln's platform struck home for Greater Cincinnatians and all Northerners. The speech was published throughout the United States, opening doors for future lectures, such as Lincoln's appearance

Right: Harriet Beecher Stowe lived in Cincinnati from 1832 to 1850. During this period, she gathered most of the background material for her world-famous novel, *Uncle Tom's Cabin* (1852). *Courtesy of the Library of Congress.*

Below: On September 17, 1859, Abraham Lincoln spoke to a large crowd at Cincinnati's Fifth Street Marketplace. Lincoln's speech here was one of the most important of his career. *Courtesy of Ohio History Connection, #AV83_B01F12_011.*

at Cooper Union in New York City. Today, many historians consider Lincoln's Cincinnati speech to be one of the most important given during his presidential campaign.[13]

On May 18, 1860, the Republican Party nominated Abraham Lincoln to run for president of the United States. In November, Lincoln won the national vote, much to the dismay of the Democratic Party, which had preached compromise on the slavery issue. Despite Cincinnati's Democratic leanings, the city showed its support for the Republican platform:

Votes for ABRAHAM LINCOLN (Republican)	12,226 (46%)
Votes for STEPHEN A. DOUGLAS (Northern Democrat)	11,135 (42%)
Votes for JOHN BELL (Constitutional Unionist)	3,090 (11%)
Votes for JOHN C. BRECKINRIDGE (Southern Democrat)	242 (1%)

Total votes cast in Cincinnati: 26,693[14]

The Southern states interpreted Lincoln's election as a final affirmation that the Federal government intended to end slavery without their consent. They responded accordingly. In December, South Carolina seceded from the Union, and over the next five months, ten more states would secede and form a new country called the Confederate States of America. Attempts at a last-minute compromise failed. On April 12, 1861, Confederate artillerists opened fire on the Federal installation of Fort Sumter at Charleston, South Carolina, forcing the Union garrison under Colonel Robert Anderson to surrender. The storm of war had come.

2

"Unshrinking Was the First Voice"

The firing on Fort Sumter sent shock waves through Cincinnati and the nation. The city's six major newspapers—the *Daily Gazette*, the *Daily Commercial*, the *Daily Enquirer*, the *Daily Times*, the *Volksblatt* and the *Volksfreund*—all headlined that the war had started. "Der Krieg ist eroeffnet!" ("The War Opens!") appeared as the April 13, 1861 headline of the *Cincinnati Volksfreund*. It continued, "Any men who have the desire not only to join a military company but to march off to the command of the Governor are sought. They should assemble at Friedrich Schmidt's on Sycamore Street. Only sound men from 26 to 35 will be accepted.... The commands will be given in German and English." The *Cincinnati Daily Times* shared the sentiment of their competitors with its headline "The War Begun!" The *Daily Commercial* added to the strain, "The War News! War Is Declared. The End of Negotiation. Who Is to Blame for War?" The time for talk was over.[15]

By 1860, a total of 161,044 residents called Cincinnati home. It was the seventh-most populous city in the United States, surpassed only by New York City, Philadelphia, Brooklyn, Baltimore, Boston and New Orleans, in that order. Cincinnati was the nation's third-largest industrial center, with only New York City and Philadelphia producing more goods. Historian Louis Leonard Tucker indicated that Cincinnati "boasted 8 tent and awning establishments, 10 brass foundries, 10 boiler yards, 2 bolt factories, 474 boot and shoemakers, 25 candle factories, 32 carriage plants, 48 wholesale warehouses, 6 gunsmiths, 10 rolling mills, 56 saddlery shops, and 3 boat works. The presence of 36 breweries and 33 major packing houses attests to the value of spirits and foodstuffs among the manufactured commodities." From the Union's perspective, Cincinnati was a vital city, and the U.S. government needed to do everything possible to keep it safe.[16]

On April 15, 1861, President Abraham Lincoln called for seventy-five thousand volunteers to put down the rebellion, and on the same day, Ohio's Governor William Dennison, a native of Cincinnati, issued a formal proclamation to the people to honor Lincoln's request. Cincinnati's response was overwhelmingly supportive. Over the next few weeks, the fervor for war reigned in Cincinnati, in its suburbs and in the streets of its Kentucky neighbors, Covington and Newport. Numerous U.S. flags purchased or sewn by local women were raised over their houses and public buildings. Citizens knew the moment had come to defend their country and their homes from a new enemy to their south.[17]

Although the war meant a loss of trade with the South, the patriotism and enthusiasm to support the Union cause rose to their highest levels ever among the citizens of either side of the Ohio River. "The excitement is becoming painfully intense," wrote a *Cincinnati Daily Commercial* reporter. "The announcement that a call would be made upon Ohio for volunteers was also applauded again and again." Crowds gathered throughout the city to listen to patriotic speeches and rhetoric. Outside the post office in Cincinnati, a fifty-year-old veteran of previous wars stood above the rowdy gathering and yelled, "I have been a Democrat for thirty years, I have fought the battles of these Southern men here in the North, and now d—n 'em, they seek to destroy the government. They can't live on this continent. I say crush them [cheers], crush them!" At the Sixth Street Market, a person sympathetic to the Southern cause spoke too loudly and was pelted with eggs. Civil War newspaper reporter and author Whitelaw Reid best summed up Cincinnati's commitment to fighting for the Union in these words:

> So clear and unshrinking was the first voice from the great conservative city of the southern border, whose prosperity was supposed to depend on the southern trade. They had reckoned idly, it seemed, who had counted on hesitation here. From the first day that the war was opened, the people of Cincinnati were as vehement in their determination that it should be relentlessly prosecuted to victory, as the people of Boston.[18]

Thousands of men mobilized for war. Cincinnatians said goodbye to their wives, mothers and families to go off to do battle with the Confederacy. Most

William Knight Harrison joined Company K, Fifth Ohio Infantry, when it organized for three months' service in April 1861. He reenlisted and served with the regiment for the remainder of the war. *Courtesy of the Public Library of Cincinnati and Hamilton County.*

thought the war would be over within a few weeks, maybe within a couple of months, at worst. They brought with them the patriotic feelings and sense of duty and honor that prevailed throughout the country—and not just in the North. As much as local citizens took action to support their beliefs to preserve the Union, there were many citizens from Greater Cincinnati who chose to fight for the South. Students from the South departed in droves from local schools such as Miami University in Oxford, Ohio, to head home and join the Confederate army. Others who would fight for the Confederacy soon evacuated to Tennessee or Virginia to search for a military unit to call their own. Covington and Newport were cities where political divisions in families were particularly commonplace. Nonetheless, the vast majority of Greater Cincinnatians chose to fight for the Union. On April 15, the *Cincinnati Gazette* predicted that within a few days Ohio would have twenty-five thousand men ready for war, and Cincinnati would contribute a great many of them. Reports from the Home Guard Headquarters at 141 Main Street indicated that over seven thousand men had been enrolled into the Cincinnati home guard by the night of the eighteenth.[19]

The men came from all walks of life. Many were the hardened river men and factory workers, plenty were the affluent businessmen and politicians and still more were the farmers and shopkeepers. Young boys yearning for adventure ran away from home to join the nearest military unit. All felt the same sense of pride and drive to enlist into the service of their state.

Among the elite class of Cincinnati were the members of the Literary Club. On April 17, the club voted to cancel literary exercises in favor of military drill. Members formed their own infantry unit called the Burnet Rifles, which did not formally leave for battle as a single group. However, fifty-one of its volunteers, including future U.S. president Rutherford B. Hayes, chose to join various Union units during the war. Most became officers. Excluding brevets, the final ranks of these Literary Club men numbered one major general, five brigadier generals, eight colonels, four lieutenant colonels, eleven majors, fourteen captains, five first lieutenants, two second lieutenants and one private. Sixty-year-old Judge Bellamy Storer organized the older men of the club into a home guard unit.[20]

Cincinnati's prewar paramilitary units quickly moved into action. Some of the more well-known of such existing home guard companies were the Guthrie Greys Battalion, the Rover Guards, the Lafayette Guards and the Continental Battalion. The city agreed on April 16 to recruit and organize the home guards by city wards. (There were seventeen wards at the time.) The home guard committee leaders of each ward designated a meeting location where citizens could enlist for three months' service. For example, the Eleventh Ward chose Dauman's Hall at Hamilton Road (today's McMicken Avenue) and Elder Street. The Rover Guards' armory on Vine Street above Fourth Street was so overwhelmed with volunteers that the recruiters had to turn many visitors away. The men who were rejected "wept because of their misfortune."[21] The *Cincinnati Volksfreund* announced that Turner Hall on Walnut Street near Fourteenth Street would be the assembly point for German American volunteers. Gustav Tafel, the president of the Cincinnati Turnverein, called for a mass meeting to occur on April 17 at Turner Hall. They were to begin the organization of an all-German regiment led by Robert L. McCook, the law partner of local German American judge Johann Bernhard Stallo. Stallo was one of the most respected leaders in the city. Other recruiting stations sprang up at Zeltner's Tavern, Lafayette Hall, Mohawk Firehouse, Weyand's Brewery, Flattich Hall, Courthouse Exchange and Schiller's Beer Garden.[22]

George Brinton McClellan, a president of the Ohio & Mississippi Railroad and a former U.S. Army officer, contacted Governor Dennison to offer his services to Ohio. Larz Anderson and William S. Groesbeck, both prominent and politically influential citizens of Cincinnati, recommended that Dennison consider McClellan to lead Ohio's troops. The thirty-four-year-old McClellan had graduated in 1846 from the U.S. Military Academy at West Point. He had reached the rank of captain in the U.S. Army before he resigned in January 1857 to become the chief engineer for the Illinois Central Railroad.

Union major general George B. McClellan of Cincinnati served as the commander of Ohio's militia before becoming commander of the Army of the Potomac. Mathew Brady took this photo in 1861. *Courtesy of the Library of Congress.*

Over time, he attained the position of vice president of the company. In 1860, McClellan became president of the Eastern Division of the Ohio & Mississippi Railroad, headquartered in Cincinnati. During this brief period of his life in Cincinnati, he made many political contacts in Ohio, including a relationship with Governor Dennison.[23]

McClellan told Dennison that "Cincinnati is the most important strategical point in the valley of the Ohio, both from its position and the resources it will furnish to the party holding it. Should the Confederate States operate west of the Alleghenies, Cincinnati will doubtless be their objective point." He also added that it would be imperative for the military to reconnoiter the ground in Northern Kentucky to decide how to use it for possible defense of the city. Even though Dennison originally preferred Ohio officer Irvin McDowell to lead the state's first troops to war, the governor took McClellan's advice to heart. With the U.S. Army's consent, Dennison appointed McClellan a major general of Ohio volunteers, effective April 23. McClellan's first assignment would be to organize the thousands of troops forming in Cincinnati.[24]

Meanwhile, on April 18, Cincinnati's first troops left the city for their training grounds. The Gibson House hotel treated the Rover Guards and Zouave Guards to complimentary meals before they boarded a Little Miami & Xenia Railroad train bound for Columbus, Ohio. The Lafayette Guards militia company joined them for the trip. These units would form the core of the Second Ohio Infantry. Thousands of Cincinnati citizens crowded around the Little Miami Railroad passenger station on Front Street to bid their farewells to the troops. One mother threw her arms around her son-turned-soldier and said, "It almost breaks my heart to part with you my dear boy, but go, go, and defend your country."[25]

On the other side of the city, the Ohio First German Regiment (later designated the Ninth Ohio Infantry) had recruited to capacity. Due to lack of space to perform their drills, the new regiment moved the next day from Turner Hall to the Cincinnati Orphan Asylum lot at the southwest corner of Fourteenth and Elm Streets. August Willich, who helped organize and drill the regiment, was elected its adjutant general. Willich would later form his own regiment, the Thirty-Second Indiana Infantry, and would lead it as its colonel. Both regiments used Prussian signals and commands spoken in German.[26]

Dr. William H. Mussey rightly predicted that sick and wounded soldiers would need attention. He wrote to Secretary of the Treasury Salmon P. Chase to gain permission to take over the abandoned U.S. Marine Hospital on Sixth Street for use as a medical facility. Chase agreed, but the expense would not fall on the Federal government. Mussey successfully raised the funds for setting up the Marine Hospital by obtaining donations from Cincinnatians. It became Greater Cincinnati's first private military hospital of the Civil War when the facility accepted sick soldiers on June 28, 1861. Mussey earned the rank of brigade surgeon and was assigned to the Marine Hospital. Later in the war, he served in the field.[27]

Thousands of recruits in downtown Cincinnati filled vacant lots and public buildings. Many more soldiers arrived on trains from various parts of

The U.S. Marine Hospital had been abandoned before the war began. Citizens reopened it in 1861 and used it for treatment of soldiers. It became Good Samaritan Hospital in 1866. *Courtesy of the National Archives.*

the state. On April 19, the state government ordered Major General William H. Lytle, commander of the First Division of Ohio Militia, to establish a camp of rendezvous and instruction at the Cincinnati Trotting Park located at the end of Vine Street, seven miles north of downtown. The Trotting Park had been the site of the U.S. Fair in recent years. The facility would be called Camp Harrison, in honor of Cincinnati war hero and U.S. president William Henry Harrison.

On the next day, the troops marched from their various locations to Camp Harrison. By April 21, the camp held 1,400 men. A large crowd of citizens followed with picnic lunches to watch the soldiers train under Cincinnatian Frederick W. Lister, a former British soldier and drill instructor. For Cincinnatians, the camp was a spectacular sight and a fun outing for the day. However, reality quickly set in. A soldier in the Franklin Guards wrote about his first night at the camp as having "given us an idea of the real life of a soldier, and having taken off a little of the romance which the gay and

Camp Harrison hosted Cincinnati's regiments from April to May 1861. The site had been the former U.S. Fairgrounds. *From* Frank Leslie's Illustrated Newspaper *(May 18, 1861).*

flashing uniforms of the citizen soldiery on Fourth of July occasions suggest to the uninitiated."[28]

On April 22, the Irish Americans of the city met at the Catholic Institute (Mozart Hall) to organize a regiment of their own. Hundreds signed up at the meeting, and more would join them, including some Anglo American and German American companies that needed a regiment to accept them. Within days, a new unit composed mainly of Cincinnati's Irish Americans formed at Camp Harrison. It would be designated the Tenth Ohio Infantry.[29]

As the new commander of Ohio's militia, Major General McClellan's first order of business was to write to Lieutenant General Winfield Scott, the general-in-chief of all Union forces, requesting he send ten thousand arms and more supplies for the troops. Without them, McClellan could not possibly defend either Cincinnati or the state. Second, he made a list of men he wanted on his staff, including Major Fitz John Porter for adjutant general, Lieutenant Orlando M. Poe for engineering and Allan Pinkerton for intelligence gathering. Lastly, McClellan ordered Brigadier General Joshua

Bates to take command of the brigade at Camp Harrison, even though Lytle outranked Bates. Although disappointed, General Lytle graciously gave up his command to Bates and, in turn, accepted the colonelcy of the Tenth Ohio Infantry.[30]

General McClellan also found a suitable camp of instruction for the new troops. A West Point–educated engineer and Cincinnati entrepreneur, Colonel William S. Rosecrans, spotted a beautiful seven-hundred-acre piece of bottomland surrounding the small, quiet town of Germany, Ohio. It was situated on the Little Miami Railroad and the Glendale-Milford Road, two excellent paths for transportation of troops and supplies. Gently flowing around the plot was the Little Miami River, a water source large enough to supply a camp throughout the year.[31]

Even better, Germany sat sixteen miles by rail from downtown Cincinnati, a distance that would discourage Cincinnatians from making trips to visit their husbands and sons. Quick-thinking businessmen had taken advantage of the attraction to Camp Harrison by opening refreshment stands along the routes from Cincinnati. Omnibus owner Medard Fels had established a new line that would carry travelers from downtown Cincinnati to Camp Harrison for twenty-five cents a person. However, the distraction that thirty thousand

Union major general William Starke Rosecrans was president of the Western Coal Oil Company in Cincinnati when the war erupted. He joined General George McClellan's staff in April 1861 and became the second commander of the Department of the Ohio in July. *Courtesy of the Library of Congress.*

visitors to Camp Harrison created on April 28 convinced the officers that something had to change. Camp Dennison would be the solution.[32]

On April 27, A.E. Ferguson and Colonel George W. Holmes successfully negotiated the leases of the land with the residents of the village of Germany. The leases would expire on March 1, 1862, and they would cost the State of Ohio twelve to thirty dollars per acre annually. McClellan ordered Colonel William S. Rosecrans to survey the land and lay out the camp site.[33] On the same day, McClellan telegraphed the headquarters of the Ohio Militia with his plan:

> *From this position* [Camp Dennison] *I can move the command rapidly to any point where it may be required. In three days I shall have seven regiments at Camp Dennison (the present camp) and four regiments at Camp Harrison, six miles from Cincinnati. By the end of the week the Cleveland and Columbus camps will be abandoned, and there will be some seventeen regiments at Camp Dennison. By the end of two weeks there*

Union major general Jacob Dolson Cox lived in Cincinnati as an Ohio state senator when the war began. He was elected governor of Ohio in October 1865. *Courtesy of U.S. Army HEC, MOLLUS Collection.*

will be twenty-four regiments in that camp, unless I find it necessary in the meantime to detach some regiments toward Marietta. My desire is to concentrate the whole command in this camp, and to thoroughly organize, discipline, and drill. By the end of six weeks I hope they will be in condition to act efficiently in any direction where they may be required. I hope that my wish can be carried out, and that I may not be required to take my men under fire until they are reduced to some order and discipline.[34]

Brigadier General Jacob D. Cox in Columbus received the order on April 29 to move his Ohio troops to Camp Dennison. Camp Harrison had been Cincinnati's largest attraction for nearly two weeks, but between May 12 and 18, it would be abandoned in favor of a new place where the art of war could be taught.

Jacob Dolson Cox was born in Montreal, Canada, in 1827, but he had spent most of his life in Ohio. He attended Oberlin Collegiate Institute, the country's best-known abolitionist school of higher education. He practiced

A view of the southwest portion of Camp Dennison as it appeared in June 1861 when Brigadier General Jacob D. Cox's brigade occupied the huts. *From* Frank Leslie's Scenes and Portraits of the Civil War *(1894).*

law in Warren, Ohio, and was elected in 1858 as a Republican to the Ohio state senate. When the war started, Governor Dennison appointed Cox to a brigadier generalship of Ohio militia. In May 1861, the U.S. government confirmed the appointment by bestowing on Cox the official rank of brigadier general of U.S. volunteers.[35]

Following McClellan's orders, Cox transferred the first soldiers to Camp Dennison. Cox recalled in his memoirs his first day at the camp:

> *It was McClellan's purpose to put in two brigades on the west side of the railway, and one on the east. My own brigade was assigned to the west side, and nearest to Cincinnati. The men of the two regiments shouldered*

their pine boards and carried them up to the line of the company streets, which were close to the hills skirting the valley, and which opened into the parade and drill ground along the railway. A general plan was given to the company officers by which the huts should be made uniform in size and shape....My own headquarters were in a little brick schoolhouse of one story, which stood (and I think still stands) on the east side of the track close to the railway. My improvised camp equipage consisted of a common trestle cot and a pair of blankets, and I made my bed in the open space in front of the teacher's desk or pulpit. My only staff officer...slept on the floor in one of the little aisles between the pupil's seats.[36]

Camp Dennison would become Ohio's largest camp in the Civil War and one of the largest in the United States. Throughout the first week of May, new regiments from other parts of Ohio poured into Camp

Dennison. Nearly fifteen thousand men occupied the camp by the end of June. At the beginning of this period, cold, rainy weather prevailed. The green soldiers were instructed to build cantonments—small wooden shanties measuring twelve by eighteen feet with dirt floors—constructed from lumber shipped from Cincinnati. Each shanty could hold twelve men. Professional carpenters and soldiers worked side by side to build the cantonments. Unfortunately, the craftsmanship was poor, and the roofs of these buildings often leaked. A soldier in the Eleventh Ohio Infantry recalled his first experience at the camp:

> *The first night spent in Camp Dennison will never be forgotten by any who had the misfortune to be there....Huddled together under their partially completed quarters, the rain coming down in torrents, with a steady drip, drip, drip, through the many crevices in the boards, mud beneath and all around them, but few closed their eyes that night.*[37]

As the war ramped up, so did the city's makers of munitions, military supplies and weapons. The factory of Samuel S. Ashcraft & Company, located on the Miami & Erie Canal, increased its production of cannon balls and shells to between three and four hundred per day. A staff of seventy-five persons churned out cannon shot ranging in weight from six to sixty-four pounds. The company could double its output, if needed. Springer & Whiteman received a government contract for supplying rations. Wells's Cincinnati Type Foundry casted thousands of barrels of Minié balls; J. Painter & Company and Holenshade, Morris & Company

Miles Greenwood's Eagle Iron Works was one of the largest weapons manufacturers in the United States during the Civil War. Confederate sympathizers tried several times to destroy it, but they failed. *From* History of Prominent Mercantile and Manufacturing Firms in the United States *(1857).*

EAGLE IRON WORKS,

M. GREENWOOD, PROPRIETOR,
Nos. 383, 384, 385, 386 & 396, Corner Walnut and Canal Streets,
CINCINNATI, OHIO.

built army wagons; and Dunn & Witt manufactured bullets and pontoon bridges. Irish American businessman David Sinton increased production of pig iron from his two furnaces in eastern Ohio and sold the metal to the government to make tools and weapons. Entrepreneur and inventor Miles Greenwood prepared his Eagle Iron Works on Walnut Street to produce rifles, cannons and other metal material for the war effort. However, a group of Cincinnati women beat the U.S. government to Greenwood's door to gain a contract with him. The ladies offered to order a number of forty-two-pounder rifled cannons to protect the hills surrounding the city. It is unknown whether Greenwood accepted the job.[38]

CINCINNATI LOOKS SOUTHWARD

Across the Ohio River, the Kentucky government hovered in an ambiguous state of neutrality to the war. Unlike its neighbor to the north, Kentucky permitted slavery, and its citizens were heavily divided over the institution that had started the conflict. After the firing on Fort Sumter, Kentucky governor Beriah Magoffin issued an official proclamation of neutrality that essentially said the state would side with neither the Union nor the Confederacy. Nonetheless, Kentuckians shared the same enthusiasm and patriotism that other Americans possessed. No statement of neutrality would stop them from joining the armies of the Confederacy or the Union.

The majority of the citizens in Kenton and Campbell Counties supported the Union cause. For example, seven of every eight soldiers from Newport joined the Union army. Most of them had been recent immigrants to the United States, and they belonged to the working class that required nothing from slaves.[39] However, the Unionists lived next to slave-owning families who thought their rights had been violated by President Lincoln's government. Fights often ensued in the streets of Covington and Newport. At the Independence Day celebration in Newport, neighbors knew which side their neighbors had chosen by how they reacted to the parade. Alcohol mixed with the political tensions of the day led to brawls, shootings and fires. The incident made it clear to everyone that only violence would settle their differences, and the men of the community reacted by leaving for war.[40]

President Lincoln clearly understood the vital importance of keeping the Bluegrass State in the Union. "I hope to have God on my side, but I must have Kentucky," Lincoln wrote. He believed that "to lose Kentucky is nearly the same as to lose the whole game. Kentucky gone, we cannot hold Missouri, nor I think Maryland. These all against us, and the job on our hands is too big for us. We would well consent to separation at once, including the surrender of this capitol [Washington, D.C.]."

In the end, Lincoln received his wish, as evidenced by the reactions within Kenton and Campbell Counties. On May 1, 1861, nearly 1,500 citizens gathered in Covington to show their support for the Union and raise Old Glory over Butcher's Hall, the Independent Union Home Guard headquarters on York Street. Recruiting for the Union forces greatly outpaced recruiting for the Confederate forces in Northern Kentucky. While Kentucky enforced its neutrality, hundreds of Bluegrass men crossed the Ohio River to join Ohio-born Kentucky units. On the other hand, Newport lawyer and states' rights advocate George B. Hodge raised only one company of Confederate soldiers from his home city and county. Serving or having served in any of the Union armed forces from April 1861 to February 1864, Kenton County boasted 1,237 men, while Campbell County counted 1,181 men. Between April 12, 1861, and April 12, 1864, the Union army recruited 822 volunteers from Kenton County, 791 volunteers from Campbell County and 165 volunteers from Boone County. By the end of the Civil War, Kentucky contributed 100,000 White and 24,000 Black men to fight for the Union, while only about 35,000 White soldiers fought for the Confederacy.[41]

The Bluegrass State's neutrality disallowed military camps, Confederate or Union, from being established on Kentucky soil. Ohio and Kentucky

Camp Clay, located at Pendleton, Ohio, held the first Kentucky Union regiments to organize during the Civil War. The camp was later renamed Camp Dick Corwine. *From* Pictorial War Record *(1881–1884).*

military officials initially respected this requirement. In the Greater Cincinnati area, they created Camp Colerain at Bevis, Ohio, and Camp Clay at Pendleton, Ohio, in late April 1861 for the purpose of organizing Kentucky recruits for the Union.

Camp Clay was named after the famous U.S. congressman and senator from Kentucky Henry Clay. It sat along the Little Miami Railroad at the eastern edge of Cincinnati's Seventeenth Ward. Some old workshops and omnibus sheds provided shelter. By May 1, the first Kentucky Unionist recruits had arrived at Camp Clay. Many of these men were residents of Louisville, Covington and Newport. Some were members of paramilitary units, such as the Woodruff Guards and the Woodruff Zouaves. However, not enough Kentuckians enlisted to meet the minimum numbers to create a regiment. Ohio called on its own recruits, mostly from Cincinnati, to fill the rosters of the Kentucky units. Over the next two months, Kentucky's first Union regiments, the First Kentucky (U.S.) Infantry and the Second Kentucky (U.S.) Infantry, would be mustered into service as a result of the support from the Buckeye State.[42]

Kentucky's neutral stance displeased Cincinnatians. Many considered it treasonous. Especially concerning to them was that weapons and military supplies produced by Cincinnati manufacturers still flowed to Kentucky consumers, knowing well that many of these items were being transported across state boundaries into the seceded Confederate states. The Cincinnati Home Guard clamored for Cincinnati mayor George Hatch to put an end to these sales. Hatch understood the predicament of supplying Kentucky as any other "friendly state" versus helping the enemy within Kentucky's borders. He contacted Governor Dennison for an official statement on how to deal with this situation.

Dennison replied to Hatch that he was strictly opposed to the shipment of Cincinnati's products to the seceded Confederate states, but he supported the sale of military items to the border states such as Kentucky. Dennison ended his letter by encouraging Hatch to use his cleverness to help keep the Bluegrass State in the Union. This message failed to bolster Hatch's relationship with his constituents. The Republicans in Cincinnati accused Hatch, a Unionist Democrat, of not being serious enough to stop the flow of goods to the South. In other words, some citizens implied that Hatch sympathized with the South. Many Cincinnatians would come to believe this accusation. Despite Dennison's and Hatch's hesitations, the U.S. government made the decision for them. Secretary of the Treasury Salmon Chase issued an order on May 2, 1861, to customs agents to seize all goods

Newport Barracks in Newport, Kentucky, as seen from the Ohio River in 1861. Built in 1804, the barracks continued to serve the U.S. Regular Army throughout the Civil War. *From* Harper's Weekly *(August 31, 1861)*.

heading to the Southern states that could be used for military gain, and in July, the U.S. Congress officially forbade all transportation of goods to the South. Cincinnati lost half its economic market in a single stroke.[43]

Before the advent of Camp Harrison, the Newport Barracks served as Greater Cincinnati's primary U.S. military post. It was established in 1804 at the mouth of the Licking River in Newport, Kentucky, to replace the decaying and insufficient Fort Washington. The Newport Barracks was built with Federal money under the direction of Newport's founder, General James Taylor. For a time, it was the fledging United States' most important western outpost, acting as a staging area for American military campaigns against the British during the War of 1812. In 1859, the installation recruited soldiers for the Department of the South. Officers in the U.S. Army often found themselves visitors to Newport Barracks. In May 1846, Lieutenant William T. Sherman brought twenty-five recruits to the barracks. In April 1858, Brigadier General William S. Harney, Colonel Joseph E. Mansfield, Colonel Robert E. Lee, Colonel Thomas T. Fauntleroy and Lieutenant Colonel George B. Crittenden came to Newport Barracks to serve at the court-martial of Major General David E. Twiggs. All these men became generals in the Civil War.[44]

Despite the establishment of Cincinnati's new camps, the Newport Barracks continued to be a critical military installation for the region. It served as a major recruiting station, and its military hospital and prison played important roles during the Civil War. Both facilities remained filled throughout the conflict. In fact, the barracks' hospital claimed the highest successful recovery percentage of any other military hospital in the nation, though the rate was unstated. Also, the camp's military band proved to be the most popular in Greater Cincinnati during the war. The band performed at numerous public functions on both sides of the river.

Before the Civil War started, great concern arose that pro-secessionist sympathizers would capture the barracks. A letter dated January 12, 1861, from Private John Clark to Lieutenant General Winfield Scott stated, "I am full satisfied that there are many persons in and about Newport, Kentucky, who hold sentiments dangerous to the Union and to the constitution, and would, if chance offered, seize the Newport Barracks and turn the guns on this city [Cincinnati]." When war finally broke out, the men stationed at the barracks split between Union and Confederate sentiments. However, those soldiers with pro-secessionist leanings resigned from the U.S. Army and traveled back to their homes to join the Confederate army.

The barracks remained firmly under Union control for the rest of the war. Lieutenant Colonel Sidney Burbank was left in charge, and Dr. Nathaniel Burger Shaler was made the chief surgeon. Burbank was reassigned to Missouri on July 16, 1861, and Major John King accepted the command of Newport Barracks. When the Fifteenth U.S. Infantry was reorganized at the barracks in October 1861, Colonel J.P. Sanderson took over the installation. Lieutenant Colonel Sidney Burbank was assigned to command again in June 1862, and Lieutenant Colonel Seth Eastman, First U.S. Infantry, succeeded him in March 1863.[45]

Newport Barracks showed signs of decay by 1861. River floods had damaged the installation's structures. During the summer, the mosquitoes, rotting debris along the riverbanks and poor ventilation in the buildings made life at the barracks somewhat unpleasant. However, the place was generally clean, and its buildings were better than tents. Colonel Glover Perin, the post surgeon who succeeded Nathaniel Shaler, described Newport Barracks' layout in great detail in 1869. The dimensions of the roughly rectangular plot of land on which the barracks stood were 288 feet along the Ohio River and 563 feet along the Licking River. The post design consisted of multiple buildings surrounding a rectangular parade ground. The average occupancy was 228 men, but during the Civil War, often that number was

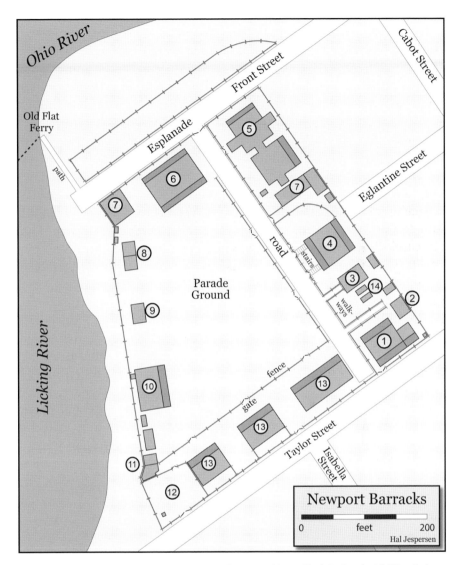

Layout of Newport Barracks in 1869, from Surgeon Glover Perin's sketch: (1) Hospital, (2) laundry and storerooms, (3) church, (4) officers' quarters, (5) general headquarters, (6) headquarters, (7) stables, (8) commissary and carpenter shop, (9) magazine, (10) guard house and prison, (11) men's sinks and washhouse, (12) wood yard, (13) barracks, (14) tents. *Author's collection.*

well exceeded, making the barracks uncomfortably crowded. On May 7, 1861, the *Cincinnati Daily Times* reported that 456 men were housed at the barracks—exactly double its normal capacity.[46]

The U.S. War Department established on May 3 the Department of the Ohio, a military zone that encompassed the states of Ohio, Indiana and Illinois. Six days later, it was extended to include western Pennsylvania and western Virginia north of the Kanawha and Greenbrier Rivers. Major General George B. McClellan became the department's first commander. He occasionally rode on horseback from his headquarters in Cincinnati to Camp Dennison to check on the progress of the department's soldiers; however, he spent most of his time in the city. Yet his men loved him, and they nicknamed him "Little Mac."[47]

By mid-May, rifles and uniforms arrived for the soldiers at Camp Harrison and Camp Dennison. On May 17, the newly equipped Sixth Ohio Infantry, known as the Guthrie Grays, marched proudly through the main thoroughfares of downtown Cincinnati when the regiment evacuated Camp Harrison en route to Camp Dennison. Crowds of citizens cheered and showered praise on the soldiers as they passed. Major Robert Anderson, the former commander and hero of Fort Sumter, had arrived in Cincinnati that day to much applause and great fanfare. He saluted the regiment when it passed the home of his brother, Larz Anderson, where the major was staying. As the Sixth Ohio men boarded their train at the Little Miami Railroad Depot, the women said their good-byes to their loved ones. The Fifth Ohio Infantry followed the next day, leaving Camp Harrison empty for good. The soldiers paraded down Sycamore Street and hopped on a train to Camp Dennison.[48]

Enlistment continued at a feverish pace. Throughout the summer and fall, military camps sprang up throughout the city and Hamilton County to handle the large numbers of recruits. In addition to camps Dennison, Clay and Colerain were camps Gurley, John McLean, Monroe and Dick Corwine. Artillerymen who had joined the Union cause stayed in barracks constructed on the Cincinnati Orphan Asylum lot. The barracks were large enough to hold nearly two thousand men. Cannons were parked in the lot, too. On the Kentucky side of the Ohio River, Camp Webster at Jamestown (now Dayton), Camp Finnell and Camp King at South Covington and Camp Bromley at the north side of Bromley served as rendezvous and training camps.[49]

Many of the three-month enlistments of the infantry regiments expired in July and August 1861. Officers and prominent men came to Camp Dennison

Guthrie's Grays marching through Cincinnati. *From* Harper's Weekly *(June 8, 1861).*

to make speeches to encourage the soldiers to reenlist for three years. Most would do so. Governor Dennison spoke to them with praise on May 26, and the next day, Major Robert Anderson of Fort Sumter fame swore in the thousands of soldiers who had chosen to fight for the Union until the war was won. Judge Stallo repeated the oath in German. The soldiers were rewarded with the knowledge that many of them would soon be heading to the front. Major General McClellan would lead them in a campaign into western Virginia to repel the Confederate forces there.[50]

On May 30, the *Cincinnati Daily Times* reported that Miles Greenwood at last had received a contract from the U.S. government to rifle 30,000 old muskets for the State of Ohio. His Eagle Iron Works would not only complete the full order in less than a year but also produce 161 bronze cannons, mostly six-pounders, for the Union war effort. Greenwood employed over five hundred workers at his facility at the beginning of the war, but that number increased to seven hundred to fulfill government contracts.[51]

Seven nuns of the Sisters of Charity in Cincinnati made their way to Camp Dennison on June 1. Mayor Hatch and Archbishop John Purcell had heard about the outbreak of measles in the camp, and they requested the sisters to tend to the sick soldiers there. The nuns' leader was Sister Anthony O'Connell, an Irishwoman by birth, who had entered the convent in 1835. She had come to Cincinnati in March 1837 to work at St. Peter's Orphanage. In 1852, O'Connell took over the management of St. John's Hospital for the Invalids, which she adapted into a soldiers' hospital early in the Civil War. The medical aid that O'Connell and her fellow sisters provided to the sick and wounded on the battlefields and in the hospitals would earn them great respect among soldiers and civilians alike. They called Sister Anthony and her compatriots the "Angels of the Battlefield."[52]

From April through June, increasing numbers of women in Cincinnati, Newport and Covington volunteered their time to help the soldiers in the local camps and hospitals. The ladies performed many different chores, ranging from providing food and drink for the hungry soldiers to stitching pants, shirts and socks for their clothing. The government often provided the ladies with raw materials for their work. On June 12, Captain Cahill, the brigade quartermaster in Cincinnati, requisitioned twelve thousand yards of flannel for the women to sew into shirts. As the war lengthened, these women joined local branches of the Soldiers' Aid Society, Ladies' Aid Society, Ladies' Christian Commission and U.S. Christian Commission. The Cincinnati branch of the U.S. Christian Commission would distribute about $300,000 worth of supplies and money and 82,627 Bibles to Union soldiers over the course of the war. The work of Cincinnati's women in the war proved invaluable to the country.[53]

Because travel by rail was still in its infancy in the United States, particularly in the South, the rivers in the western theater served as the major highways of the Civil War era. Although railroads existed throughout the South and quickly became military targets for both sides, steamboats provided the most efficient form of mass transportation for the armies. Consequently, the U.S. military knew it had to control the major navigable rivers of the West, especially the Ohio, Mississippi, Missouri, Tennessee, Cumberland, Arkansas, White, Yazoo and Red Rivers. The most critical of these was the Mississippi River, which handled the heaviest boat traffic west of the Appalachians and formed a natural inroad for invading forces. To take these waterways from the Confederates, the U.S. military needed special armed river craft that could navigate the shallows during the summer months. The U.S. Army would fund and build the new boats, but the U.S. Navy would staff and weaponize them. Time was of the essence, because the Confederacy had begun to build gunboats for this purpose. Thus, in May 1861, Secretary of the Navy Gideon Welles ordered

Captain John Rodgers II, U.S. Navy, helped chart the North Pacific Ocean prior to the war. After serving in Cincinnati, he went east, where he won acclaim for his capture of the CSS *Atlanta*. *Courtesy of Naval History and Heritage Command, #NH46934.*

Commander John Rodgers II to Cincinnati to begin work immediately on a new fleet of armed vessels known as the U.S. Western Gunboat Flotilla, or the "Brown Water Navy."[54]

John Rodgers II was born in Maryland in 1812. He had followed in the footsteps of his father by joining the U.S. Navy in 1828. Rodgers's experience with deep-water ships was unquestionable, as he had spent over thirty years of his career in the Brazilian, Mediterranean and Pacific squadrons. However, when it came to riverboats, Commander Rodgers had much to learn. Rodgers consulted with engineer James B. Eads, a salvage expert and inventor who had proposed to President Lincoln a strategy for using shallow-draft armored gunboats to win the western waters. Eads's plan looked promising, and Lieutenant General Winfield Scott incorporated it into his overall Federal strategy for executing the war, called the "Anaconda Plan." Welles assigned Rodgers and Eads to Major General George McClellan of the U.S. Army, who gave Rodgers full control over the job of purchasing and refitting three civilian steamboats into gunboats. McClellan added to his staff a steamboat expert, William J. Kountz, for advice and purchasing assistance. Rodgers similarly requested a naval construction expert, Samuel M. Pook, to help him build the first three armored gunboats for the Union navy.[55]

Rodgers naturally chose Cincinnati as the place where he would convert the three civilian steamboats into gunboats. The Queen City had been one of the largest producers of steamboats in the United States. It had plenty of skilled craftsmen who could do the unusual work of armoring a steamboat at one of the well-established boatyards in the region, such as the John Litherbury Company, the Marine Railway and Dry Dock Company or the Samuel T. Hambleton & Company. Also, the city harbored an abundance of the raw materials, particularly lumber and iron, that were needed for the job. Cincinnati was destined to become the birthplace of America's western navy during the Civil War.[56]

With McClellan's approval, Rodgers, Kountz and Pook bought three civilian steamers at a total cost of $62,200. The team estimated that an additional $41,000 would be needed to convert the steamers into the final products. On June 8, Rodgers awarded the refitting contract to Daniel H. Morton, who owned his own steamboat yard as well as a share of the Marine Railway and Dry Dock Company located upriver in the suburb of Fulton. The contract stipulated that the conversions would need to be completed within nineteen days, or else Morton would incur financial penalties for each subsequent day. At the same time, Rodgers ordered heavy artillery for the three gunboats. Despite the politics between the

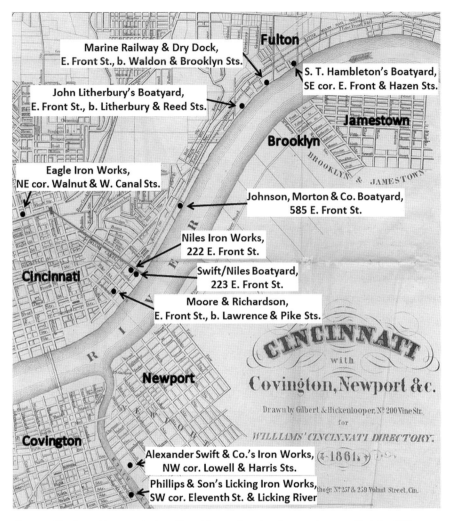

Greater Cincinnati boatyards, iron foundries and engine factory that supplied the U.S. Navy during the Civil War. Locations are overlaid on an 1861 map from *Williams' Cincinnati Directory. Author's collection.*

army and navy concerning Rodgers's aggressiveness, McClellan fully supported Rodgers's quick actions throughout the project. Eventually, the War Department would be impressed, too.[57]

Using Pook's blueprints, Morton's boat carpenters removed the frills from the civilian steamers to reduce weight, and then they added a five-inch-thick layer of oak to the sides of the boats, which lent them their nickname "timberclad." The builders also constructed portholes for the cannons and

Timberclad USS *Tyler* docked for refitting. This Cincinnati-built and refitted gunboat saw significant combat on the Western rivers. *Courtesy of Naval History and Heritage Command, #NH49975.*

a pilot house on the salon deck of each boat. Unfortunately, Morton's work was poorly done, and Rodgers demanded repairs. However, due to rapidly falling water depths in the Ohio River, McClellan and Rodgers agreed to send the unfinished boats downstream to Louisville rather than risk them being stranded in the mud at Cincinnati.[58]

Under the army's orders, the USS *Tyler* left Cincinnati on June 24 for final outfitting at Louisville, and the USS *Lexington* and USS *Conestoga* followed the next morning. The three timberclads would see the most combat of all the gunboats of the western theater. In July, the U.S. Navy set up an office in Cincinnati at 5–7 East Front Street to recruit sailors for the gunboats. The response to the recruiting effort was slow, but the boats would have full crews before summer's end. In fact, over the course of the Civil War, Cincinnati contributed several thousand sailors to the Union navy.[59]

General McClellan and the regiments at Camp Dennison began their move to the front in mid-June. McClellan left Cincinnati on June 20 and traveled to western Virginia via Marietta, Ohio. He took eighty-six men from the Fourth U.S. Artillery to serve as his bodyguard. His wife and mother-in-law stayed in Cincinnati to await his return. By mid-July, most of the regiments had left Camp Dennison. One observer thought it looked like a "deserted village."[60]

TABLE 1

RESIDENTS OF CINCINNATI OR HAMILTON COUNTY, OHIO, WHO ENLISTED INTO THE U.S. NAVY DURING THE CIVIL WAR BETWEEN APRIL 12, 1861, AND FEBRUARY 24, 1864		
TOWNSHIP OR TOWN OF RESIDENCE	NUMBER OF MEN WHO ENLISTED INTO THE U.S. NAVY	STATE OF OHIO CREDITS
First Congressional District of Ohio		
Cincinnati, First Ward	138	49
Cincinnati, Second Ward	22	7
Cincinnati, Third Ward	497	240
Cincinnati, Fifth Ward	77	46
Cincinnati, Seventh Ward	44	14
Cincinnati, Ninth Ward	104	35
Cincinnati, Tenth Ward	56	19
Cincinnati, Eleventh Ward	55	22
Cincinnati, Thirteenth Ward	362	168
Cincinnati, Seventeenth Ward	94	51
Anderson Township	34	13
Mill Creek Township	25	9
Spencer Township	10	4
TOTAL	1,518	677
Second Congressional District of Ohio		
Cincinnati, Sixth Ward	10	4
Cincinnati, Eighth Ward	83	23
Cincinnati, Twelfth Ward	57	33
Cincinnati, Fourteenth Ward	70	26
Cincinnati, Fifteenth Ward	50	44
Cincinnati, Sixteenth Ward	69	40

TOWNSHIP OR TOWN OF RESIDENCE	NUMBER OF MEN WHO ENLISTED INTO THE U.S. NAVY	STATE OF OHIO CREDITS
Mill Creek Township (Lick Run Precinct)	3	1
Mill Creek Township (Clifton Recinct)	5	2
Mill Creek Township (Corryville Precinct)	7	3
Storrs Township	13	10
Springfield Township	21	9
Harrison Township	3	3
Miami Township	1	1
TOTAL	392	199
GRAND TOTAL	1,910	876

Source: Ohio State Archives Series 123: *Naval Credits Recorded by the Cincinnati Provost Marshal Prior to February 24, 1864.*

The importance of Cincinnati as a transportation hub compelled military units from other Union states to use the city as a launch pad to the South. On each visit, Cincinnatians gave these troops a warm reception, as if they were their own boys headed off to battle. Colonel Lew Wallace's Eleventh Indiana infantrymen, arrayed in their ornate Zouave uniforms, paraded through the city on June 7. The citizens met them with much fanfare. A few days later, the Eighth and Tenth Indiana Infantry regiments passed through Cincinnati on their way to war. The people of Cincinnati greeted them with cheers and a complimentary meal at the Fifth Street Market House. A flag flying over the Coles & Hopkins store at Fifth and Vine Streets read, "Cincinnatians Welcome the Noble Sons of Indiana. God Speed and Bless You." After eating, the regiments marched off. They would be the first of many non-Cincinnati regiments to receive the same treatment at the Fifth Street Market and other city establishments.[61]

Quartermaster General Montgomery C. Meigs assigned command of the burgeoning Cincinnati military supply depot to Captain John H. Dickerson, who quickly went to work furnishing the Union regiments throughout the western theater. On July 10, Cincinnati depot quartermaster David Waddle McClung reported that his office had sent nine hundred muskets to the Eagle Iron Works to be rifled. Soldiers in the field would call these modified muskets the "Greenwood Rifle," after the owner of the ironworks. Greenwood's factory would complete the rifling of four thousand muskets by the first week of August at a cost twenty dollars cheaper per gun than the purchase of an Enfield rifle. McClung's department had also purchased from Cincinnati vendors 2,000 horses, 3,900 sets of harness and 850 wagons for the army. The government contracted with Proctor & Gamble Company to supply the army's candles and soap, while Charles Kahn Jr. filled large orders for beef to feed the troops. The city's slaughterhouses, which had dominated the nation's pork production for years—thus earning Cincinnati the nickname "Porkopolis"—soon fulfilled Union army orders for lard, salted pork, bacon and ham. Hard bread, rice, sugar, salt, potatoes and Rio coffee were other popular items that Cincinnati's wholesalers sold to the government. In addition, Cincinnati became the U.S. Army's primary quartermaster depot for supplying clothing to its soldiers in the western theater. In August 1861 alone, the Union army ordered 100,000 uniforms to be finished in two weeks. Cincinnati's predominately Jewish American clothiers, particularly Mack & Brothers, Stadler, Brother & Company and Glaser & Brothers, worked together to fulfill the demand.[62]

Except for the clothing industry, Cincinnati's economic future looked grim. The *Annual Statement of the Commerce of Cincinnati* for the year ending August 1861 painted a bleak picture. "Merchants condensed and contracted their business to suit the worst, as far as possible," the report stated. "Debts due by merchants to the seceded States were generally repudiated, and consequently those Northern merchants who did a Southern business, in whole or part, were made hopelessly bankrupt." Speculation ended in all areas of commerce. The U.S. government's prevention of shipments to the South, including Kentucky, had placed nearly all industries into an economic depression. The largest stockpile of pork in the West lay rotting in Cincinnati warehouses. Sales of dry goods, manufactured foods, footwear and liquor dropped dramatically. Even the iron and lumber industries suffered. Furniture exports dropped from forty-two thousand pieces sold between April and September 1860 to fifteen pieces sold between the same months in 1861. It was no wonder that the City of Cincinnati allocated a fund to help destitute families of soldiers. Yet Cincinnati's economy took less of a hit from the war than the larger cities in the East, and the future would offer new opportunities for businesses to flourish.[63]

News from the war front was encouraging at first. McClellan's troops, most of whom had been at Camp Dennison, scored several victories in western Virginia, which, at the time, seemed to be large affairs. However, the reality of war fell heavily onto Cincinnati's doorstep. The first casualties trickled into the city from the battlefields in the East. Then, on July 22, 1861, the details of the First Battle of Bull Run, Virginia, appeared in the Cincinnati newspapers. The *Cincinnati Daily Times* reported the next day that "the entire city was intensely agitated yesterday upon the receipt of the news from Washington, in regard to the reverse met with by our army in Eastern Virginia.…Thousands thronged to the corners near the newspaper offices." At the same time, telegraph dispatches posted in the windows of the *Cincinnati Daily Gazette* office announced that General McClellan would take command of the Union army in Virginia. This news brought a deafening roar from the crowd "of not less than 5,000" that had gathered outside the office. The great battle that would end the Civil War had not occurred. The war would go on longer than anyone expected.[64]

4

FORTIFYING THE QUEEN CITY

When Cincinnati city officials acknowledged that the Civil War would not end quickly, they realized the immediate need to defend the city from possible Confederate attack. The city council recorded in its minutes for August 28, 1861, that it had entertained the idea of appropriating funds for building earthworks and obtaining artillery to protect the city. The next step would be to investigate what this meant physically. Council swore in Colonel Adolphus E. Jones, the future provost marshal of Cincinnati (Ohio First District), to delve deeper into the matter.[65]

In April 1861, George McClellan and his Cincinnati comrade, Captain John Pope of the U.S. Corps of Topographical Engineers and future major general, had expressed their concerns to Ohio governor William Dennison about defending Cincinnati by land. They had concluded that a proper defense could only be done through the fortification of Northern Kentucky. However, Dennison's hands were tied. Dennison met with Kentucky governor Magoffin at the Burnet House in Cincinnati to propose the fortifications, but the outcome did not go well. Magoffin refused to allow any troops—Union or Confederate—to step foot in his state, let alone construct forts in it.

Despite this answer, McClellan ordered one of his staff, Lieutenant Orlando M. Poe, a West Point–trained engineer, to scout and survey the land in Northern Kentucky that lay between Bromley on the west and the mouth of the Little Miami River on the east. On May 15, Poe returned with a detailed topographic map of the region. McClellan and Poe could

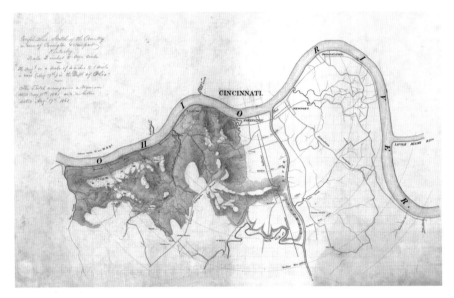

"Unfinished Sketch of the Country in rear of Covington & Newport, Kentucky." Surveyed by Lieutenant Orlando M. Poe on May 15, 1861, this is the first map that Poe, a famous cartographer, created during the Civil War. *Courtesy of the National Archives.*

easily envision the line of earthworks that could be built along an arc of hills located three miles south of the city and anchored at both ends by the Ohio River. Not only could this fortified line protect Cincinnati, but it also could shield the city's most important neighbors—Covington and Newport. Unfortunately, McClellan was powerless to act until he received approval from Governor Dennison or the U.S. War Department.[66]

On September 3, 1861, everything changed in Kentucky. On that day, Confederate major general Leonidas Polk violated the Bluegrass State's neutrality by seizing the key Mississippi River towns of Hickman and Columbus, Kentucky. Brigadier General Ulysses S. Grant, an Ohio native who had been raised just east of Greater Cincinnati, moved his Union troops from Illinois and occupied Paducah, Kentucky, on the Ohio River. These military actions immediately voided the neutrality act. Thus, the door opened for Cincinnatians to put into action their plans to defend the hills of Northern Kentucky.

With McClellan's departure to the Army of the Potomac in Virginia, the Department of the Ohio required a new leader. Brigadier General William S. Rosecrans took command on July 25. In September, at the request of Governor Dennison, President Lincoln appointed Cincinnati brigadier general Ormsby M. Mitchel to take over the department and to set up

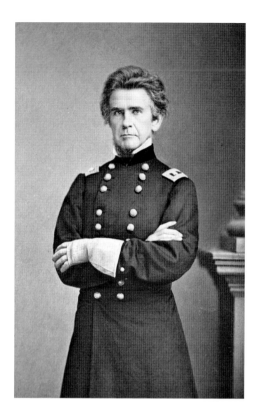

Union brigadier general Ormsby MacKnight Mitchel was the third commander of the Department of the Ohio. He died of yellow fever in South Carolina in 1862. Fort Mitchell, Kentucky, is named for him. *Courtesy of the Library of Congress.*

its defense. On September 4, General Mitchel, Governor Dennison and Colonel Adolphus Jones inspected Camp Dennison. They determined that the artillery units should be moved from other parts of the city to the camp. On the following day, Mitchel met with the public in Cincinnati to discuss ideas for protecting the city. He quickly grasped from both events the large deficiencies in the department's capabilities to guard against a Confederate attack. However, Mitchel was an excellent organizer and persuader, having successfully established in Cincinnati in April 1845 America's first professional astronomical observatory. He was an experienced U.S. Army engineer, too, which allowed him to appreciate the need for military earthworks in Northern Kentucky. Mitchel's qualifications made him an ideal choice to make the fortification of Cincinnati a reality.[67]

On September 19, the War Department extended the Department of the Ohio to incorporate the portion of Kentucky within fifteen miles of Cincinnati, which permitted Mitchel to begin construction of earthworks in that region. The next day, General Mitchel ordered Colonel Charles Whittlesey, commander of the newly formed Twentieth Ohio Infantry, to report to Cincinnati for special duty. Whittlesey was a fellow West Pointer and a famed surveyor, archaeologist, geologist and engineer. He and Mitchel had known each other for many years through their shared interest in science. Mitchel explained the dire situation of Cincinnati's defenses, and he put Whittlesey to work rectifying it. Using Lieutenant Poe's map as a guide, Whittlesey personally surveyed the hills surrounding Cincinnati, Covington and Newport. During this survey, he noted the most important locations to place forts and batteries. On September 25, Whittlesey sent a proposal to Mitchel that listed the types of guns needed at each battery site. Mitchel approved, and the next day, Whittlesey requisitioned two hundred men and tools for the job of constructing earthworks. Cincinnati City Council agreed to pay Mitchel $10,000 to build the fortifications, $7,930 to buy cannons from Miles Greenwood and $5,000 to pay for the services of Benjamin Eggleston, the chairman of the Committee for City Defenses. Construction began immediately.[68]

The day after receiving Whittlesey's proposal, General Mitchel spoke to a crowd of about 10,000 citizens at the Fifth Street Market to explain the plan for building batteries on the surrounding hills. The people responded enthusiastically. On September 28, about 275 hired men under Samuel Stokes began work on the three Cincinnati batteries that Whittlesey's three civil engineers—Michael Rittner, Geoffrey Stengel and W.H. Searles—had mapped and designed. The laborers built the Mount Adams Battery in the southern portions of Lots 84 and 87 of Kirby's subdivision, while they constructed the North Battery on the eastern tip of Butcher's Hill (later called Shelter House Hill). The Price's Hill Battery followed a two-platform design that took advantage of Daniel V. Goodhue's quarry and the southern tip of the hill. On the nights of October 1, 2 and 3, Confederate guerrillas fired on the Cincinnati Battery guards stationed at the Price's Hill Battery. This was the first recorded skirmishing near Cincinnati during the war. Nonetheless, by October 3, all three batteries were complete, and their artillery pieces were in place. Secretary of War Simon Cameron visited Cincinnati on October 10 to review the troops at Camp Dennison and Newport Barracks and to inspect the batteries on the Ohio side of the river, and three days later, nearly 5,000 curious citizens visited the battery on Mount Adams.[69]

After the batteries on the Cincinnati side of the river were complete, Stokes's men started construction of the works in Northern Kentucky. On November 9, General Mitchel resigned from his post, and Brigadier General Don Carlos Buell assumed command of the Department of the Ohio, which now included all of Kentucky east of the Cumberland River.

Mount Adams (Observatory Hill) Battery at Cincinnati in October 1861. On one Sunday, over 5,000 curious onlookers visited the fortification. *From* Harper's Weekly *(November 16, 1861).*

Buell moved the departmental headquarters to Louisville, Kentucky. With Mitchel's departure to the front, Colonel Whittlesey stopped all further work on the Northern Kentucky fortifications. Unfortunately, due to lack of time and manpower, of the seventeen Kentucky fortifications that Whittlesey had proposed, only Fort Mitchel and eight batteries were finished by December 1861.[70]

Meanwhile, on November 27, 1861, Dr. John S. Newberry and a group of prominent men from the Queen City, including Robert W. Burnet and George Hoadly, founded the Cincinnati Branch of the U.S. Sanitary Commission. The national organization was the predecessor of the American Red Cross. The commission sent out inspectors to the Union armies in the field to determine their healthcare needs and to ensure that medical supplies were properly allocated to the men. Its volunteers looked out for the comfort of the soldiers and saved thousands of lives.[71]

As a way to raise funds for its cause, the Cincinnati Branch of the U.S. Sanitary Commission staged the Great Western Sanitary Fair in late 1863. Major General William S. Rosecrans and Mayor Leonard Harris led the committee that organized the event. Mozart Hall, Greenwood Hall and two bazaar buildings constructed in the Fifth Street and Sixth Street marketplaces served as exhibit halls for displays of war memorabilia, relics, curiosities and horticultural tools as well as buildings to sell local produce, clothing, merchandise, artwork, crafts, prints, poems and letters. Citizens, politicians, generals, authors and artists donated the items. Entry into the halls required a paid admission. A refreshment saloon at the Palace Garden, formerly the Burbank Barracks located on the west side of Vine Street between Fourth and Fifth Streets, sold overpriced food to guests. In addition, the commission arranged public tours of the two fascinating monitor gunboats *Catawba* and *Oneota* being constructed at the Swift & Niles Boatyard. The Great Western Sanitary Fair opened on December 21, 1863, and lasted until January 4, 1864. By the time the extraordinary fair ended, the commission netted $235,406.62 for its soldiers' relief fund.[72]

The Cincinnati branch produced an amazing list of accomplishments. The commission chartered several hospital steamboats and established a Cincinnati soldiers' home and eight military hospitals scattered throughout Cincinnati and Covington. The branch also distributed $1,079,975.38 worth of supplies and other aid to thousands of sick, wounded and disabled soldiers, all at a total cost of only $18,147.36 incurred over three years of war. As an organization focused on the well-being of soldiers, the Cincinnati contingent of the U.S. Sanitary Commission exceeded expectations.[73]

As the war progressed into the spring of 1862, good news from the battlefront arrived in Cincinnati. Federal victories at Mill Springs, Kentucky, and at Fort Henry and Fort Donelson, Tennessee, brought hope that the Union cause was not lost. However, the situation changed on April 6, 1862, when the Battle of Shiloh (Pittsburg Landing), Tennessee, erupted. The

The Great Western Sanitary Fair at the Fifth Street Market Bazaar building in Cincinnati. The two-week charity event raised $235,400 for the U.S. Sanitary Commission. *From* Harper's Weekly *(January 9, 1864).*

Mary Ann Ball "Mother" Bickerdyke nursed hundreds of sick and wounded soldiers during the Civil War. Her tireless efforts won her the praise of soldiers and officers alike. *Courtesy of the Library of Congress.*

bloody two-day battle resulted in a casualty list that surmounted the total number of casualties from all of America's previous wars combined. The people of the United States had never experienced war at this scale before. The large number of dead and wounded shocked the nation.

Worst of all, the field hospitals were inadequately staffed and equipped to handle the astounding numbers of wounded. Mary Ann Bickerdyke, a forty-four-year-old former Cincinnatian who had joined the Chicago branch of the U.S. Sanitary Commission, witnessed the carnage firsthand at Shiloh. She resolved to redouble her efforts to accomplish the necessary tasks required to properly care for the sick and wounded. She focused on cleanliness first by organizing field laundry teams among volunteers and liberated enslaved persons. She sent letters to the various branches of the commission in the North to obtain for the field hospitals necessary tools and supplies such as kettles, blankets, bandages and tents. Bickerdyke also harried local generals to provide the military orders to allow her and her staff to use government facilities and transportation to get the supplies to the battlefields. Major Generals Ulysses S. Grant and William T. Sherman became well acquainted with Bickerdyke, and over the years, they came to respect her cause. By the end of the war, she had set up over three hundred field hospitals and had attended to the wounded at nineteen different battlefields. The soldiers of the western theater nicknamed her "Mother," and they honored her in May 1865 by allowing her to ride at the head of the Union XV Corps during the Grand Review in Washington, D.C.[74]

When the wounded and sick overcrowded the field hospitals in Tennessee, Grant ordered thousands of the soldiers to be shipped to Northern cities for treatment. Among them were scores of Confederate wounded. Hundreds of citizens of the Queen City, including the Sisters of Charity and Sisters of Mercy, accompanied the chartered steamboats headed for Pittsburg Landing to retrieve the wounded. In preparation to receive the soldiers, Major General Henry Halleck ordered Camp Dennison to be converted into a military hospital. The camp's sixty-seven permanent barracks that teams of carpenters had constructed the previous November served the purpose well.

Greater Cincinnati became a primary military medical center because of its established hospitals. Throughout 1862, temporary hospitals were set up in vacant structures, such as the Fourth Street Military Hospital at 10 East Fourth Street in Cincinnati, the York Street Hospital in the James Caldwell building in Newport and the Odd Fellows Hall and James C. Blick building in Covington. However, after the wounded arrived in Greater Cincinnati on April 16, it became apparent that the hospitals in Cincinnati, Newport and Covington could not handle the extraordinarily numerous casualties. Thus, Camp Dennison General Hospital, which boasted 2,300 beds, accepted the largest numbers of wounded and sick soldiers sent to Greater Cincinnati. The camp continued in this capacity over the remaining years of the war. Camp Dennison reported its peak volume on August 27, 1863, at over 2,900 patients. It was one of the largest and finest hospitals in the North.[75]

Encouraged by early Northern naval successes in both theaters of the war, Congress appropriated $15 million in mid-February 1862 to invest in a new weapon: metal-encased gunboats, called "ironclads." The U.S. Navy had created an Ironclad Board in 1861 to lead the construction efforts behind these innovative, fast, heavily armed riverine vessels. Captain Joseph Brown, a self-taught Missouri steamboat designer and contractor, showed President Lincoln his blueprints for an armored steamboat. Upon Lincoln's recommendation, on April 14, 1862, the Navy Department awarded Brown the contracts for the Cincinnati boatyards to build two of his three ironclad gunboats: the USS *Chillicothe* and the USS *Indianola*. Brown assigned the work to the Cincinnati Marine Railway and Dry Dock Company. He set up his headquarters at the Burnet House and supervised the building of the gunboats.

The *Chillicothe* was the first ironclad to be completed, and it left Cincinnati on August 10. The *Indianola* followed its counterpart on January 1, 1863. Their successful development ultimately led to more work for Brown. Union navy rear admiral David D. Porter would trust Brown's gunboats so much that Porter gave many conversion contracts to him over the course of the Civil War. In fact, by the end of the conflict, Brown had converted forty-six of the sixty-six tinclads (thinly iron-plated gunboats) that the U.S. Navy had sponsored during the war. Brown performed the refitting work at the Cincinnati Marine Railway, whose achievement made the boatyard one of the most important construction yards in the U.S. Navy's history.[76]

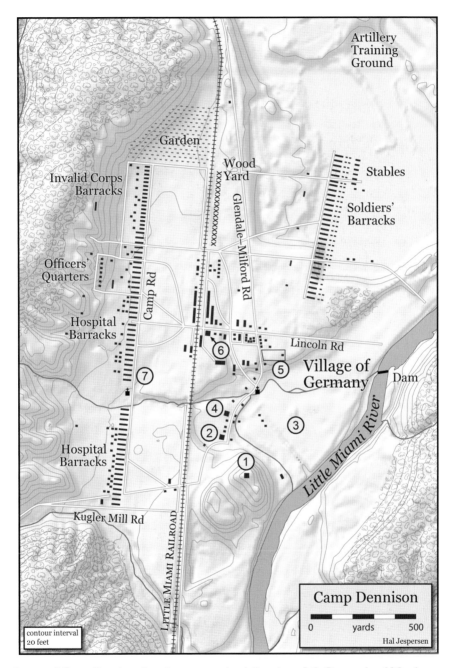

Layout of Camp Dennison, based on a survey by civil engineer L.S. Cotton, dated March 18, 1862. Today's remains: (1) water reservoir, (2) guard house, (3) paper mill and sawmill site initially occupied by the soldiers, (4) temporary camp headquarters [Waldschmidt House], (5) camp cemetery, (6) permanent camp headquarters, (7) camp road. *Author's collection.*

Confederate brigadier general John Hunt Morgan and his men conducted four raids in the vicinity of Cincinnati that created panic among its citizens. He was killed at Greeneville, Tennessee, on September 4, 1864. *Courtesy of the Library of Congress.*

Confederate victories in the eastern theater created distressing headlines at the home front during the summer of 1862. In addition, a new threat emerged that would catch Cincinnati by surprise. Confederate colonel John Hunt Morgan from Lexington, Kentucky, commanded a group of experienced cavalry raiders who operated primarily behind Union lines in central Tennessee and Kentucky. Cincinnatians referred to these cavalrymen as "guerrillas," a term that came with a negative connotation in that era.

In July, Morgan executed a raid on Central Kentucky's Union outposts that caused panic among the citizens of Greater Cincinnati. Cincinnati and Covington authorities called up their home guards to protect the cities, and they sent troops, including Cincinnati's police and firemen, south to engage the Confederate raiders. However, no troops were available to man the fortifications in Northern Kentucky. During the exciting period of July 17– 18, Morgan reached as close to the Queen City as the cities of Cynthiana, Paris and Lexington in Kentucky. At each place, he defeated the Union defenders and captured hundreds of prisoners, many of whom were from Cincinnati. Having no intentions of attacking Cincinnati with his small force, Morgan retreated into Tennessee within a few days. Nonetheless, Morgan's incursion highlighted the city's vulnerability to Confederate attack.[77]

No ethnic groups felt the loss of trade with the South more than Cincinnati's Irish Americans and African Americans. The steamboat industry depended highly on the transport of goods to New Orleans, but with the Mississippi River closed to commerce, the river shipments dropped 27 percent, and fewer stevedores were needed. Poor Irish Americans and African Americans comprised most of the levee workers who competed with one another for river work. The Irish Americans wanted to dominate the levees, and both ethnic groups lived with increased frustration over the lack of jobs.

That frustration boiled and finally exploded on July 10, when a brawl between White and Black dockworkers broke out near the wharves. The fight grew into a riot that required the Cincinnati police to intervene and stop it. However, on July 13, as the city's tensions rose from John Hunt Morgan's raid, the rioting renewed with a fury. Violence and destruction permeated the lower city, particularly around the Bucktown neighborhood and along the waterfront. The riot finally subsided on July 18 after home guardsmen were called out to patrol the streets and arrest perpetrators. It had been the largest race riot in Cincinnati since the mid-antebellum years.[78]

5

"Citizens for Labor, Soldiers for Battle"

The success of Morgan's raid in Kentucky helped convince General Braxton Bragg, commander of the Confederate Army of Mississippi at Chattanooga, Tennessee, to invade the Bluegrass State. He hoped to win new recruits for his army and take back territory that had been lost to the Federals earlier in the year. The largest Union army defending the state was the Army of the Ohio under Major General Don Carlos Buell. Bragg coordinated his movement with Major General Edmund Kirby Smith's Confederate forces stationed at Knoxville, Tennessee.

The Kentucky Campaign began when Kirby Smith's division entered Kentucky in late August 1862, and on the thirtieth, Smith attacked Union major general William "Bull" Nelson's division at Richmond, Kentucky, only ninety miles from Cincinnati. Smith's Confederates emerged amazingly victorious. Practically the entire Union force was killed, wounded or captured. A division of Confederate troops under Brigadier General Henry Heth joined Smith's command the next day. Together, they headed north and captured the cities of Lexington and Frankfort in the Department of the Ohio.[79]

Although the Department of the Ohio had been dissolved on March 11, 1862, it was reinstated on August 19 to encompass Michigan and Wisconsin in addition to Ohio, Indiana, Illinois, and the portion of Kentucky east of the Tennessee River. The department's newly appointed commander was Brevet Major General Horatio Gouverneur Wright. The forty-two-year-

Union major general Horatio Gouverneur Wright was the fifth commander of the Department of the Ohio. He later led the VI Corps of the Army of the Potomac. *Courtesy of the Library of Congress.*

old West Point graduate had spent much of his career with the Corps of Engineers in Florida. During the first year of the Civil War, he served as an engineer at the battles of First Bull Run, Virginia, and at Port Royal, South Carolina. After Wright led troops in the disastrous Battle of Secessionville, South Carolina, the War Department assigned him to the Department of the Ohio. He had just settled down into his headquarters at Cincinnati when General Smith invaded eastern Kentucky, within the new boundaries of Wright's department.[80]

Wright quickly understood the gravity of the situation facing him. With the destruction of Nelson's division at Richmond, Kentucky, the door stood wide open for a Confederate attack on Greater Cincinnati. The *Cincinnati Daily Gazette* observed, "The pen of man does not suffice to describe the sudden shock that befell our people when they learned that Confederate forces were received with open arms in Kentucky's Blue Grass....This dreadful war which had seemed so far from this area, suddenly gives promise of moving to our doorsteps....Cincinnati was known to be practically defenseless against such an invasion." Wright ordered Major General Lewis "Lew" Wallace, stationed at Paris, Kentucky, to immediately catch the next train to the Queen City and assume command of its regional defenses.[81]

General Lew Wallace was an intelligent, energetic Hoosier general who had been wrongly accused of mismanaging his division at the Battle of Shiloh. Wallace wanted to wash the stain of that day from his record, and now he had an opportunity to do so. Upon his arrival in Cincinnati, he set up headquarters at the Burnet House. General Wallace quickly cobbled together a large staff of available officers and volunteers, many of whom were merchants, engineers and even entertainers. Wallace also had at his disposal the Chief Topographical Engineer of the Department of the Ohio, Major James Hervey Simpson. Simpson was a famous army engineer from the prewar days who had resigned his colonelcy of the Fourth New Jersey Infantry to rejoin the U.S. Corps of Topographical Engineers. Simpson's experiences from the Peninsula Campaign in Virginia convinced him of the value of fortifications. He called Charles Whittlesey out of retirement to help design the new entrenchments that would be needed to fill the gaps that Whittlesey had left behind in 1861.[82]

On September 2, after meeting with Mayor Hatch and the mayors of Covington and Newport, Wallace declared martial law over the three cities. All businesses were closed. All able-bodied men were to report to their nearest rendezvous location to be sworn in as militiamen to defend their homes. The newspaper headlines read, "The willing will be properly credited—The unwilling will be promptly visited. The principle adopted is 'Citizens for labor; soldiers for battle.'" The *Cincinnati Daily Gazette* added, "TO ARMS! TO ARMS! The time for playing war has passed." Thousands of Greater Cincinnati's citizens from all walks of life and all ages flocked to the defense of the three cities. Men from across Ohio poured into the Queen City. Because these "minute men" were mostly farmers who carried old guns from their homes, the media called these brave home guards the "Squirrel Hunters." By the next morning, the Squirrel Hunters and three Cincinnati regiments totaling fifteen thousand men crossed the Ohio River into Northern Kentucky to begin work on Simpson's earthworks. Over the course of the next two weeks, they would repair old batteries, build new fortifications, dig connecting trenches, construct military roads and fell trees for clearing fields of fire and creating barricades.[83]

Among the Cincinnati volunteers who came to the aid of the city were African American citizens. Initially, the Cincinnati police refused to allow these Black men to freely join the cause. "It's a White man's war," the policemen reasoned. Then, without warning or respect, they forcibly rounded up at gunpoint a contingent of four hundred African Americans to dig entrenchments in Kentucky. The next day, when Wallace heard

Right: Union major general Lewis "Lew" Wallace organized the defense of Cincinnati during the September 1862 crisis. After the war, he authored the world-renowned novel *Ben Hur: A Tale of the Christ* (1880). *Courtesy of the Library of Congress.*

Below: The Squirrel Hunters wait to be fed at the Fifth Street Market House on September 6, 1862. *From* Frank Leslie's Illustrated Newspaper *(September 27, 1862).*

of this outrage, he sent Colonel William M. Dickson of Cincinnati to retrieve the kidnapped men and form a volunteer military unit composed of African American enlisted men led by White and Black officers. The forced laborers of the previous day, spurred by their patriotism and call to duty, joined the new unit to a man. A total of about one thousand Black volunteers formed three regiments that became known collectively as the Black Brigade. They immediately marched to the front to continue their work on the fortifications, and they earned a reputation for being the most productive and reliable among all the soldiers. The Black Brigade was the first paid volunteer Union military unit of African Americans who served at the front during the Civil War.[84]

Wallace also used his political connections to persuade Governor Oliver Morton of Indiana and Governor David Tod of Ohio to rapidly transport to Cincinnati all of the available units from across their states. Dozens of raw volunteer regiments, artillery batteries and Squirrel Hunter units streamed into the city by the four major railroads that served it. Troops arrived from Kentucky, Indiana, Ohio and Michigan. To speed up the flow of troops across the Ohio River, Wallace authorized Wesley Cameron, a Cincinnati architect, to build a pontoon bridge over the waterway. Cameron completed the unthinkable feat in only thirty hours. By September 11, about 60,000 Squirrel Hunters, 2,300 Cincinnati Reserve Militia and 22,500 enlisted soldiers defended the city. After feeding them at the Cincinnati market houses, Wallace sent them across the river into Northern Kentucky to add their weight to the work forces and to provide firepower.

To cover the river fords, the general hastily rounded up sixteen steamboats, including the incomplete ironclad gunboat USS *Indianola*. He assigned them to Captain John A. Duble and loaded them with artillery to patrol the Ohio River. The hodgepodge force of armed boats plying the river, along with artillery and infantrymen ensconced behind earthworks, looked formidable to any enemy.[85]

General Kirby Smith sent Brigadier General Henry Heth with eight thousand seasoned Confederate infantry, artillery and cavalry north from Lexington, Kentucky, with orders to threaten Cincinnati, but not to bring on a general engagement. Heth's objective was to contain the Union forces to Cincinnati so that they would not reinforce Buell's army in Kentucky. On the night of September 9, Heth's scouts arrived before the fortifications in Northern Kentucky. The next morning, Heth personally observed over seventy thousand Union men with guns bristling above extensive lines of earthworks, albeit incomplete. In a matter of three days,

Brigadier General Henry Heth commanded the Confederate force that threatened Cincinnati from September 10 to the 12, 1862. He later gained fame for opening the Battle of Gettysburg, Pennsylvania. *Courtesy of the Library of Congress.*

the Squirrel Hunters had thrown up nearly eight miles of works. Except for some skirmishing on September 10 about a mile south of Fort Mitchel, Heth did little to test the defenses. General Smith ordered Heth to return to Frankfort, and the Confederates withdrew from Northern Kentucky on the night of September 11.[86]

The so-called "Siege of Cincinnati" was over. In celebration, nearly seventy thousand men, accompanied by multiple regimental bands, sang "John Brown's Body" in unison. The music could be heard over the hills and valleys of Northern Kentucky for miles. The city rejoiced as the Squirrel Hunters and other soldiers paraded through the crowd-lined streets of Cincinnati. They marched in columns of fours over the pontoon bridge. It was an awesome scene. On September 14, the *Cincinnati Gazette* wrote, "Thanks to the promptitude of Generals Wright and Wallace, and the patriotism, courage and valor of the people, the Rebel movement toward Cincinnati has been frustrated and rolled back....Cincinnati is a large and wealthy city, attractive as a prize to the enemy. Hereafter, it must not be undefended as hitherto; we must have troops for home defense."[87]

Major Simpson tried to do just that. By November 1862, Simpson and as many as 1,780 hired men finished twelve forts and batteries in addition to the nine that Whittlesey had built the year before. The laborers completed the line of batteries, forts and connecting entrenchments of Northern Kentucky in November 1863. Promoted to lieutenant colonel, Simpson remained chief engineer of the defenses for the duration of the Civil War. Although he managed to mount a proper number of artillery pieces for a majority of the thirty batteries and forts, he struggled to maintain even a regiment-sized guard for the eight-mile defensive line. Experienced troops were needed elsewhere. Simpson improvised by borrowing convalescents from the tri-state's hospitals to serve as his guards and artillerists. However,

Union lieutenant colonel James Hervey Simpson served as chief topographical engineer for the Department of the Ohio. Before the war, he was famous for surveying the route that the Forty-Niners followed to the California gold fields. *Courtesy of the Library of Congress.*

his plan failed to stop Rebel guerrillas from spiking several of the guns and burning barracks at the Northern Kentucky fortifications. Without the necessary troops, Cincinnati stood vulnerable to Confederate raiders throughout the war.[88]

COPPERHEADS AND RAIDERS

Soon after the Battle of Antietam, Maryland, on September 17, 1862, President Abraham Lincoln issued his highly controversial Emancipation Proclamation, which went into effect on January 1, 1863. The proclamation permanently freed all enslaved peoples found within the seceded Confederate states; however, the border states, such as Kentucky, were immune to the law. In fact, Newport, Kentucky, continued to enforce the Fugitive Slave Act for the rest of the war, until the Thirteenth Amendment of the U.S. Constitution passed. Kentuckians generally opposed the proclamation, but Cincinnatians expressed mixed feelings.

One of the stipulations of the Emancipation Proclamation indicated that the Union army could formally recruit African Americans into its ranks. In February, Governor John A. Andrew of Massachusetts called for African Americans to form new "colored" regiments in his state. Cincinnati's Black residents read about the call in the newspapers, and many of these men, some veterans of the Black Brigade, traveled to Massachusetts to sign up. They would help form the 54th and 55th Massachusetts infantry regiments. From July through November, several hundred Black Cincinnatians joined Ohio's first African American regiment, designated the 127th Ohio Infantry. It was later renamed to the 5th U.S. Colored Infantry. It saw severe combat in Virginia in 1864, when the regiment received four Congressional Medals of Honor from its soldiers' extraordinary bravery at the Battle of Chaffin's Farm.[89]

On March 12, 1863, the U.S. Senate refused Horatio Wright's July 1862 appointment to the rank of major general. Wright was reduced to a brigadier general in command of the Department of the Ohio. Wright responded to the decision with a communication to Army Chief of Staff G.W. Cullum:

> *The recent action of the Senate, in refusing my confirmation as major-general, of which I presume there is no doubt, can be looked upon only as a condemnation of my administration of the affairs of this department, and will naturally occasion in the public mind a want of confidence which will seriously impair my usefulness in my present position. In this view of the case, I feel bound to suggest to the military authorities at Washington my removal from this command, by the assignment thereto of someone who shall fully command the confidence of the people and the troops in the department, and to ask that no unnecessary delay be permitted in adopting this suggestion.*[90]

Accordingly, the War Department ordered Wright to leave his Cincinnati post and report to Virginia for a field assignment in the Army of the Potomac. President Abraham Lincoln appointed a Rhode Island businessman and West Point graduate, Major General Ambrose E. Burnside, to fill the vacated position. Burnside had been praised as a national hero for his success in the Roanoke Island campaign in January 1862. However, in December, Burnside's failure as the leader of the Army of the Potomac at the Battle of Fredericksburg, Virginia, and in the disastrous "Mud March" that followed, had forced Lincoln to relieve the general of command. Nevertheless, Lincoln chose Burnside to head the Department of the Ohio during its most intense political turmoil.[91]

When Burnside arrived at Cincinnati headquarters on March 24, 1863, Wright briefed him on the situation in the department. He informed Burnside of the growing number of forays by Confederate raiders in Kentucky and that a Confederate attack on the Bluegrass State was imminent. He also indicated that he had few men in the department to defend its borders. However, Wright's biggest concerns at the moment were the Copperheads and the public's resistance to the recently passed Federal draft.[92]

The mounting casualties of the Civil War and the institution of the Emancipation Proclamation allowed the anti-war politicians, known as Peace Democrats or "Copperheads," to gain support throughout the North. Southwest Ohio was a stronghold for the Copperheads, who were led by the vociferous U.S. representative Clement L. Vallandigham from Dayton, Ohio. Only three days before Burnside's arrival, Vallandigham

Left: Union sergeant Powhatan Beaty was a veteran of Cincinnati's Black Brigade before he enlisted into Company G, Fifth U.S. Colored Infantry. He received the Medal of Honor for his actions at the Battle of Chaffin's Farm, Virginia. *Courtesy of the Library of Congress.*

Right: Union major general Ambrose E. Burnside, the sixth commander of the Department of the Ohio, is best known for giving the English language the word *sideburns* from his unusual whiskers. *Courtesy of the Library of Congress.*

and several Peace Democrat politicians, including Cincinnati's U.S. representative George H. Pendleton, had held a large political rally at Hamilton, Ohio. Thousands had come out to hear speeches about making peace with the Confederacy, ending the war through compromise and removing the Republican government from office due to their "attempt… to perpetuate their existence upon unlawful grounds." Many Northerners considered this public rhetoric treasonous, but the First Amendment of the U.S. Constitution allows such talk.[93]

Nonetheless, in wartime, laws are often undermined. Burnside believed that any criticism of President Lincoln's policies was traitorous because it gave encouragement to the Confederate cause. On March 30, Burnside wrote to Secretary of War Edwin Stanton, "There are some persons in this town [Cincinnati] who want to go south and who ought to be sent there, for they are doing harm here, and yet there is no positive proof or excuse for arresting them.…I think it is important that they should be sent, and the earlier the better. Can I have an answer from this tonight?" Stanton approved their removal. Burnside was determined to stop the Copperhead movement in any way possible, and he would target its leader next.[94]

In the meantime, Cincinnati's critical April mayoral election proceeded as normal. The winner was thirty-seven-year-old Leonard A. Harris, the former colonel of the battle-hardened Second Ohio Infantry and a veteran brigade commander at the Battle of Perryville, Kentucky. He had resigned from the army the previous December because of poor health. Harris ran as a pro-war Republican and defeated the Copperhead Democratic candidate Joseph Torrence.

The people of Cincinnati grew to love Harris during his two terms as their mayor. His greatest accomplishment was the administration of discipline and political tolerance into the Cincinnati police force. The Society of the Army of the Cumberland equally remembered Harris with great praise. "His conduct in that office [of mayor] was marked by the same vigor and efficiency as had distinguished him on the field," the society recalled. "So highly were his services appreciated, that he was presented a house, in which he lived to the day of his death." Harris also proposed the law that resulted in the formation of the "Hundred Days' Men," a series of regiments recruited in 1864 to guard Federal lines of communication against Confederate raiders. As colonel and acting mayor, he led one of those Hundred Days regiments, the 137th Ohio Infantry, into service in Maryland. In 1866, President Andrew Johnson appointed him collector of internal revenue in Cincinnati.[95]

The election of Harris as Cincinnati's mayor bolstered Burnside's scheme to rid his department of Vallandigham. On April 13, Burnside issued General Orders Number 38, which stated: "The habit of declaring sympathy for the enemy will not be allowed in this department. Persons committing such offenses will be at once arrested, with a view to being tried as above stated or sent beyond our lines into the lines of their friends. It must be understood that treason expressed or implied will not be tolerated in this

Union colonel Leonard A. Harris, the second of Cincinnati's mayors in the Civil War. He ably led a brigade in the heavy fighting at Perryville, Kentucky. *From* Portraits of Companions of the Commandery of the State of Ohio MOLLUS *(1893)*.

department." Vallandigham responded defiantly on May 1 with a two-hour speech at Mount Vernon, Ohio, in which he criticized Burnside and termed the general's order as a "base usurpation of authority." The congressman encouraged Ohioans to resist the order through their votes.[96]

Vallandigham's speech at Mount Vernon was the last straw. Burnside ordered the congressman's arrest in Dayton on May 4. Soldiers took Vallandigham into custody the next morning and imprisoned him in Kemper Barracks on Second Street, between Sycamore Street and Broadway in Cincinnati. His supporters in Dayton rioted and burned down several buildings there before Burnside quelled the violence with troops from the 117th Ohio Infantry. A few days later, a military court tried Vallandigham for his anti-government words spoken at Mount Vernon. George Pendleton and George Pugh defended him, but the evidence was too damning. The commission convicted Vallandigham on May 7 and sentenced him to be incarcerated at Fort Warren near Boston, Massachusetts, for the duration of the war. Before Vallandigham could be moved, Lincoln commuted his sentence to banishment to Confederate lines in Tennessee.[97]

Vallandigham traveled from the South to Canada later in the year and ran his campaign for Ohio governor from there. He lost handily to the War Democrat candidate John Brough in the October 1863 elections. Burnside's decisive actions surrounding Orders Number 38 not only destroyed the momentum of the Copperhead movement in Cincinnati and the rest of the Midwest but also quelled any wholesale opposition to abide by the Federal draft within his department. The Copperheads had been the draft's largest detractors. Without their voice, military conscription remained relatively safe.[98]

The Queen City would experience one more major Confederate threat before the war ended. In the opening days of July, Cincinnatians rejoiced over the news of the major Union victories at Gettysburg, Pennsylvania, and Vicksburg, Mississippi. It was at this same time that Brigadier General John Hunt Morgan led 2,460 seasoned Confederate cavalrymen with four artillery pieces on a raid through Kentucky, Indiana, and Ohio. Burnside assigned command of the Union cavalry division chasing them to Brigadier General Edward Hobson, a battle-hardened Kentucky cavalry commander known for his determination and leadership skill. What resulted was a campaign known as the Indiana-Ohio Raid, or the Great Raid. Traversing 947 miles, it was the longest cavalry raid of the Civil War.[99]

On July 8, Morgan and his men crossed the Ohio River just south of Corydon, Indiana. General Burnside and the Department of the Ohio sprang into overdrive. Indiana's governor Oliver Morton called up sixty-five thousand militia and regular troops to stop the Confederate raider, but Morgan's troopers outpaced them, and by July 12, the Confederates reached Sunman, Indiana, only eighteen miles from the Ohio border. After discussing the critical situation with Ohio governor David Tod, General Burnside declared martial law in Cincinnati, Covington, and Newport. Simultaneously, the governor called out the Ohio militia from thirty-two counties. Nearly sixty thousand Buckeye militiamen and regulars would be mobilized to confront Morgan's raiders.[100]

Mirroring the September 1862 crisis, Cincinnatians responded to Tod's call in great numbers. By the time Morgan's two thousand cavalrymen entered Ohio on July 13 at the village of Harrison, nearly ten thousand citizens had gathered in downtown Cincinnati and its neighboring city to the north, Hamilton. However, Burnside and his District of Ohio commander, Jacob D. Cox, failed to halt Morgan's lightning-speed movements. Purposefully avoiding the cities, the Confederate general led his division on a daring eighty-five-mile, thirty-five-hour night ride from Sunman in Dearborn County, across northern Hamilton County and through Clermont County to Williamsburg, Ohio. Hobson's exhausted Union cavalrymen with artillery lagged eight hours in rear of Morgan's soldiers. During the night march around Cincinnati, Morgan's troopers fought a small skirmish at Miamitown and then threatened Camp Dennison the next morning. However, thanks to camp commander George W. Neff's gallant defense at the Little Miami Railroad Bridge skirmish, the Confederates continued on their eastward journey without causing any damage.[101]

Mayor Harris formed a volunteer cavalry company to chase the raiders, while over 1,000 Union cavalrymen under Brigadier General Henry Judah departed Cincinnati on steamboats to head off the invaders. At the same time, Lieutenant Commander LeRoy Fitch of the Mississippi Squadron led several gunboats upstream to prevent Morgan's crossing of the Ohio River. Judah, Hobson and Fitch eventually engaged Morgan's men at the decisive Battle of Buffington Island, Ohio, on July 19, when nearly half of the Confederate force was destroyed. Morgan escaped with the remnants, but he and 364 of his men were finally captured near West Point, Ohio, on July 26. Union cavalry organized by Major George Rue at Covington Barracks were responsible for the capture.[102]

General Morgan, his officers and most of the Confederate enlisted men captured in Ohio were shipped by steamboat and train to Cincinnati, and from there, they were transferred to Northern prison camps. Thousands

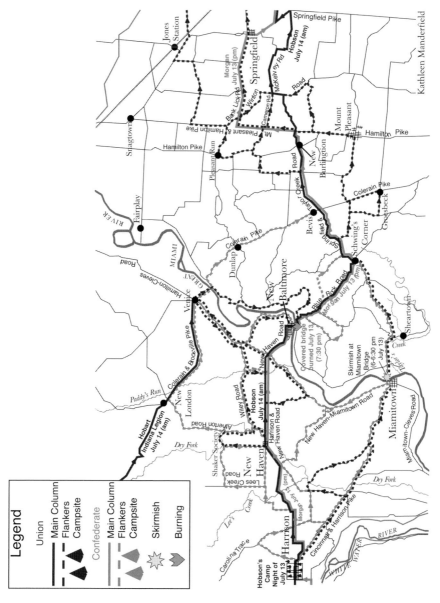

Map of Morgan's and Hobson's routes through western Hamilton County, Ohio, July 13–14, 1863. *Author's collection.*

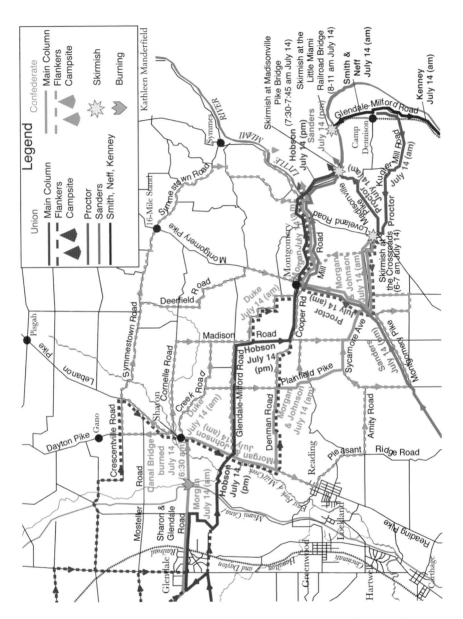

Map of Morgan's route and the paths of his Union pursuers in eastern Hamilton County, July 14, 1863. *Author's collection.*

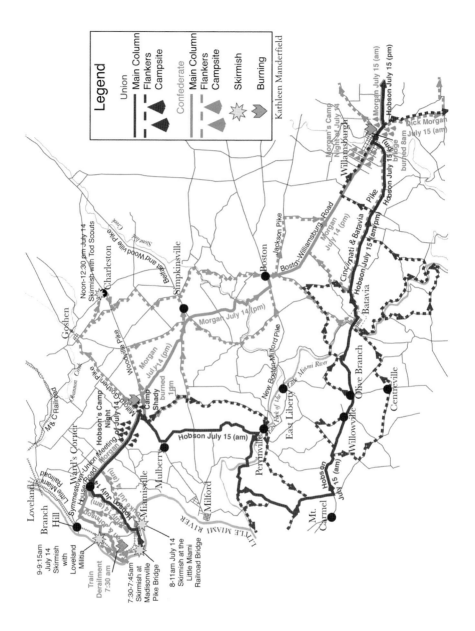

Map of Morgan's and Hobson's routes through Clermont County, Ohio, July 14–15, 1863.
Author's collection.

of spectators met the raiders at the public landing. Most Cincinnatians, angered by the way Morgan's troopers had confiscated horses and other private property along their path, jeered and ridiculed the soldiers as they were marched to the City Prison situated at the northeast quadrant of Ninth Street, between Plum Street and Central Avenue. However, many citizens cheered the raiders, for they had achieved the remarkable feat of diverting nearly 130,000 Federal troops over the course of three weeks. The raid had also delayed Burnside's launch of his newly reformed Army of the Ohio into East Tennessee. After shipping Morgan and his troopers off to prisons across the North, Burnside was able to begin his field work with the Army of the Ohio in late August.[103]

While Burnside led the Army of the Ohio in the Knoxville Campaign in Tennessee, the Department of the Ohio needed a new commander to accept its daily responsibilities. On November 16, the War Department ordered Major General John G. Foster to fill the seat. Forty-year-old Foster had graduated from West Point in the same class as George B. McClellan. Foster had served under Burnside in North Carolina and in Tennessee, and he was Burnside's choice to be his successor. The department added to its territory the eastern section of Tennessee occupied by Burnside's Army of the Ohio. Foster set up his headquarters in Cincinnati, but he would not stay in the Queen City for long. Foster was severely injured when his horse fell on top of him, and he resigned from his command in February 1864 to recover.[104]

The War Department decided to detach the Department of the Ohio with the Union XXIII Corps (Army of the Ohio) and create a new military district called the Northern Department, effective January 12, 1864. It consisted of the states of Ohio, Michigan, Indiana and Illinois, and its headquarters moved to Columbus, Ohio. Major General Samuel Peter Heintzelman, a West Pointer who had seen extensive combat in Virginia for most of the war, was named the Northern Department's first leader. During his tenure as department commander, he often worked out of the Spencer House in Cincinnati. On October 1, 1864, Major General Joseph Hooker took charge of the department after Major General William Sherman relieved him of command of the XX Corps near Atlanta, Georgia. Hooker was the Army of the Potomac's former commander whom General Robert E. Lee had disgraced at the Battle of Chancellorsville, Virginia, in May 1863. Hooker moved the department headquarters to 114 West Fourth Street in Cincinnati. Fate intervened for "Fighting Joe" while he was stationed in the Queen City. Here, Hooker met the prominent Olivia Groesbeck, sister of former U.S. congressman William S. Groesbeck. Fifty-year-old Joseph courted forty-year-old Olivia while he performed his military duties in the Queen City. They married on October 3, 1865, at Olivia's home at the northeast corner of Seventh and Plum Streets in Cincinnati.[105]

THE SLAUGHTER HAS ENDED

B y April 1864, two Union generals with Cincinnati connections had become household names in the United States: Lieutenant General Ulysses S. Grant and Major General William T. Sherman. President Lincoln placed his hope and trust in these two men to bring a swift end to the Civil War. They had rightly earned that trust through their successful war records in the West. In March, Lincoln promoted Grant to lieutenant general with the role of general-in-chief of all Union armies in the field, and Sherman inherited from Grant the command of the major armies in the western theater. The two stalwarts met at the Burnet House in Cincinnati on March 20 to plan the spring campaigns. Sherman recalled his meeting with Grant. "He was to go for Lee," Sherman wrote. "And I was to go for Joe Johnston. That was the plan."[106]

The Federals' successful war effort had allowed Cincinnati's economy to recover from its collapse in 1861. By late 1862, nearly all the city's manufacturing facilities and foodstuff suppliers were in full production, serving not only the Union army but also the foreign countries that had relied on the South for certain goods. Many of these companies expanded over the course of the war as the growing Union armies created increased demand and profitability. The growth of Cincinnati's economy during the war is seen in the annual chamber of commerce records in Table 2.[107]

From May 1861 through June 1865, the Cincinnati Quartermaster Depot supplied the Union army with 345,823 uniform coats, 1,473,603 uniform trousers, 2,350,000 shirts, 5,000,000 stockings, 1,317,000 canteens,

Union lieutenant general Ulysses S. Grant (*left*) often performed business in Cincinnati as a young man. Major General William T. Sherman (*right*) sent his daughter to school in Reading, Hamilton County, Ohio. Together, these men successfully ended the Civil War. *Courtesy of Library of Congress.*

1,008,000 haversacks and many more items. The city manufactured the most military wagons and ambulances in the North. James C.C. Holenshade's company produced as many as 6,000 army wagons per year, along with pickaxes, wheelbarrows, camp kettles, mess pans, bolts and tin cups. As Cincinnati grew into the largest supplier of the Union armies in the western theater, the U.S. Quartermaster's facilities grew with it. By 1864, the Quartermaster Department owned or leased dozens of houses, buildings and lots in Cincinnati and in Covington, Kentucky.

Here follows a list with brief descriptions of the U.S. Quartermaster Department structures in both cities as of July 1864. Accompanying the 1864 quartermaster depot report was a Cincinnati street map that marked the exact locations of the buildings, which allowed each location to be translated into GPS coordinates. Street numbers are given as Civil War–era numbers, not modern ones. All address numbers within Cincinnati's city limits changed in 1895.

TABLE 2

TOTAL VALUE OF CINCINNATI'S IMPORTS AND EXPORTS (FINANCIAL YEAR STARTING SEPTEMBER 1 AND ENDING AUGUST 31)		
FINANCIAL YEAR	IMPORTS (U.S. DOLLARS)	EXPORTS (U.S. DOLLARS)
1858–1859	$94,213,247	$66,007,707
1860–1861	$90,198,136	$67,123,126
1861–1862	$103,292,893	$76,449,862
1862–1863	$144,189,213	$102,397,171
1863–1864	$389,790,537	$239,079,825
1864–1865	$307,552,397	$293,730,317

CINCINNATI'S U.S. QUARTERMASTER BUILDINGS

ORDNANCE WAREHOUSE
Address | 49–51 Sycamore Street
GPS Coordinates | 39.098283°, -84.507521°
Date Built and Primary Construction Material | 1849, brick
Capacity | Not given
Description of Use | Storage of ammunition, artillery ordnance, harness, and other items. Captain Franklin A. Perdue, 104th Ohio Infantry, managed the building in April 1864.

ORDNANCE WAREHOUSE
Address | 17 Sycamore Street
GPS Coordinates | 39.097231°, -84.507196°
Date Built and Primary Construction Material | 1852, brick
Capacity | Not given
Description of Use | Storage of arms and horse equipment. Captain Franklin A. Perdue managed the building in May 1863.

WOODRUFF HOUSE
Address | 91 Sycamore Street, between Third and Fourth Streets
GPS Coordinates | 39.099893°, -84.507920°
Date Built and Primary Construction Material | 1853, brick
Capacity | Not given

Ordnance Warehouse at 49–51 Sycamore Street, Cincinnati, circa mid-1864. *Courtesy of the National Archives.*

Description of Use | Quartermaster's headquarters, paymasters' offices and surgeons' offices. Colonel Thomas Swords, assistant quartermaster general, managed the building in May 1864.

COMMISSARY DEPARTMENT WAREHOUSE AND OFFICE
Address | 32 Vine Street, at Commerce Street
GPS Coordinates | 39.096471°, -84.511519°
Date Built and Primary Construction Material | 1860, brick
Capacity | Not given
Description of Use | Inspection of stored goods. Major Beekman DuBarry, U.S. Army Commissary of Subsistence, managed the building in June 1864.

COMMISSARY DEPARTMENT
Address | Commerce Street, in rear of 32 Vine Street
GPS Coordinates | 39.096471°, -84.511519°
Date Built and Primary Construction Material | 1848, brick
Capacity | Not given
Description of Use | Storage of military provisions. Major Beekman DuBarry managed the building in June 1864.

GARESCHE BARRACKS
Address | Corner of Seventh Street and Sycamore Street
GPS Coordinates | 39.104669°, -84.508600°
Date Built and Primary Construction Material | 1863, rough boards
Capacity | 100 men and officers
Description of Use | Housing for soldiers. The 156th Ohio Infantry occupied the barracks on May 21, 1864.

MEDICAL PURVEYOR'S BUILDING
Address | 71 Vine Street
GPS Coordinates | 39.097517°, -84.512415°
Date Built and Primary Construction Material | 1857; brick
Capacity | Not given
Description of Use | Storage of medicines and hospital supplies. Captain Henry N. Rittenhouse, U.S. Army medical storekeeper, managed the building in April 1864.

INSPECTOR'S WAREHOUSE
Address | Corner of Second and Vine Streets
GPS Coordinates | 39.097366°, -84.511850°
Date Built and Primary Construction Material | 1855, brick
Capacity | Not given
Description of Use | Inspection of clothing, camp equipment and garrison equipment. Captain Charles W. Moulton, assistant quartermaster, managed the building in April 1864.

STOREHOUSE
Address | 116 Third Street
GPS Coordinates | 39.098754°, -84.513740°
Date Built and Primary Construction Material | 1856, brick
Capacity | Not given
Description of Use | Storage of clothing and camp equipment. Opened on November 10, 1863. Captain William H. Gill, U.S. Army military storekeeper, managed the building in May 1864.

GOVERNMENT WAGON YARD
Address | Corner of Eighth and Freeman Streets
GPS Coordinates | 39.103327°, -84.533764°
Date Built and Primary Construction Material | 1864, rough boards
Capacity | Not given
Description of Use | Wagon park. Captain David W. McClung, assistant quartermaster, managed the yard in 1864.

Garesche Barracks at Seventh and Sycamore Streets, Cincinnati, circa mid-1864. It was named in honor of Lieutenant Colonel Julius P. Garesche, who was killed at Stone's River, Tennessee, and whose funeral was held at St. Xavier Church on Sycamore Street. *Courtesy of the National Archives.*

Government Wagon Yard at Eighth and Freeman Streets, Cincinnati, circa mid-1864. *Courtesy of the National Archives.*

TENT MANUFACTORY
Address | Corner of Court and Sycamore Streets
GPS Coordinates | 39.107107°, -84.509263°
Date Built and Primary Construction Material | 1857, brick
Capacity | Not given
Description of Use | Manufacture of tents and cutting of clothing.
  Captain Charles W. Moulton managed the building in May 1864.

HARNESS DEPARTMENT
Address | 377 Main Street
GPS Coordinates | 39.106083°, -84.511113°
Date Built and Primary Construction Material | 1845, brick
Capacity | Not given
Description of Use | Storage of harness, camp cooking utensils, and
  equipment for horses and mules. Captain David W. McClung managed
  the building in April 1864.

HARNESS WAREHOUSE
Address | 393 Main Street
GPS Coordinates | 39.106547°, -84.511227°
Date Built and Primary Construction Material | 1850, brick
Capacity | Not given
Description of Use | Storage of harness. Captain David W. McClung
  managed the building in May 1864.

MILITARY COMMANDANT HEADQUARTERS
Address | 108 Broadway, at corner of Arch Street
GPS Coordinates | 39.100303°, -84.505773°
Date Built and Primary Construction Material | 1832, brick
Capacity | Not given
Description of Use | Military Commander's headquarters, clerks' offices
  and judge advocate's office. Colonel Thomas Swords managed the
  building in May 1864.

MILITARY HEADQUARTERS STABLE
Address | In rear of 135 Broadway
GPS Coordinates | 39.101327°, -84.507047°
Date Built and Primary Construction Material | 1859, brick
Capacity | Four horses
Description of Use | Shelter for horses. Colonel Thomas Swords managed
  the building in May 1864.

Harness Warehouse at 393 Main Street, Cincinnati, circa mid-1864. *Courtesy of the National Archives.*

Washington Park Hospital
Address | Corner of Fourteenth and Elm Streets, and north of Twelfth Street
GPS Coordinates | 39.109324°, -84.519216°
Date Built and Primary Construction Material | 1837, brick
Capacity | 150 patients
Description of Use | Hospital for sick and wounded soldiers. Surgeon
  Joseph Bird Smith managed the building on July 1, 1862.

Washington Park Hospital Additional Building
Address | Corner of Fourteenth and Elm streets
GPS Coordinates | 39.109324°, -84.519216°
Date Built and Primary Construction Material | Not given
Capacity | Not given
Description of Use | Dead room, dry room, storeroom, tent wards and
  guard room.

WASHINGTON PARK HOSPITAL STABLES
Address | Corner of Fourteenth and Elm Streets
GPS Coordinates | 39.109324°, -84.519216°
Date Built and Primary Construction Material | 1863 and 1864, rough boards
Capacity | Seven hundred horses
Description of Use | Shelter for horses. It contained a dead room, stable
    yard, corn crib, veterinary hospital, forage rooms, saddle room, office
    and room for inspection of horses. Captain David W. McClung managed
    the building in 1864.

LYTLE BARRACKS
Address | Sixth Street below Harriet Street
GPS Coordinates | 39.100117°, -84.538260°
Date Built and Primary Construction Material | 1862, rough boards
Capacity | Seven hundred men and officers in barracks, eleven horses in stable
Description of Use | Prison for deserters and stragglers, stable, lodging for
    men being transferred to and from the army. Included officers' quarters,
    commissary, clerks' rooms, guard room, kitchens and outdoor water
    closets. Closed on October 28, 1865. Companies B, C, E and F of the
    156th Ohio Infantry occupied the barracks on May 21, 1864.

CLOTHING, CAMP AND GARRISON EQUIPAGE WAREHOUSES
Address | 86–90 and 96–106 Second [Columbia] Street
GPS Coordinates | 39.097251°, -84.512684° and 39.097159°,
    -84.513327°
Date Built and Primary Construction Material | 1859, brick
Capacity | Not given
Description of Use | Storage of clothing, camp equipment and garrison
    equipment. Opened on November 10, 1863. Captain William H. Gill
    managed the building in June 1864.

WEST END HOSPITAL BARRACKS
Address | George Street, above Freeman Street
GPS Coordinates | 39.101294°, -84.532657°
Date Built and Primary Construction Material | 1864, rough boards
Capacity | 125 men and officers
Description of Use | Housing for soldiers. The Veteran Reserve Corps
    occupied the building in March 1864.

WEST END HOSPITAL
Address | George Street, above Freeman Street
GPS Coordinates | 39.101294°, -84.532657°

Lytle Barracks at Sixth and Harriet Streets, Cincinnati, circa mid-1864. The complex was named for Brigadier General William H. Lytle, a Cincinnatian who fell at the Battle of Chickamauga, Georgia, on September 20, 1863. *Courtesy of the National Archives.*

West End Hospital (or George Street Hospital), at George and Freeman Streets, Cincinnati, was established in early 1862. This photo was taken circa mid-1864. *Courtesy of the National Archives.*

Date Built and Primary Construction Material | 1846, brick
Capacity | 120 patients
Description of Use | Hospital for sick and wounded soldiers. Opened March 1, 1862, closed on May 21, 1865. Surgeon William H. Gobrecht managed the building in May 1864.

Marine Hospital
Address | Corner of Lock, Sixth and Baum Streets
GPS Coordinates | 39.105420°, -84.503340°
Date Built and Primary Construction Material | 1859, brick
Capacity | 250 patients
Description of Use | Hospital for sick and wounded soldiers. Dr. F. Grabe, U.S. Volunteers, managed the building in September 1861.

Marine Hospital Stable and Drying House
Address | Adjacent to Marine Hospital
GPS Coordinates | 39.105420°, -84.503340°
Date Built and Primary Construction Material | Stable (1859), Drying House and Carpenter Shop (May 1864), rough boards and stone
Capacity | Three horses
Description of Use | Stable—shelter for horses; Drying House—laundry and carpenter's shop.

Marine Hospital Barracks and Barracks Stable
Address | Corner of Sixth and Baum Streets
GPS Coordinates | 39.105420°, -84.503340°
Date Built and Primary Construction Material | 1864, rough boards
Capacity | Ninety men and officers in barracks, four horses in stable
Description of Use | Barracks—Commanding officers' office and housing for soldiers. The Veteran Reserve Corps occupied the building on February 20, 1864. Stable-Shelter for officers' horses.

Marine Hospital Chapel
Address | On grounds of Marine Hospital
GPS Coordinates | 39.105420°, -84.503340°
Date Built and Primary Construction Material | March 16, 1864, wood
Capacity | Not given
Description of Use | Soldiers' chapel.

INSPECTOR'S WAREHOUSE
Address | Corner of Court Street and Broadway
GPS Coordinates | 39.107417°, -84.507413°
Date Built and Primary Construction Material | 1863, brick
Capacity | Not given
Description of Use | Inspection and storage of materials for
    manufacturing soldiers' clothes. Captain Charles W. Moulton managed
    the building in November 1863.

KELTON BARRACKS
Address | Abigail Street
GPS Coordinates | 39.110170°, -84.505252°
Date Built and Primary Construction Material | 1862 and 1863, rough
    boards
Capacity | Four hundred men and officers
Description of Use | Housing for soldiers. Included a coal house. Closed
    on October 28, 1865. Companies D and H of the 156th Ohio Infantry
    occupied the barracks on May 19, 1864.

Kelton Barracks on Abigail Street in Cincinnati, circa mid-1864. The installation was
named for Union assistant adjutant general John C. Kelton of the Department of the
Mississippi. *Courtesy of the National Archives.*

Military Prison
Address | 264 Third Street, between Central Avenue and John Street
GPS Coordinates | 39.097883°, -84.519642°
Date Built and Primary Construction Material | 1846, brick
Capacity | One hundred prisoners
Description of Use | Confinement of political prisoners and rebels. Contained a room for men being transferred to the U.S. Navy, as well as prisoner rooms, guard rooms, bedrooms, hospital room, ration storage room, dining room and outdoor privy. Opened in May 1863.

Fair Bazaars at Fifth Street Marketplace and at Sixth Street Marketplace
Address | Fifth Street Bazaar located on Fifth Street, between Main and Walnut Streets; Sixth Street Bazaar located on Sixth Street, between Plum and Elm Streets
GPS Coordinates | Fifth Street Bazaar: 39.101508°, -84.510554°; Sixth Street Bazaar: 39.101931°, -84.517402°
Date Built and Primary Construction Material | December 1863, rough boards
Capacity | Six hundred men and officers for the Fifth Street Bazaar
Description of Use | Housing for soldiers passing through the city. The Fifth Street Bazaar (formerly "Ladies' Bazaar") included soldiers' quarters, kitchen, storeroom, coal room and storage for old clothes. The Sixth Street Bazaar (formerly "Produce and Merchandise Hall") hosted soldiers' quarters, officers' room, sentinel room, stable and indoor water closet. The Great Western Sanitary Fair occupied the buildings from December 21, 1863, through January 4, 1864, immediately after which the U.S. government confiscated them. The military formally purchased the buildings from the U.S. Sanitary Commission on January 21, 1864.

Warehouses
Address | 86–90 Second Street, between Race and Vine Streets
GPS Coordinates | 39.097251°, -84.512684°
Date Built and Primary Construction Material | 1863, brick
Capacity | Not given
Description of Use | Storage of military goods. Five-story structure contained water hydrants and sinks in the cellar, and on each floor were offices, well holes and hoist ways for loading and unloading goods. Major Beekman DuBarry managed the building in May 1864.

U.S. Commissary Building at 82–84 East Second Street near Broadway, Cincinnati, circa mid-1864. *Courtesy of the National Archives.*

U.S. COMMISSARY BUILDING
Address | 82–84 East Second Street, near Broadway
GPS Coordinates | 39.098376°, -84.505105°
Date Built and Primary Construction Material | 1854, brick
Capacity | Not given
Description of Use | Storage of military goods. Captain Joseph J. Slocum, U.S. Army Commissary of Subsistence, managed the building in June 1864.[108]

COVINGTON'S U.S. QUARTERMASTER BUILDINGS

U.S. QUARTERMASTER BARRACKS, OFFICERS' QUARTERS, AND OFFICES
Address | One mile south of Ohio River, on the east side of the Banklick Pike (Independence Pike)
GPS Coordinates | 39.074178°, -84.504363°
Date Built and Primary Construction Material | September 1862, rough boards

Capacity | Two thousand men and officers
Description of Use | Housing and offices for enlisted men and officers.
The 162nd Ohio Infantry and recruits for the 117th U.S. Colored Infantry
occupied the buildings in August 1864.

U.S. QUARTERMASTER BARRACKS FOR U.S. COLORED TROOPS AND LABORERS
Address | One mile south of Ohio River, on the east side of the Banklick
Pike, adjoining the government stables
GPS Coordinates | 39.074178°, -84.504363°
Date Built and Primary Construction Material | December 1864, rough
boards
Capacity | 120 men
Description of Use | Housing for laborers working in the Northern
Department's Quartermaster Depot. The 124th U.S. Colored Infantry
occupied the buildings in December 1864, and Captain George P.
Webster, assistant quartermaster, managed the barracks complex.

U.S. QUARTERMASTER BLACKSMITH SHOP, WAGON SHOP, PRINT SHOP AND
HARNESS SHOP
Address | One mile south of Ohio River, on the east side of the Banklick
Pike, just south of the quartermaster barracks
GPS Coordinates | 39.074178°, -84.504363°
Date Built and Primary Construction Material | October 1862, rough boards
Capacity | Thirty mechanics
Description of Use | Workshops for mechanics in the employment of the
U.S. government. Captain George P. Webster managed the buildings in
October 1862.

MILITARY PRISON
Address | One mile south of Ohio River, on the east side of the Banklick
Pike
GPS Coordinates | 39.074178°, -84.504363°
Date Built and Primary Construction Material | September 1863, rough boards
Capacity | One hundred officers, guards and prisoners
Description of Use | Confinement of indicted soldiers, political prisoners
and rebels.

GOVERNMENT STABLES
Address | One and one-quarter mile south of Ohio River, on the east side
of the Banklick Pike
GPS Coordinates | 39.074178°, -84.504363°

Date Built and Primary Construction Material | October 1862 (auxiliary sheds were built after July 1864), rough boards
Capacity | 1,500 animals or 1,000 horses
Description of Use | Shelter for horses and mules. Captain George P. Webster's government animals were placed in this facility.

U.S. QUARTERMASTER'S FORAGE HOUSE
Address | Corner of Fourth and Greenup Streets
GPS Coordinates | 39.087666°, -84.507718°
Date Built and Primary Construction Material | Rented December 1, 1862, dressed boards
Capacity | 115,200 cubic feet
Description of Use | Storage of government forage. Captain George P. Webster managed the building in December 1862.

MAIN STREET GENERAL HOSPITAL
Address | Encompassed by Main, Fourth, Third and Bakewell Streets (former Elliston House hotel)
GPS Coordinates | 39.087036°, -84.518099°
Date Built and Primary Construction Material | Rented from Benjamin H. Elliston on March 20, 1862, brick and frame
Capacity | Three hundred patients
Description of Use | Hospital for sick and wounded soldiers. Closed on June 16, 1865.

SEMINARY U.S. GENERAL HOSPITAL
Address | Encompassed by Eleventh, Madison and Robbins Streets and Kentucky Central Railroad (former buildings of the Western Baptist Theological Institute, or Judsonian Seminary)
GPS Coordinates | 39.079114°, -84.509818°
Date Built and Primary Construction Material | Rented from S.A. Haines on September 10, 1862, brick
Capacity | 158 patients
Description of Use | Hospital for sick and wounded soldiers. Closed on May 2, 1865.

GOVERNMENT WAREHOUSE AND STABLE
Address | Corner of Madison and Eighth Streets
GPS Coordinates | 39.082426°, -84.509578°
Date Built and Primary Construction Material | Rented from James C. Blick on September 29, 1863, brick

Capacity | Warehouse—116,368 cubic feet; Stable—24 horses
Description of Use | Storage for quartermaster's goods, clothing, camp
  equipment and garrison equipment. Contained the office of the post
  quartermaster. Captain George P. Webster, assistant quartermaster,
  managed the building in September 1863.[109]

The last Confederate offensive against Cincinnati occurred in early June 1864. Brigadier General John H. Morgan, who had escaped from prison by way of Cincinnati the previous November, led about 2,700 Confederate cavalry and artillery from southwest Virginia into southeast Kentucky on what would be called his "Last Kentucky Raid." When Morgan's men captured Lexington and Georgetown in Kentucky, panic set in among Greater Cincinnatians.

Brigadier General Edward Hobson again came to the rescue of the Queen City. He transported two Ohio Hundred-Days' regiments and a hodgepodge of Kentucky units by train from Covington, Kentucky, to Keller's Bridge north of Cynthiana, Kentucky. The resulting battle with Morgan's troops on June 11 ended in defeat for the outnumbered Union detachment, but Hobson delayed Morgan by several crucial hours that allowed Union brigadier general Stephen Burbridge's veteran two-thousand-man cavalry force to catch up to Morgan the next morning. The Second Battle of Cynthiana practically disabled Morgan's force, and the Confederate general retreated hastily back to Virginia. The enemy never threatened Cincinnati again for the rest of the war.

The crucial presidential election of 1864 weighed heavily on Northerners. The Democrats chose Cincinnatians George B. McClellan and George H. Pendleton to run for president and vice president, respectively. They ran on the platform of seeking peace with the Confederacy through compromise. Their opponents, Abraham Lincoln and his running mate Andrew Johnson, sought to bring the Union together through the total defeat of the Confederacy. Sherman's and Grant's victories in Georgia and Virginia brought renewed hope to Cincinnati's voters, especially to the soldiers, that the war would soon end. On September 24, the largest political rally in Cincinnati's history up to that time was held at several locations in the business district. During the event, Salmon P. Chase and other Republican supporters spoke in front of joyous crowds estimated at 150,000. Cincinnati and Hamilton County showed their faith in Lincoln when they reelected him with 4,148 more votes than McClellan out of the 35,474 votes cast in those jurisdictions. The *Cincinnati Daily Times* quipped, "And so the great Democratic farce of 1864 is over."[110]

U.S. representative George H. Pendleton was a leader of the Copperhead movement in Cincinnati. He ran for vice president with George B. McClellan in the 1864 presidential election. *Courtesy of the Library of Congress.*

While the Civil War raged on distant fronts, Cincinnatians sought escape from its horrors through entertainment. The theater was perhaps the most prized enjoyment of the period. The three main theaters in Cincinnati were Pike's Opera House, Wood's Theater and the National Theater. These establishments served as entertainment houses as well as places for public gatherings. After the firing on Fort Sumter, all the theaters closed their doors until the autumn of 1861. When they reopened, Wood's Theater and Pike's Opera House hosted the city's operas, minstrel shows and variety shows, which proved to be the most popular performances of the era. The National Theater held the only ballet appearances during the war. Counting all the shows the three theaters staged from April 12, 1861, through June 30, 1865, the following is the list of the top-ten plays and their numbers of performances during the Civil War, with no. 1 being the most popular play:

1. *The Seven Sisters* (musical burlesque extravaganza, fifty-nine showings)
2. *Mazeppa* (melodramatic burlesque, fifty-five showings)
3. *Fanchon the Cricket* (romantic melodrama, fifty-two showings)
4. *The French Spy* (melodrama, fifty-one showings)
5. *Camille* (romantic tragedy, thirty-eight showings)

6. *Uncle Tom's Cabin* (historical melodrama, thirty-one showings)
7. *Jack Sheppard* (historical melodrama, thirty showings)
8. *Chimney Corner* (domestic drama, twenty-six showings)
9. *Macbeth* (historical tragedy, twenty-five showings)
10. *Hamlet* (historical tragedy, twenty-four showings)[111]

The war seemed to drag on, but Cincinnatians remained faithful to their cause until the end. Good news finally arrived when the Confederacy's capital city of Richmond, Virginia, formally surrendered on April 2, 1865, to Cincinnatian major general Godfrey Weitzel, who marched his troops into the city the next morning. The beginning of the war's conclusion came on April 9, the day Confederate general Robert E. Lee surrendered the Army of Northern Virginia to Lieutenant General Ulysses S. Grant at Appomattox Court House, Virginia. When the news broke in Cincinnati at 9:30 p.m. that evening, General Hooker gave a speech to a crowd gathered outside of his Fourth Street headquarters. Word quickly spread, and the people of Cincinnati reacted joyously with bonfires, cannon salutes and fireworks. Bells rang from all corners of the city. President Lincoln declared April 14 a day of thanksgiving. On that day, Cincinnati closed its businesses and celebrated the end of the war with religious services, speeches, a ten-mile-long torchlight parade and fireworks at the Fifth Street Market and the courthouse. Just as the festive night wound to a close, Confederate extremist John Wilkes Booth assassinated President Lincoln in Washington, D.C.[112]

The news of Lincoln's death reached Cincinnati in the evening of April 15. Cincinnati mourned its president with black cambric draped on buildings and houses and flags flown at half-mast. Memorial services were observed over the next few days in the Queen City, Covington and Newport. The country was in shock. The bloody war had taken yet another life.[113]

Over 620,000 Union and Confederate lives had been lost in the Civil War. They had given their "last full measure of devotion"[114] to their causes. Congress understood the depth of bravery, courage and devotion that had been required to bring the Civil War to a close. The government recognized a small number of Federal soldiers for their exceptional conduct on the battlefield. The Civil War introduced the first Congressional Medals of Honor in the nation's history, and some of them were given to residents of Cincinnati and Hamilton County. Here is a list of those men and the actions for which they received the country's highest military honor.

ALBERT, CHRISTIAN
Rank and organization | Private, Company G, Forty-Seventh Ohio Infantry.
Action Place and Date | At Vicksburg, Mississippi, May 22, 1863. Entered
   service at —————.
Place of birth | Cincinnati, Ohio.
Date of Issue and Citation | August 10, 1895. Gallantry in the charge of
   the "volunteer storming party."

BEATY, POWHATAN
Rank and organization | First Sergeant, Company G, Fifth U.S. Colored
   Infantry
Action place and date | At Chaffin's Farm, Virginia, September 29, 1864.
   Entered service at Delaware County, Ohio.
Place of birth | Richmond, Virginia
Date of issue and citation | April 6, 1865. Took command of his company,
   all the officers having been killed or wounded, and gallantly led it.

BOYNTON, HENRY V.N.
Rank and organization | Lieutenant Colonel, Thirty-Fifth Ohio Infantry.
Action place and date | At Missionary Ridge, Tennessee, November 25,
   1863. Entered service in Ohio.
Place of birth | West Stockbridge, Massachusetts
Date of issue and citation | November 15, 1893. Led his regiment in the
   face of a severe fire of the enemy, was severely wounded.

BROWN, JOHN H.
Rank and organization | First Sergeant, Company A, Forty-Seventh Ohio
   Infantry.
Action place and date | At Vicksburg, Mississippi, May 19, 1863. Entered
   service at Cincinnati, Ohio.
Place of birth | Boston, Massachusetts
Date of issue and citation | August 24, 1896. Voluntarily carried a verbal
   message from Colonel A.C. Parry to General Hugh Ewing through a
   terrific fire and in plain view of the enemy.

BUHRMAN, HENRY G.
Rank and organization | Private, Company H, Fifty-Fourth Ohio Infantry.
Action place and date | At Vicksburg, Mississippi, May 22, 1863. Entered
   service at —————.
Place of birth | Cincinnati, Ohio.
Date of issue and citation | July 12, 1894. Gallantry in the charge of the
   "volunteer storming party."

COOK, JOHN
Rank and organization | Bugler, Battery B, Fourth U.S. Artillery.
Action place and date | At Antietam, Maryland, September 17, 1862.
  Entered service at Cincinnati, Ohio.
Place of birth | Hamilton County, Ohio.
Date of issue and citation | June 30,1 894. Volunteered at the age of
  fifteen years to act as a cannoneer, and as such volunteer served a gun
  under a terrific fire of the enemy.

DAVIDSON, ANDREW
Rank and organization | Assistant Surgeon, Forty-Seventh Ohio Infantry.
Action place and date | At Vicksburg, Mississippi, May 3, 1863. Entered
  service at Cincinnati, Ohio.
Place of birth | Middlebury, Vermont
Date of issue and citation | October 17, 1892. Voluntarily attempted to
  run the enemy's batteries.

DORMAN, JOHN
Rank and organization | Seaman, U.S. Navy. Born: 1843, Cincinnati,
  Ohio. Accredited to: Ohio. G.O. No.: 32, April 18, 1864.
Citation | Served on board the USS *Carondelet* in various actions of that
  vessel. Carrying out his duties courageously throughout the actions of the
  Carondelet, Dorman, although wounded several times, invariably returned
  to duty and constantly presented an example of devotion to the flag.

FORCE, MANNING F.
Rank and organization | Brigadier General, U.S. Volunteers.
Action place and date | At Atlanta, Georgia, July 22, 1864. Entered service
  at Cincinnati, Ohio.
Place of birth | Washington, D.C.
Date of issue and citation | March 31, 1892. Charged upon the enemy's
  works and, after their capture, defended his position against assaults of
  the enemy until he was severely wounded.

GRAY, JOHN
Rank and organization | Private, Company B, Fifth Ohio Infantry.
Action place and date | At Port Republic, Virginia, June 9, 1862. Entered
  service at: Hamilton County, Ohio.
Place of birth | Scotland.
Date of issue and citation | March 14, 1864. Mounted an artillery horse
  of the enemy and captured a brass six-pound piece in the face of the
  enemy's fire and brought it to the rear.

HOFFMAN, HENRY
Rank and organization | Corporal, Company M, Second Ohio Cavalry.
Action place and date | At Sailors Creek, Va., 6 April 1865. Entered
 service at ———.
Place of birth | Germany
Date of issue and citation | May 3, 1865. Capture of flag.

JARDINE, JAMES
Rank and organization | Sergeant, Company F, Fifty-Fourth Ohio
 Infantry.
Action place and date | At Vicksburg, Mississippi, May 22, 1863. Entered
 service at Hamilton County, Ohio.
Place of birth | Scotland.
Date of issue and citation | April 5, 1894. Gallantry in the charge of the
 "volunteer storming party."

McGINN, EDWARD
Rank and organization | Private, Company F, Fifty-Fourth Ohio Infantry.
Action place and date | At Vicksburg, Mississippi, May 22, 1863. Entered
 service at ———.
Place of birth | New York, New York
Date of issue and citation | June 28, 1894. Gallantry in the charge of the
 "volunteer storming party."

MURPHY, JOHN P.
Rank and organization | Private, Company K, Fifth Ohio Infantry.
Action place and date | At Antietam, Maryland, September 17, 1862.
 Entered service at Cincinnati, Ohio.
Place of birth | Ireland.
Date of issue and citation | September 11, 1866. Capture of flag of
 Thirteenth Alabama Infantry (CSA).

SEARS, CYRUS
Rank and organization | First Lieutenant, Eleventh Battery, Ohio Light
 Artillery.
Action place and date | At Iuka, Mississippi, September 19, 1862. Entered
 service at Cincinnati [mistakenly listed as Bucyrus], Ohio.
Place of birth | Delaware County, New York
Date of issue and citation | December 31, 1892. Although severely
 wounded, fought his battery until the cannoneers and horses were nearly
 all killed or wounded.

TYRRELL, GEORGE WILLIAM
Rank and organization | Corporal, Company H, Fifth Ohio Infantry.
Action place and date | At Resaca, Georgia, May 14, 1864. Entered
  service at Hamilton County, Ohio.
Place of birth | Ireland.
Date of issue and citation | April 7, 1865. Capture of flag.

WELSH, EDWARD
Rank and organization | Private, Company D, Fifty-Fourth Ohio Infantry.
Action place and date | At Vicksburg, Mississippi, May 22, 1863. Entered
  service at Cincinnati, Ohio.
Place of birth | Ireland.
Date of issue and citation | May 11, 1894. Gallantry in the charge of the
  "volunteer storming party."[115]

The last Confederate soldiers surrendered in Indian Territory on June 23, 1865. The bloodiest war in American history had cost the lives of 35,475 Ohioans out of the 319,659 the state had enlisted. Many were the Cincinnatians who never came home. Thousands of Cincinnati soldiers were maimed or paid the ultimate price. Yet their sacrifice had not been in vain. Through their blood, sweat and tears, the Union had been preserved and an enslaved people had been freed. Historian Louis Leonard Tucker appropriately summed up Cincinnati's role in the Civil War in these words:

> *As Lincoln's death marked the end of an epoch in American history, so, too, did it close another chapter in the history of Cincinnati. The Civil War had brought profit to some Cincinnatians, tragedy to others, change to all. For most, if not all, the transcendent consideration was that the slaughter had ended, and for this they were grateful. Equally important, the Union had been preserved.*[116]

Appendix A

U.S. Navy Steamers Built, Refit or Purchased in Cincinnati

Cincinnati played a large role in developing the U.S. Navy on the western rivers. Cincinnati's boatyards, particularly the Marine Railway and Dry Dock, remained busy fulfilling navy contracts throughout the Civil War.

The table that follows contains a list of U.S. Navy–commissioned gunboats, supply boats, transports and other purposed boats that were built, refit, purchased or commissioned in Cincinnati. The name of the vessel,

The USS *Chillicothe* was the first metal-clad river vessel ever built in Cincinnati. *Courtesy of Naval History and Heritage Command, #NH264.*

its alternate name in brackets and its corresponding identification number, if applicable, are given. If the Cincinnati boatyard that performed the building or refitting of the vessel is known, that information is shown. Also presented are the boat's propulsion and class design as well as the vessel's initial complement of artillery.

Numerous Union military steamboats that were purchased, built or refitted in Cincinnati are not listed here because they were not posted onto the "Index of Union Vessels" in the *Official Records of the Union and Confederate Navies*, series II, volume 1. However, Cincinnati newspapers during the Civil War often mentioned these boats in their articles. Among Cincinnati's unlisted Civil War military vessels are the transports *R.J. Lockland* and *Dew Drop* (both built in Cincinnati), the *Cottage* (purchased on November 19, 1862), the *Express* and *Golden Era* (both purchased on March 10, 1863), the *New Transfer* (purchased on November 13, 1863), the *Alice* (purchased on August 16, 1864, and refitted by September 28, 1864), and the *Norse*, *Virginia Barton*, *Lotus*, *D.C. Horton* and *Majestic* (all built or refitted between August 4 and October 12, 1864).[117]

TABLE 3

Vessel Name USS __ (with Vessel Number)	Vessel Description [A, B] (With Design and Use)	Date of Purchase (P), Refit Done (R), Building Complete (B), or Commission (C) in Cincinnati	Builder (B) or Refitter (R) in Cincinnati	Initial Armament [C]
Abeona (No. 32)	STS, I, W (tinclad gunboat)	1864 (B); Dec. 21, 1864 (P); Apr. 10, 1865 (R)	Marine Railway (R)	2 30-pdr-r; 2 24-pdr-sb; 2 12-pdr-r
Argosy (No. 27)	STS, I, W (tinclad gunboat, supply boat)	Mar. 10, 1863 (P)	—	6 24-pdr-sb; 2 12-pdr-r
Carrabasset (No. 49)	SWS, I, W (tinclad gunboat, tugboat, transport)	Dec. 1863 (P); Mar. 1864 (R)	Marine Railway (R)	2 32-pdr-sb; 4 24-pdr-sb
Catawba	SCS, I, W (ironclad monitor)	Apr. 13, 1864 (B); Mar. 1, 1865 (R)	Swift/Niles Works (B); Swift/Niles Works (R)	2 XV-inch-sb

Appendix A

Vessel Name USS __ (with Vessel Number)	Vessel Description [A, B] (With Design and Use)	Date of Purchase (P), Refit Done (R), Building Complete (B), or Commission (C) in Cincinnati	Builder (B) or Refitter (R) in Cincinnati	Initial Armament [C]
Champion II (No. 24) [*Champion No. 4*]	SWS, I, W (tinclad gunboat, tugboat, transport, dispatch boat)	1859 (B); Mar. 10, 1863 (P); Apr. 1863 (R)	Marine Railway (R)	2 30-pdr-r; 1 24-pdr-sb; 2 12-pdr-sb
Chillicothe	SWS, I (ironclad gunboat)	Aug. 10, 1862 (B)	Marine Railway (B)	2 XI-inch-sb
Clara Dolsen [CSS *Clara Dolsen*]	SWS (supply boat, transport, receiving boat)	1861 (B)	John Litherbury (B)	1 32-pdr-sb
Collier (No. 29) [*Allen Collier*]	STS, I, W (tinclad gunboat)	1864 (B); Dec. 7, 1864 (P); Mar. 1865 (R)	Marine Railway (R)	2 20-pdr-r; 1 12-pdr-r; 6 24-pdr-sb
Colossus (No. 25)	STS, I, W (tinclad gunboat)	Dec. 6, 1864 (P); Feb. 1865 (R)	Marine Railway (R)	2 30-pdr-r; 4 24-pdr-sb; 1 12-pdr-sb
Conestoga	SWS, W (timberclad gunboat)	June 1, 1861 (P); June 25, 1861 (R)	S.T. Hambleton (R)	4 32-pdr-sb
Covington (No. 25) [*Covington No. 2*]	SWS, I, W (tinclad gunboat)	1862 (B); Feb. 13, 1863 (P); Mar. 1863 (R)	Marine Railway (R)	4 24-pdr-sb; 2 30-pdr-r; 2 50-pdr-r
Cricket (No. 6) [*Cricket No. 2*]	STS, I, W (tinclad gunboat)	Nov. 14, 1862 (P); Nov. 1862 (R)	Marine Railway (R)	6 24-pdr-sb
Curlew (No. 12) [*Florence*]	STS, I, W (tinclad mortar gunboat)	Dec. 17, 1862 (P); Jan. 25, 1863 (R)	Marine Railway (R)	6 32-pdr-sb; 1 20-pdr-r
Elfin (No. 52) [*W.C. Mann*]	SWS, I, W (tinclad gunboat)	Feb. 23, 1864 (P); Mar. 1864 (R)	Marine Railway (R)	8 24-pdr-sb
Elk (No. 47) [*Countess*]	SWS, I, W (tinclad gunboat)	1863 (B); Dec. 8, 1863 (P); Feb. 1864 (R)	Marine Railway (R)	2 32-pdr-sb; 4 24-pdr-sb

Vessel Name USS __ (with Vessel Number)	Vessel Description [A, B] (With Design and Use)	Date of Purchase (P), Refit Done (R), Building Complete (B), or Commission (C) in Cincinnati	Builder (B) or Refitter (R) in Cincinnati	Initial Armament [C]
Exchange (No. 38)	STS, I, W (tinclad gunboat)	Apr. 6, 1863 (P); Apr. 30, 1863 (R)	Marine Railway (R)	2 32-pdr-sb; 4 24-pdr-sb
Fairy (No. 51) [*Maria*]	STS, I, W (tinclad gunboat, ammunition boat)	1861 (B); Mar. 7, 1864 (P); Mar. 1864 (R)	Marine Railway (R)	8 24-pdr-sb
Fawn (No. 30) [*Fanny Barker*]	STS, I, W (tinclad gunboat, transport, dispatch boat)	1863 (B); Apr. 3, 1863 (P); Apr. 24, 1863 (R)	Marine Railway (R)	6 24-pdr-sb
Forest Rose (No. 9)	STS, I, W (tinclad gunboat, transport, dispatch boat)	Nov. 5, 1862 (P); Nov. 1862 (R)	Marine Railway (R)	2 30-pdr-r; 4 24-pdr-sb
Fort Hindman (No. 13) [*James Thompson; Manitou*]	SWS, I, W (tinclad gunboat, transport)	Apr. 24, 1863 (R)	Marine Railway (R)	6 VIII-inch-sb
Gamage (No. 60) [*Willie Gamage*]	STS, I, W (tinclad gunboat)	1864 (B); Dec. 22, 1864 (P); Mar. 1865 (R)	Marine Railway (R)	6 24-pdr-sb; 2 20-pdr-r; 1 12-pdr-r
Gazelle (No. 50) [*Emma Brown*]	SWS, I, W (tinclad gunboat, dispatch boat)	Nov. 21, 1863 (P); Jan. 1864 (R)	Marine Railway (R)	6 12-pdr-r
General Price [*Laurent Millaudon; Milledon*; CSS *General Sterling Price*]	SWS, W (cottonclad ram, gunboat, transport)	1856 (B)	—	4 IX-inch-sb
Glide I	STS, I, W (tinclad gunboat, supply boat)	Dec. 23, 1862 (R)	Marine Railway (R)	6 24-pdr-sb
Glide II (No. 43)	STS, I, W (tinclad gunboat)	Nov. 30, 1863 (P); Dec. 17, 1863 (R)	Marine Railway (R)	2 32-pdr-sb; 4 24-pdr-sb

APPENDIX A

Vessel Name USS __ (with Vessel Number)	Vessel Description [A, B] (With Design and Use)	Date of Purchase (P), Refit Done (R), Building Complete (B), or Commission (C) in Cincinnati	Builder (B) or Refitter (R) in Cincinnati	Initial Armament [C]
Grampus [*Ion*]	SWS (receiving boat for Cincinnati's navy recruits)	July 22, 1863 (P)	—	none
Great Western	SWS, W (ammunition boat, gunboat, supply boat, receiving boat)	1857 (B); Feb. 10, 1862 (P)	—	1 12-pdr-sb; 1 32-pdr-sb; 1 6-pdr-r
Grossbeak (No. 8) [*Fanny*; *Grosbeak*]	SWS, I, W (tinclad gunboat)	1864 (B); Dec. 3, 1864 (P); Dec. 30, 1864 (R)	Marine Railway (R)	2 20-pdr-r; 2 30-pdr-r; 1 12-pdr-sb; 2 24-pdr-sb
Hastings (No. 15) [*Emma Duncan*]	SWS, I, W (tinclad gunboat, transport)	Mar. 11, 1863 (P)	—	2 30-pdr-r; 2 32-pdr-sb; 4 24-pdr-sb
Huntress (No. 58)	STS, I, W (tinclad gunboat, ammunition boat)	May 1864 (R)	Marine Railway (R)	2 30-pdr-r; 4 24-pdr-sb
Ibex (No. 10) [*Ohio Valley*]	STS, I, W (tinclad gunboat)	Dec. 9, 1864 (P)	—	2 30-pdr-r; 2 12-pdr-r; 4 24-pdr-sb
Indianola	SWS, SCS, I (ironclad gunboat)	Premature launch Sep. 4, 1862 (B); Dec. 27, 1862 (B)	Marine Railway (B)	2 XI-inch-sb; 2 IX-inch-sb
Judge Torrence	SWS (ammunition boat)	1857 (B); Feb. 10, 1862 (P)	—	2 24-pdr-sb
Juliet (No. 4)	STS, I, W (tinclad gunboat, minesweeper)	Nov. 1, 1862 (P)	—	6 24-pdr-sb
Kate (No. 55) [*Kate B. Porter*]	STS, I, W (tinclad gunboat, salvage boat)	Dec. 22, 1864 (P); Mar. 1865 (R)	Marine Railway (R)	2 20-pdr-r; 6 24-pdr-sb; 2 12-pdr-sb

Appendix A

Vessel Name USS __ (with Vessel Number)	Vessel Description [A, B] (With Design and Use)	Date of Purchase (P), Refit Done (R), Building Complete (B), or Commission (C) in Cincinnati	Builder (B) or Refitter (R) in Cincinnati	Initial Armament [C]
Kenwood (No. 14)	STS, I, W (tinclad gunboat, transport)	Apr. 3, 1863 (B); Apr. 1863 (P); Apr. 30, 1863 (R)	Marine Railway (R)	2 32-pdr-sb; 4 24-pdr-sb
Klamath [*Harpy*]	STS, I, W (ironclad monitor)	Apr. 20, 1865 (B)	S.T. Hambleton (B)	2 XI-inch-sb
Kosciusko [*Lancaster*; *Lancaster No. 3*]	SWS, W (ram, gunboat)	1855 (B); Apr. 5, 1862 (P); Apr. 20, 1862 (R)	Marine Railway (R)	1 24-pdr-sb
Lexington	SWS, W (timberclad gunboat)	June 1, 1861 (P); June 25, 1861 (R)	John Litherbury (R)	2 32-pdr-sb; 4 VIII-inch-sb
Linden (No. 10)	SWS, I, W (tinclad gunboat)	Nov. 20, 1862 (P); Dec. 27, 1862 (R)	Marine Railway (R)	6 24-pdr-sb
Maria Denning	SWS (receiving boat, supply boat, transport)	1858 (B)	—	none
Meteor (No. 44) [*Sciota*]	STS, I, W (tinclad gunboat, transport)	1863 (B); Nov. 10, 1863 (P); Dec. 24, 1863 (R)	Marine Railway (R)	2 32-pdr-sb; 4 24-pdr-sb
Mist (No. 26)	STS, I, W (tinclad gunboat)	Dec. 23, 1864 (P)	—	2 20-pdr-r; 4 24-pdr-sb; 1 12-pdr-sb
Monarch	SWS, W (cottonclad ram, minesweeper)	1853 (B); Apr. 20, 1862 (P)	—	1 30-pdr-r; 3 12-pdr-sb
Moose (No. 34) [*Florence Miller No. 2*]	STS, I, W (tinclad gunboat)	March 1863 (B); May 20, 1863 (P); June 15, 1863 (R)	Marine Railway (R)	6 24-pdr-sb
Naiad (No. 53) [*Princess*]	STS, I, W (tinclad gunboat)	Mar. 3, 1864 (P); Mar. 1864 (R)	Marine Railway (R)	8 24-pdr-sb

Vessel Name USS __ (with Vessel Number)	Vessel Description A, B (With Design and Use)	Date of Purchase (P), Refit Done (R), Building Complete (B), or Commission (C) in Cincinnati	Builder (B) or Refitter (R) in Cincinnati	Initial Armament C
Naumkeag (No. 37)	STS, I, W (tinclad gunboat)	1863 (B); Apr. 14, 1863 (P); Apr. 17, 1863 (R)	Marine Railway (R)	2 30-pdr-r; 4 24-pdr-sb
New Era (No. 7)	STS, I, W (tinclad gunboat, transport)	Oct. 27, 1862 (P)	—	6 24-pdr-sb
New National	SWS, W (transport, supply boat, receiving boat, dispatch boat)	1851 (B)	—	1 12-pdr-r
Nyanza (No. 41)	STS, I, W (tinclad gunboat)	Nov. 4, 1863 (P); Dec. 12, 1863 (R)	Marine Railway (R)	6 24-pdr-sb
Nymph (No. 54) [*Cricket No. 3*]	STS, I, W (tinclad gunboat)	1863 (B); Mar. 8, 1864 (P); Apr. 1864 (R)	Marine Railway (R)	12 24-pdr-sb
Oneota	SCS, I, W (ironclad monitor)	May 21, 1864 (B); Mar. 1, 1865 (R)	Swift/Niles Works (B); Swift/Niles Works (R)	2 XV-inch-sb
Oriole (No. 52) [*Florence Miller No. 3*]	STS, I, W (tinclad gunboat, towboat)	1864 (B); Dec. 7, 1864 (P); Mar. 1865 (R)	Marine Railway (R)	2 30-pdr-r; 1 12-pdr-r; 6 24-pdr-sb
Peosta (No. 36)	SWS, I, W (tinclad gunboat)	1857 (B)	—	3 30-pdr-r; 3 32-pdr-sb; 6 24-pdr-sb; 2 12-pdr-sb
Peri (No. 57) [*Reindeer*]	STS, I, W (tinclad gunboat, towboat)	1863 (B); Apr. 30, 1864 (P)	—	1 30-pdr-r; 6 24-pdr-sb
Petrel (No. 5) [*Duchess*]	STS, I, W (tinclad gunboat)	Dec. 13, 1862 (P); Jan. 25, 1863 (R)	Marine Railway (R)	8 24-pdr-sb
Prairie Bird (No. 11) [*Mary Miller*]	STS, I, W (tinclad gunboat)	Dec. 19, 1862 (P); Jan. 25, 1863 (R)	Marine Railway (R)	8 24-pdr-sb

Vessel Name USS __ (with Vessel Number)	Vessel Description [A, B] (With Design and Use)	Date of Purchase (P), Refit Done (R), Building Complete (B), or Commission (C) in Cincinnati	Builder (B) or Refitter (R) in Cincinnati	Initial Armament [C]
Queen City (No. 26) [*Queen City No. 3*]	SWS, I, W (tinclad gunboat)	Jan. 1863 (B); Feb. 13, 1863 (P); Apr. 3, 1863 (R); Apr. 1, 1863 (C)	Marine Railway (R)	2 30-pdr-r; 2 32-pdr-sb; 4 24-pdr-sb
Queen of the West [CSS *Queen of the West*]	SWS, W (cottonclad ram, minesweeper)	1854 (B); Apr. 11, 1862 (P); Apr. 28, 1862 (R)	Marine Railway (R)	1 30-pdr-r; 1 20-pdr-r; 3 12-pdr-sb
Rattler (No. 1) [*Florence Miller*]	STS, I, W (tinclad gunboat)	1862 (B); Nov. 11, 1862 (P); Nov. 1862 (R)	Marine Railway (R)	2 30-pdr-r; 4 24-pdr-sb
Reindeer (No. 35) [*Rachel Miller*]	STS, I, W (tinclad gunboat, dispatch boat, supply boat, transport)	1863 (B); May 21, 1863 (P); June 18, 1863 (R); July 25, 1863 (C)	Marine Railway (R)	6 24-pdr-sb
Rodolph (No. 48)	STS, I, W (tinclad gunboat, minesweeper, tugboat)	1863 (B); Dec. 31, 1863 (P); Feb. 1864 (R)	Marine Railway (R)	2 32-pdr-sb; 4 24-pdr-sb
Romeo (No. 3)	STS, I, W (tinclad gunboat)	Oct. 31, 1862 (P)	—	6 24-pdr-sb
Sibyl (No. 59) [*Hartford*]	SWS, I, W (tinclad gunboat, dispatch boat, towboat)	1863 (B); Apr. 27, 1864 (P); June 8, 1864 (R)	Marine Railway (R)	2 30-pdr-r; 2 24-pdr-sb
Silver Lake (No. 23) [*Silver Lake No. 2*]	STS, I, W (tinclad gunboat)	Nov. 15, 1862 (P); Dec. 24, 1862 (R); Dec. 24, 1862 (C)	Marine Railway (R)	6 24-pdr-sb
Siren (No. 56) [*White Rose*]	STS, I, W (tinclad gunboat, receiving boat)	Mar. 11, 1864 (P); Apr. 1864 (R)	Marine Railway (R)	2 24-pdr-sb

Vessel Name USS __ (with Vessel Number)	Vessel Description [A, B] (With Design and Use)	Date of Purchase (P), Refit Done (R), Building Complete (B), or Commission (C) in Cincinnati	Builder (B) or Refitter (R) in Cincinnati	Initial Armament [C]
Springfield (No. 22) [*W.A. Healy*]	SWS, I, W (tinclad gunboat)	1862 (B); Nov. 19, 1862 (P); Nov. 1862 (R)	Marine Railway (R)	6 24-pdr-sb
Stockdale (No. 42) [*J.T. Stockdale*]	STS, I, W (tinclad gunboat, tugboat)	Nov. 13, 1863 (P); Dec. 16, 1863 (R)	Marine Railway (R)	2 30-pdr-r; 4 24-pdr-sb
Switzerland	SWS, W (ram, transport)	1854 (B); Apr. 11, 1862 (P)	—	10 brass howitzer guns
Tallahatchie (No. 46) [*Cricket No. 4*]	STS, I, W (tinclad gunboat)	1863 (B); Dec. 1863 (P); Feb. 24, 1864 (R)	Marine Railway (R)	2 32-pdr-sb; 4 24-pdr-sb
Tempest (No. 1)	SWS, I, W (tinclad gunboat)	Dec. 29, 1864 (P); Apr. 15, 1865 (R)	Marine Railway (R)	2 30-pdr-r; 2 20-pdr-r; 2 24-pdr-sb; 2 12-pdr-sb
Tensas (No. 39) [*Sam Sugg*; CSS *Tom Sugg*]	SWS, I, W (tinclad gunboat, transport)	1860 (B)	—	2 24-pdr-sb
Tippecanoe [*Vesuvius*; *Wyandotte*]	SCS, I, W (ironclad monitor)	Dec. 22, 1864 (B); Mar. 10, 1865 (R)	John Litherbury (B); John Litherbury (R)	2 XV-inch-sb
Tyler [*A.O. Tyler*]	SWS, W (timberclad gunboat)	1857 (B); June 1, 1861 (P); June 24, 1861 (R)	Marine Railway (R)	1 32-pdr-sb; 6 VIII-inch-sb
Undine (No. 55) [*Ben Gaylord*]	STS, I, W (tinclad gunboat)	1863 (B); Mar. 7, 1864 (P); Apr. 28, 1864 (R); Apr. 1864 (C)	Marine Railway (R)	8 24-pdr-sb

VESSEL NAME USS __ (WITH VESSEL NUMBER)	VESSEL DESCRIPTION [A, B] (WITH DESIGN AND USE)	DATE OF PURCHASE (P), REFIT DONE (R), BUILDING COMPLETE (B), OR COMMISSION (C) IN CINCINNATI	BUILDER (B) OR REFITTER (R) IN CINCINNATI	INITIAL ARMAMENT [C]
Victory (No. 33) [*Banker*]	STS, I, W (tinclad gunboat, dispatch boat)	1863 (B); May 21, 1863 (P); June 21, 1863 (R); July 8, 1863 (C)	Marine Railway (R)	6 24-pdr-sb
Wave (No. 45) [*Argosy No. 2*; CSS *Wave*]	STS, I, W (tinclad gunboat, supply boat)	Nov. 14, 1863 (P); Dec. 24, 1863 (R)	Marine Railway (R)	6 24-pdr-sb
Yuma [*Tempest*]	STS, I, W (ironclad monitor)	May 30, 1865 (B)	S.T. Hambleton (B)	2 XI-inch-sb

[A] Boat Propulsion Type: SWS=side-wheel steamer; STS=stern-wheel steamer; SCS=screw-steamer
[B] Boat Armor: W=wood; I=iron
[C] Cannon Type: r=rifled cannon; sb=smoothbore cannon; pdr=pounder (projectile weight)

Appendix B

CIVIL WAR FORTIFICATIONS
CONSTRUCTED IN GREATER CINCINNATI

From 1861 to 1864, the U.S. Army's engineers designed earthen fortifications to protect Cincinnati from possible land and river attack. In 1861, locally funded work details constructed batteries (earthworks to protect artillery) on the east and west ends of the city on the Buckeye side of the Ohio River. Union strategists intended to use these fortifications to defend the Queen City from enemy gunboats and from land forces approaching along the riverbanks.

From September 1861 through November 1863, thousands of enlisted men and hired crews built earthen batteries, forts, rifle trenches, and military roads on the Bluegrass side of the river. Most of them were constructed during, or within a month after, the September 1862 "Siege of Cincinnati" crisis. This intricate arc of defenses, stretching from Bromley, Kentucky, on the west to modern Fort Thomas, Kentucky, on the east, allowed Union land forces with artillery to defend Cincinnati from Confederate troops who advanced by the six main roads leading from central Kentucky. Those roads, listed from west to east, were as follows: the Burlington Turnpike, Lexington Turnpike, Independence Turnpike, Licking River Turnpike, Alexandria Turnpike and the Ohio River Turnpike. Cincinnati became the heaviest fortified Union city west of the Appalachian Mountains. The enemy never tested its defenses except briefly during the Siege of Cincinnati.

Lieutenant Colonel James Simpson, the chief topographical engineer for the Department of the Ohio, supplied Cincinnati's batteries and forts with large-caliber siege artillery, twelve-pounder field guns and small mortars.

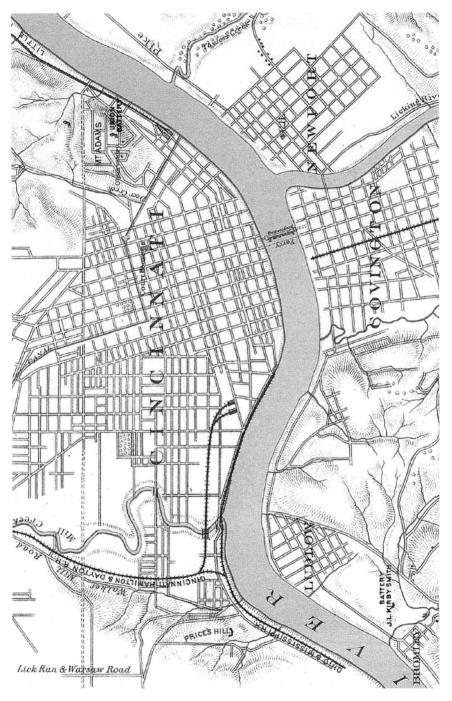

Defenses of Cincinnati on the Ohio side of the Ohio River. *From* Atlas to Accompany the Official Records of the Union and Confederate Armies *(1895), Plate CIII.*

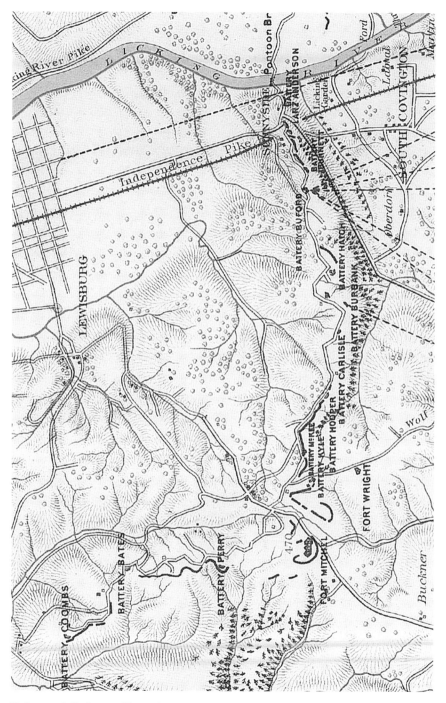

Defenses of Covington, Kentucky, south of the Ohio River. *From* Atlas to Accompany the Official Records of the Union and Confederate Armies *(1895), Plate CIII.*

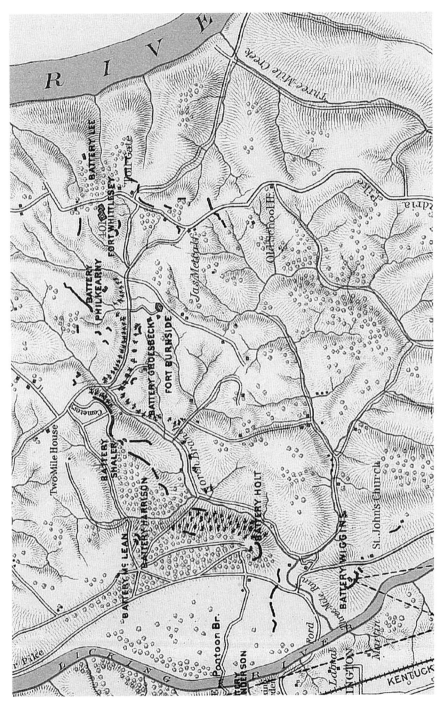

Defenses of Newport, Kentucky, south of the Ohio River. *From* Atlas to Accompany the Official Records of the Union and Confederate Armies *(1895), Plate CIII.*

The artillerists assigned to Cincinnati's defenses never fired these cannons in battle. Nonetheless, Greater Cincinnati residents frequently heard cannon booms throughout the war. Soldiers would often fire the artillery for training, target practice, weaponry tests and Union victory celebrations. The military removed all the guns from Cincinnati's defenses by June 27, 1865, and in December, it sold off the barracks, officers' quarters and cook houses located at the fortifications.

The table that follows provides a summary of all the major batteries and forts erected to defend Greater Cincinnati from Confederate incursions. Each battery's location is also given in GPS coordinates, since only nine of the thirty fortifications show extant traces of their original earthworks. The first column shows the most popular name of each earthwork, along with its alternate names in brackets. The table also presents the person or place for which the fortification was named, the year it was built, the year it was finished, its type of engineering design and its condition as of the year 2020.[118]

TABLE 4

FORTIFICATION NAME	PERSON/PLACE THE FORTIFICATION WAS NAMED AFTER	YEAR BUILDING BEGAN	YEAR BUILDING FINISHED	TYPE OF FORTIFICATION	CONDITION IN 2020, WITH APPROXIMATE GPS LOCATION
Cincinnati (Ohio) Fortifications, Listed from West to East					
Price's Hill Battery: No. 1 [Point of Hill] No. 2 [Quarry]	Price family, who owned much of the hill overlooking the west side of the Mill Creek valley.	1861	1861	Dual-platform battery: No. 1: southern platform, lunette No. 2: northern platform, two-sided redan, with one short side	Destroyed (No. 1: 39.099857°, -84.557761°) (No. 2: 39.100657°, -84.557309°)

Fortification Name	Person/Place The Fortification Was Named After	Year Building Began	Year Building Finished	Type of Fortification	Condition in 2020, With Approximate GPS Location
Mount Adams Battery [Observatory Hill; Catholic Church]	Mount Adams, an eastern downtown Cincinnati neighborhood.	1861	1861	three-sided redan with an extended pan coupe	Destroyed (39.107722°, -84.495850°)
Butcher's Hill Battery [North]	A hill overlooking many of Cincinnati's Deer Creek slaughterhouses.	1861	1861	lunette	Destroyed (39.111275°, -84.494548°)
Covington (Kentucky) Fortifications, Listed from West to East					
Battery J.L. Kirby Smith	Colonel J.L. Kirby Smith, 43rd Ohio Infantry, mortally wounded Oct. 4, 1862, at the Second Battle of Corinth, MS.	1862	by mid-1863	two-sided redan, obtuse angle	Destroyed (39.084575°, -84.554074°)
Battery Coombs [Ludlow Hill]	Major General Leslie Coombs, a Kentucky native, War of 1812 veteran and staunch Unionist.	1861	1861	three-sided redan, with short north flank wall and a traverse jutting forward from the south flank wall	Extant, Devou Park (39.078600°, -84.551598°)
Battery Bates	Brigadier General Joshua H. Bates, retired, organized Ohio volunteers for Sept. 1862 crisis.	1862	by mid-1863	three-sided redan with an extended pan coupe	Extant, Devou Park (39.073521°, -84.544876°)

Fortification Name	Person/Place The Fortification Was Named After	Year Building Began	Year Building Finished	Type of Fortification	Condition in 2020, With Approximate GPS Location
Battery Rich [Riggs; Old Battery]	Stephen Rich, the owner of the property.	1861	1861	two-sided redan	Destroyed (39.068049°, -84.545761°)
Battery Perry [Haystack]	Aaron F. Perry of Cincinnati, agent who organized the local labor force.	1862	by mid-1863	three-sided redan with an extended pan coupe	Destroyed (39.065682°, -84.545294°)
Fort Mitchel	Brigadier General Ormsby M. Mitchel, commander of the Department of the Ohio in 1861, died Oct. 30, 1862, at Beaufort, SC.	1861	early 1862	square fort with four bastions and a ravelin adjoined to the east wall	Destroyed (39.058620°, -84.544348°)
Battery Kyle	Robert Samuel Kyle, the owner of the property.	1862	by mid-1863	two-sided redan, obtuse angle	Destroyed (39.057385°, -84.538064°)
Battery McRae	Captain Alexander McCrae, 3rd U.S. Cavalry, who was killed Feb. 21, 1862, at the Battle of Valverde, NM Territory.	1862	by mid-1863	two-sided redan, with one short side	Destroyed (39.057571°, -84.534439°)
Fort Wright	Major General Horatio G. Wright, U.S. Engineers, commander of the Department of the Ohio in Sept. 1862.	1863	by mid-1863	redoubt, hexagonal in plan but pentagonal in shape, 619 ft. along interior crest	Destroyed (39.053512°, -84.536291°)

Fortification Name	Person/Place The Fortification Was Named After	Year Building Began	Year Building Finished	Type of Fortification	Condition in 2020, With Approximate GPS Location
Battery Hooper [(Old) Kyle's]	William Hooper, who gave money for construction of the fortifications.	1861	1861, modified in 1863	three-sided redan	Subsurface features only, owned by City of Ft. Wright (39.055310°, -84.526968°)
Battery Carlisle	George Carlisle of Cincinnati, who gave money for construction of the fortifications.	1862	end of 1863	three-sided redan	Destroyed (39.055673°, -84.524392°)
Battery Burbank	Lieutenant Colonel Sidney Burbank, 2nd U.S. Infantry, military commander of Cincinnati in September 1862.	1862	end of 1863	three-sided redan with an extended pan coupe and an internal traverse	Destroyed (39.053829°, -84.520545°)
Battery Hatch [Brick Yard; Brick Yard Knob]*	George H. Hatch, the mayor of Cincinnati in September 1862.	1862	end of 1863	two-sided redan, obtuse angle	Extant, private property (39.054677°, -84.517566°)
Battery Buford	Kentucky half-brothers Brigadier General Napoleon B. Buford, a Union infantry commander, and Major General John Buford, a Union cavalry leader who died Dec. 16, 1863.	1863	end of 1863	three-sided redan, closed at the gorge with a stockade	Extant, private property (39.056594°, -84.508639°)

Fortification Name	Person/Place the Fortification Was Named After	Year Building Began	Year Building Finished	Type of Fortification	Condition in 2020, With Approximate GPS Location
Battery Burnet [Quarry]	Robert W. Burnet, president of the Cincinnati Branch of the U.S. Sanitary Commission in September 1862.	1861	1861	a three-sided redan with an extended pan coupe	Extant, private property (39.056732°, -84.506609°)
Battery Larz Anderson [Tunnel]+	Larz Anderson of Cincinnati, who gave money for construction of the fortifications.	1861	1861	lunette	Extant traces, private property (39.057981°, -84.501804°)
Newport (Kentucky) Fortifications, Listed from West to East					
Battery Wiggins [John's Hill; St. John's Catholic Church]	Samuel Wiggins, of Cincinnati, gave money for construction of the fortifications.	1862	end of 1863	unknown, from family description probably three-sided redan with an extended pan coupe and internal traverse	Destroyed (39.049360°, -84.488215°)
Battery Holt [Three Mile Creek; Licking Point; Stuart]	Colonel Joseph Holt, a Kentuckian and President Lincoln's judge advocate general of the U.S. Army.	1861	1861, later modified	rounded earthwork to fit topographic setting, probably based on lunette	Extant, private property (39.055489°, -84.483935°)

APPENDIX B

Fortification Name	Person/Place The Fortification Was Named After	Year Building Began	Year Building Finished	Type of Fortification	Condition in 2020, With Approximate GPS Location
Battery McLean [Upper Locust Hill]	Major Nathaniel H. McLean, assistant adjutant general U.S. Army and chief of staff, Department of the Ohio.	1862	by mid-1863	modified lunette	Destroyed (39.067411°, -84.485229°)
Battery Harrison [Pike Harrison; Lower Locust Hill]	Lieutenant Montgomery Pike Harrison, 5th U.S. Infantry, killed by Native Americans at the Colorado River, Texas, in 1849.	1862	by mid-1863	three-sided redan with an extended pan coupe	Destroyed (39.064859°, -84.482129°)
Battery Shaler	Dr. Nathaniel B. Shaler, the property owner and chief surgeon at Newport Barracks, KY.	1861	1861	three-sided redan and an advanced lunette outwork	Extant, in private cemetery (39.065493°, -84.472967°)
Battery Groesbeck: No. 1 (south) No. 2 (north)	William S. Groesbeck of Cincinnati, who gave money for construction of the fortifications.	1863	by mid-1863	unknown, but likely No. 1 was a lunette, and No. 2 was a modified lunette with a traverse jutting from the east wall; both served as outworks of Fort Burnside	Destroyed (No. 1: 39.061975°, -84.460120°) (No. 2: 39.063264°, -84.460226°)

APPENDIX B

Fortification Name	Person/Place The Fortification Was Named After	Year Building Began	Year Building Finished	Type of Fortification	Condition in 2020, With Approximate GPS Location
Fort Burnside	Major General Ambrose E. Burnside, commander of the Department of the Ohio in 1863.	1863	end of 1863	redoubt, hexagonal in shape, 684 ft. diameter along interior crest.	Destroyed (39.061862°, -84.458462°)
Battery Phil Kearny [Beech Wood]	Major General Philip Kearny, who was killed at the Battle of Chantilly, VA, Sept. 1, 1862.	1861	1861	three-sided redan with an extended pan coupe	Destroyed (39.065979°, -84.457310°)
Fort Whittlesey	Colonel Charles Whittlesey, 20th Ohio Infantry, and chief engineer during 1861 fortification construction.	1862	by mid-1863	two square redoubts and connecting stockade	Fragments exist as landforms in yards (39.066988°, -84.447945°)
Battery Lee [R. W. Lee]	Rensselaer W. Lee of Covington, "who has ever by his hospitality shown himself the Union soldier's friend."	1863	end of 1863	probably three-sided redan with an extended pan coupe	Destroyed (39.070735°, -84.439722°)

* Fort Henry (39.055219°, -84.517251°), located northeast of Battery Hatch, served as Major General Lew Wallace's field headquarters during the September 1862 crisis. Fort Henry was not an earthwork; it was the house of winery owner E.A. Thompson. The house no longer exists, but a shallow undulation in the ground surface marks the site of the structure.

+ A military pontoon bridge (39.059297°, -84.497522°) spanned the Licking River northeast of the Larz Anderson Battery. The bridge connected the Covington and Newport defenses. A remnant of the military road leads down to the pontoon bridge crossing from the entrance to the Meinken Field parking lot.

Price's Hill Battery on the west side of Cincinnati, October 1861. The city is visible in the distance. Cincinnati's first shots of the war occurred here. *From* Frank Leslie's Illustrated Newspaper *(November 16, 1861).*

Appendix C

Civil War Sites in Greater Cincinnati

C incinnati, Newport and Covington are wonderful cities in which to spend time and explore. They offer many things to do besides just visiting their historical locations. Professional and college sports teams, special events, museums, theaters and many other forms of entertainment abound.

With that in mind, here follows a list of some of the most important Civil War and Underground Railroad sites in the Greater Cincinnati region. Because the focus of this study is on Cincinnati, the sites are limited to Hamilton County (Ohio), the city of Cincinnati (Ohio), the city of Covington (Kentucky), the city of Newport (Kentucky) and the portions of Kenton County (Kentucky) and Campbell County (Kentucky) that fall within the Interstate 275 beltway. A few sites in Clermont County (Ohio) that lie along the border with Hamilton County are also included. The neighboring counties—Boone County (Kentucky), Dearborn County (Indiana), Butler County (Ohio), Warren County (Ohio) and Clermont County (Ohio)—offer their own excellent lists of Civil War and Underground Railroad sites, but they are not covered here for the sake of space and emphasis on Cincinnati.

Many of the sites do not exist anymore. As the cities grew into modernized business and industrial centers in the twentieth century, many of the Civil War–era structures were lost to progress. Therefore, it is a treat when one finds an original structure or landscape from the period that is still present today.

The list is broken down into east and west regions, starting with the cities and then ending with the counties. For the Kentucky counties, only their northern regions are given. Those counties naturally separate themselves as east versus west along the line of the Licking River; Campbell County lies to the east of the river, while Kenton County lies to the west. The regions are divided into specific neighborhoods or park areas. Beneath the neighborhoods are the site names, with a present-day address or a general location accompanying each site. The "Additional Notes" indicate whether the site is private or public and whether it is marked or not. Finally, a short description of the site's significance is given.

Western Downtown Cincinnati, Ohio (west of Vine Street)

Central Business District

Burnet House Hotel Marker (39.098827°, -84.512497°)
Address | Northwest corner of West Third Street and Vine Street
Additional Notes | The marker is accessible to the public. The location is private property.

At the time the luxurious 340-room building opened on May 3, 1850, the *Illustrated London News* called it "the finest hotel in the world." It hosted dozens of Union generals and famous persons. Among those of Civil War fame who lodged here were John C. Breckinridge, Andrew Johnson, Edwin Stanton, Salmon P. Chase, Horace Greeley, Phil Sheridan, George H. Thomas, James G. Blaine, Ambrose Burnside, Lew Wallace, Stephen A. Douglas and Jefferson Davis. Abraham Lincoln stayed here on February 12, 1861, on his way to Washington, D.C., to be inaugurated president; he gave a speech from the hotel balcony to a joyous Cincinnati crowd. In March 1864, Generals Ulysses S. Grant and William T. Sherman planned the Atlanta Campaign in Parlor A of the establishment. Long after the war had ended, Parlor A served as a meeting room for the local Sons of Union Veterans. The Burnet House was torn down in 1926. A historical marker is attached to the corner wall of the present-day building, on whose tenth floor is a small exhibit dedicated to the history of the former hotel.[119]

Burnet House was the most luxurious hotel in the West when it opened in 1850. Many important meetings of the Civil War occurred here, including the planning for the Atlanta Campaign of 1864. *Courtesy of the Library of Congress.*

CUSTOM HOUSE & POST OFFICE SITE (39.099734°, -84.512880°)
Address | 1 West Fourth Street
Additional Notes | Unmarked. The location is private property.

This is the site of the former post office and customhouse of Cincinnati, a place of social gatherings and political demonstrations during the Civil War. The original building was three stories tall and was constructed of hewn sandstone blocks adorned with Corinthian columns.[120]

JOHN SHILLITO & CO. SITE (39.099661°, -84.513338°)
Address | 15 West Fourth Street
Additional Notes | Unmarked. The location is private property.

John Shillito's store occupied this site during the Civil War. The company was a leading supplier of flags to Union regiments, including the Fifty-Fourth Massachusetts Infantry, and Shillito's large storefront windows often displayed the banners proudly for passersby to view. The upper three stories of the modern building retain the original design of the Shillito store façade from the 1860s.[121]

LEVI COFFIN'S "DISPATCHER'S OFFICE" SITE (39.102186°, -84.516764°)
Address | Northwest corner of West Sixth Street and Elm Street
Additional Notes | Unmarked. The location is private property.

Sometime after 1847, Levi Coffin, the Quaker who was labeled the "President of the Underground Railroad," used his store here as a major safe haven for runaway slaves on their flight to freedom. The building, which earned the nickname the "Dispatcher's Office," contained tunnels that led from its cellar to the Ohio River. Runaway slaves navigated through the network of tunnels to move undetected beneath the city streets. Coffin is said to have helped three thousand slaves in their escape. Neither Coffin's store nor the tunnels remain.[122]

MCLEAN BARRACKS / THIRD STREET MILITARY HOSPITAL SITE (39.097883°, -84.519642°)
Address | North side of West Third Street, halfway between Central Avenue and John Street
Additional Notes | Unmarked. The location is private property.

On this lot once stood the McLean Barracks, a collection of buildings from among several that made up the Convent of the Divine Will of the Sisters of Mercy. The convent was also known as the German Orphanage. The U.S. government rented the structures from the Sisters of Mercy from October 21, 1861, until August 2, 1865. In addition to military housing, the buildings served as a soldiers' hospital and a prison. The Sisters of Mercy helped tend to the soldiers here until the hospital closed on May 15, 1863, to be converted into a prison.[123]

NORTHERN DEPARTMENT HEADQUARTERS SITE (39.099915°, -84.514025°)
Address | Approximately 28 West Fourth Street
Additional Notes | Unmarked. The location is private property.

The Northern Department headquarters occupied Roderick McCormack's residence here from October 12, 1864, until July 5, 1865. The headquarters had been temporarily located in a house on Fifth Street (39.101830°, -84.507484°) since October 6, 1864. Major General Joseph Hooker moved

Military Prison (*center*) at McLean Barracks, located between Central Avenue and John Street, Cincinnati, circa mid-1864. The Third Street Hospital occupied the building until May 1863. *Courtesy of the National Archives.*

the headquarters of the department from Columbus, Ohio, to Cincinnati because he felt the Queen City was "more convenient and central for the dispatch of business."[124]

OHIO MECHANICS INSTITUTE AND U.S. SANITARY COMMISSION HEADQUARTERS SITE (39.102222°, -84.513563°)
Address | Southwest corner of West Sixth Street and Vine Street
Additional Notes | Unmarked. The location is private property.

On this site sat the second Ohio Mechanics Institute building in Cincinnati. Miles Greenwood was a president of the institute, which focused on vocational training, one of the first of its kind in the United States. The building also hosted Greenwood Hall and the headquarters of the Cincinnati Branch of the U.S. Sanitary Commission from December 1861 until the end of the Civil War. In his youth, inventor and industrialist Thomas Edison read profusely at the institute's Apprentice

Library while he was working in Cincinnati as a telegraph operator toward the end of the war.[125]

On the south side of the OMI stood the Catholic Institute, which contained Mozart Hall (39.101988°, -84.513595°), where many political rallies, military celebrations and public meetings were held during the war. On December 21, 1863, the Great Western Sanitary Fair opened at Mozart Hall, which offered entertainment, exhibits, and art during the event. The Catholic Institute also served as the final location of Cincinnati's provost marshal's office. Colonel Adolphus E. Jones occupied it from July 11 to December 19, 1865. Jones was the last provost marshal of the First and Second Ohio Districts, which encompassed all of Hamilton County, and he was the war's last volunteer Union officer on duty in the city.

SAINT JOHN'S HOSPITAL SITE (39.098247°, -84.517661°)
Address | Northwest corner of Third Street and Plum Street
Additional Notes | Unmarked. The location is private property.

Sister Anthony O'Connell and the Sisters of Charity operated the hospital here that had been opened in 1855. Its 75-bed facility could accommodate 150 patients. It treated many hundreds of Union and Confederate soldiers over the duration of the Civil War. After the war, it was renamed the Hospital of the Good Samaritan. The building no longer stands.[126]

SAINT PETER IN CHAINS CATHOLIC CATHEDRAL (39.103588°, -84.519035°)
Address | Southwest corner of Eighth Street and Plum Street
Additional Notes | The location is accessible to the public.

The cathedral was completed in 1845. At the time of the Civil War, the cathedral's 221-foot steeple was the tallest man-made structure in Cincinnati. On April 15, 1861, Archbishop John Purcell attached an American flag to the steeple as a symbol of hope and patriotism for the country. It served as a landmark that was visible from miles away; many a soldier longed to see it when they returned to Cincinnati from the war.[127]

ZION BAPTIST CHURCH (39.098133°, -84.514784°)
Address | South side of Third Street, between Race Street and Elm Street
Additional Notes | Unmarked. The location is accessible to the public.

This is the site of the Zion Baptist Church, which formed in 1841 after some members from the African Union Baptist Church left its congregation over the question of focus on abolitionism. The Zion members were active Underground Railroad conductors, and the church basement served as a station. Abolitionist Laura Smith Haviland taught African American children here. The church's deacon, John Hatfield, once presided over a mock funeral to mask the sounds of twenty-eight escaped slaves who were hidden in the cellar. Construction of the expressway obliterated the site.[128]

Piatt Park

PRESIDENT JAMES A. GARFIELD MONUMENT (39.104493°, -84.514063°)
Address | Piatt Park, Garfield Place at Vine Street
Additional Notes | The location is accessible to the public.

This 1887 monument sculpted by Charles A. Niehaus remembers Ohio's Civil War general and U.S. president James A. Garfield. The park hosted the August 1, 1861, "welcome home" banquet for Cincinnati's three months' men of the Second Ohio Infantry. They had just returned from the First Battle of Bull Run, Virginia.

Washington Park

CINCINNATI ORPHAN ASYLUM AND CITY BARRACKS / ELM STREET BARRACKS SITE (39.109324°, -84.519216°)
Address | 1241 Elm Street
Additional Notes | Unmarked. The location is accessible to the public.

Across Elm Street from Washington Park, in the space that Music Hall occupies today, was the site of the Cincinnati Orphan Asylum. Barracks large enough to accommodate 2,000 men were constructed there in 1861. Throughout the Civil War, tens of thousands of soldiers called the barracks home. In 1861 alone, about 17,000 soldiers and 250 prisoners quartered there. The old asylum building, where the south wing of Music Hall now stands, was converted on February 22, 1862, into the Washington Park Hospital, which treated 4,789 soldiers over the course of the war. The hospital

Washington Park Hospital, the former Cincinnati Orphan Asylum, at the corner of Fourteenth and Elm Streets, Cincinnati, mid-1864. The Orphan Asylum Barracks surround the building. *Courtesy of the National Archives.*

closed on May 25, 1865. Artillerymen trained for war in its adjoining lot to the south (39.108618°, -84.518867°), including Standart's Ohio Battery and the Cincinnati Battery, later known as Dilger's Battery I, First Ohio Light Artillery. The lot was also used as an army wagon and ambulance park and as a tent hospital.

Two blocks east, at 1313 Vine Street, stands Flattich Hall (39.109954°, -84.515475°), a Civil War military meeting place.[129]

COMMERCIAL (CINCINNATI) HOSPITAL SITE (39.107715°, -84.520287°)
Address | 1223 Central Parkway
Additional Notes | Unmarked. The location is private property.

The modern surface parking lot marks the site of the Commercial Hospital, later renamed the Cincinnati Hospital, which was built here in 1823 at the request of Dr. Daniel Drake. During the war, the hospital was one of eight hospitals in downtown Cincinnati that served wounded and sick soldiers. It had a capacity of 150 beds. The world's first known hospital-based civilian ambulance service began here in 1865. The Civil War–era buildings were torn down in 1867. The hospital's adjoining lot opposite Grant Street (39.108298°, -84.520390°) hosted the April 20, 1861 launch of Thaddeus S. Lowe and his balloon *Enterprise* on their nine-hundred-mile flight to South Carolina. During the Civil War, Lowe formed America's first aerial reconnaissance corps and became the world's first aerial observer to direct artillery fire in battle. The Cincinnati Reserve Militia's headquarters occupied the lot May through September 1861, before the headquarters moved to the Orphan Asylum.[130]

FRIEDRICH HECKER MONUMENT (39.108681°, -84.517802°) AND COLONEL ROBERT L. McCOOK MONUMENT (39.108887°, -84.517850°)
Address | Washington Park, directly across Elm Street from the Hamilton County Memorial Building
Additional Notes | The location is accessible to the public.

These two monuments remember two well-respected Civil War leaders of German American troops.

Friedrich Hecker was an influential agitator during the Prussian Revolution of 1848, and his political actions eventually forced him to flee Germany in 1849. He immigrated to the United States and bought a farm in Illinois. Hecker joined the Union army at the beginning of the Civil War. He served with distinction as colonel of the Twenty-Fourth Illinois Infantry and later of the Eighty-Second Illinois Infantry. He won the respect of Cincinnati Germans for helping to establish in their city America's first Turner Society (Turnverein) on November 21, 1848. For his political defense of the middle class and for his endearing personal qualities, Hecker's followers erected this monument in 1883 in his honor.

Robert Latimer McCook, one of Ohio's famous "Fighting McCooks," joined the Union army shortly after the first shots were fired at Fort Sumter. He helped raise the Ninth Ohio Infantry, a German American regiment composed mostly of Cincinnatians, and he was made its colonel. McCook's regiment participated in many of the major battles of the Western Theater. The Ninth Ohio earned a reputation for hard fighting. McCook was promoted to brigadier general on March 21, 1862, in recognition of the bravery and skill he had shown at the Battle of Mill Springs, Kentucky, one of the first major Union victories in the Civil War. During the initial movements of the Union army in the Kentucky Campaign of autumn 1862, McCook became severely ill and was forced to ride in an open ambulance as his men marched across northern Alabama. On August 5, 1862, Confederate cavalrymen attacked his column, and one of them shot McCook as he lay in his ambulance. He died the next day and was buried in Spring Grove Cemetery in Cincinnati. Veterans of the Ninth Ohio Infantry erected this monument in 1878 to McCook's memory.[131]

HAMILTON COUNTY MEMORIAL HALL (BUILDING) (39.108624°, -84.518429°)
Address | 1225 Elm Street
Additional Notes | The location is accessible to the public.

A local chapter of the Grand Army of the Republic (GAR), a national Civil War veterans' organization, raised the money to build this Beaux-Arts Classical Revival structure that honors Cincinnati's soldiers from all wars. Samuel Hannaford designed and completed the memorial in 1908. Excerpts from several of Abraham Lincoln's most famous speeches are etched into the exterior of the building, and inside are exhibits of art and war relics, including the wreath that decorated Lincoln's casket when his funeral train passed through Columbus, Ohio.[132]

West End

ANDREW HICKENLOOPER HOUSE (39.118434°, -84.528463°) AND MAYOR GEORGE HATCH HOUSE (39.118425°, -84.528247°)
Address | 838 Dayton Street and 830 Dayton Street
Additional Notes | The buildings are private property.

Civil War artillerist Brevet Brigadier General Andrew Hickenlooper owned the house at 838 after the war; it was built in 1871. The circa 1850 house next door at 830, derisively known as "Hatch's Folly," was the home of soap and candle manufacturer George Hatch, Cincinnati's first Civil War mayor. He sold the house before the war started. Farther down the street at 812 is the mansion formerly owned by Civil War brewer John Hauck.[133]

CINCINNATI MUSEUM CENTER AT UNION TERMINAL (39.109939°, -84.537534°) AND JEWISH HOSPITAL site (39.109897°, -84.525429°)
Address | 1301 Western Avenue and the intersection of Laurel Park Circle and Laurel Park Drive
Additional Notes | The locations are accessible to the public.

This expansive cluster of museums housed in a 1933 Art Deco–style railroad terminal contains the Cincinnati History Library/Archives and the Cincinnati History Museum. The historical museum presents artifacts and exhibits on the history of the Cincinnati region, including a section on the Civil War in Cincinnati. In front of Union Terminal Fountain is a monument marking the site of Union Grounds (1867–70), the first ball field of America's first professional baseball team, the Cincinnati Red Stockings.

Nearby, in Laurel Park, is the site of the Jewish Hospital at wartime 90 Betts Street. Here stood America's first Jewish hospital (circa 1850), which opened its doors to sick and wounded soldiers on October 29, 1861.

PROCTOR & GAMBLE COMPANY SITE (39.117239°, -84.523184°)
Address | Northeast corner of York Street and Central Avenue
Additional Notes | Unmarked. The location is private property.

At the time of the Civil War, this lot was the location of the Proctor & Gamble Company factory. The company produced soap and candles for the Union army, and it was here in 1863 that P&G's "floating soap," marketed as Ivory Soap in 1879, was first formulated. After the war, the factory moved to its famous Ivorydale location near the Saint Bernard neighborhood of Cincinnati.[134]

West Riverfront

CINCINNATI, HAMILTON & DAYTON RAILROAD PASSENGER STATION SITE (39.099305°, -84.531171°)
Address | West Fifth Street (Hudepohl Street), northwest of its intersection with Linn Street
Additional Notes | Unmarked. The location is private property.

The Cincinnati, Hamilton & Dayton Railroad funneled thousands of Union troops between Cincinnati and the upper Midwest states. In 1864, a new passenger depot (39.099125°, -84.530264°) opened adjacent to the original. These stations, now gone, marked the southern terminus of the rail line.

OHIO & MISSISSIPPI RAILROAD PASSENGER STATION SITE (39.095254°, -84.527865°)
Address | Northwest corner of West Pete Rose Ray and West Mehring Way
Additional Notes | Unmarked. The location is private property.

The railroad passenger station that stood here in the Civil War era witnessed many famous persons pass through it, including Abraham Lincoln on several occasions, and thousands of soldiers and officers, such as Lieutenant General Ulysses S. Grant and Major General George B. McClellan.

EASTERN DOWNTOWN CINCINNATI, OHIO (EAST OF VINE STREET)

The Banks District

NATIONAL UNDERGROUND RAILROAD FREEDOM CENTER (39.097703°, -84.511244°)
Address | 50 East Freedom Way
Additional Notes | The location is accessible to the public.

This museum presents displays, artifacts and interactive exhibits that "reveal the stories of freedom's heroes, from the era of the Underground Railroad to contemporary times." Perhaps the museum's most impressive artifact is an early antebellum slave pen that was moved here from a farm in Mason County, Kentucky.[135]

Central Business District

ABRAHAM LINCOLN'S 1859 SPEECH SITE (39.101663°, -84.510607°)
Address | Northern center point of Government Square, Fifth Street
Additional Notes | The marker is accessible to the public. The location is private property.

Near the midpoint of the Federal Building on Fifth Street is the site of E. & D. Kinsey's silverware store. On the night of September 17, 1859, Abraham Lincoln stood on the store's second-floor balcony and delivered a two-and-a-half-hour speech to citizens from Cincinnati, Newport and Covington. Lincoln's Cincinnati speech was the most important one that he delivered during his presidential campaign. In front of bus terminal A nearby is a marker that indicates this as the site of Lincoln's speech. Government Square was also the site of the Fifth Street Bazaar that figured prominently in the Great Western Sanitary Fair.[136]

Fifth Street Market Bazaar building on Fifth Street, between Main and Walnut Streets, Cincinnati, circa mid-1864. The Great Western Sanitary Fair used this building to display donated items for sale. *Courtesy of the National Archives.*

A.H. Pugh's Printing Company Site (39.102509°, -84.503663°)
Address | 400 Pike Street
Additional Notes | Unmarked. The location is private property.

This building stands on the site where Achilles H. Pugh ran a printing shop. Pugh printed James G. Birney's weekly abolitionist newspaper, *The Philanthropist*, at this location. The highly influential publication gained national attention, and most Cincinnatians at the time, including Nicholas Longworth Sr., opposed its views. In the riots of July 1836, Cincinnati mobs twice broke into the shop, destroyed the printing press, and threatened Pugh's life and those of his colleagues for their support of the antislavery movement. Reluctantly, Pugh and his staff continued their efforts. The paper was published in Cincinnati until October 1843.[137]

Appendix C

Allen Temple Site (39.103325°, -84.506519°)
Address | Southeast corner of Sixth Street and Broadway
Additional Notes | Unmarked. The location is private property.

This is the site of a Jewish synagogue that was built in 1852 and became the home of the African Methodist Episcopal Church in 1870. The Black Brigade of Cincinnati assembled here on September 5, 1862. The temple sat at the western edge of Bucktown, which at the time of the Civil War housed the city's slums. Many free African Americans lived in the Bucktown neighborhood, and former enslaved persons "hid in plain sight" there. Consequently, the Underground Railroad scene in Cincinnati was most active in the Bucktown blocks currently bounded by Sixth Street on the south, Culvert Street on the east, Seventh Street on the north and Broadway on the west.[138]

Ambrose Burnside's Headquarters Site (39.105570°, -84.513693°)
Address | 24 East Ninth Street
Additional Notes | Unmarked. The location is accessible to the public.

Major General Ambrose E. Burnside occupied a three-story brick girls' school at this site (currently the children's library) while he was commander of the Department of the Ohio in 1863. He moved his personal staff to this location on June 14, 1863, and they remained here until they left for the front on August 10, 1863. Burnside kept a telegraph in the house from which he and his staff sent dispatches day and night during Confederate brigadier general John Hunt Morgan's Indiana-Ohio Raid in July 1863.[139]

Baker Street Baptist Church Site (39.099381°, -84.511634°)
Address | East end of East Ogden Place, on the south side of the street
Additional Notes | Unmarked. The location is private property.

Established on July 21, 1831, the African Union Baptist Church was the first African American Baptist church in Cincinnati. Members moved their place of worship to this site in 1840 and named it the Baker Street Baptist Church. It was used until 1864. The church harbored runaway slaves in antebellum times, and famous abolitionists William Lloyd Garrison and Frederick Douglass spoke here. During the Civil War, many of its congregation joined the Union army when the first African American units formed in the United States, including the Cincinnati Black Brigade, the Fifty-Fourth Massachusetts Infantry and the Fifty-Fifth Massachusetts Infantry. The building no longer exists.[140]

CHRIST EPISCOPAL CHURCH CATHEDRAL (39.101049°, -84.507143°) AND FOURTH STREET MILITARY HOSPITAL (39.100800°, -84.508747°)
Address | 318 East Fourth Street and 220 East Fourth Street
Additional Notes | The church is accessible to the public, but the other sites are private property.

The current edifice at 318 was completed in 1957, but Christ Church has maintained a place of worship here since 1835. The Civil War–era church stood at the present-day entrance to the main sanctuary, adjacent to the parish house on Fourth Street. On October 22, 1863, Brigadier General William Haines Lytle's funeral occurred here with several hundred persons in attendance.

At 220 is the site of the Fourth Street Military Hospital, which the Sanitary Commission opened on February 20, 1862, to accept wounded soldiers from the Battle of Fort Donelson, Tennessee. The five-story brick building could shelter three hundred patients. The hospital closed on June 30, 1862. A Union army tent manufacturer stood directly across Fourth Street from the hospital.[141]

DEPARTMENT OF THE OHIO HEADQUARTERS (1861) SITE (39.098768°, -84.510134°)
Address | South side of East Third Street, between Walnut and Main Streets
Additional Notes | Unmarked. The location is accessible to the public.

On May 3, 1861, Major General George B. McClellan established the Department of the Ohio headquarters in the Duhme and Morton Buildings, located across Third Street from the Masonic Hall. Today's expressway occupies the Duhme and Morton sites. Staffs of Generals George McClellan, William Rosecrans and Ormsby Mitchel managed the department from here until November 9, 1861. Ulysses S. Grant visited here on June 10 and 11, 1861, to request a position on General McClellan's staff, but McClellan did not meet him. Grant returned to Springfield, Illinois, where the command of an Illinois regiment awaited him. In 1863, the Morton Building also contained the Medical Department office for the Department of the Ohio.

DEPARTMENT OF THE OHIO HEADQUARTERS (1862–1864) SITE (39.100550°, -84.507130°)
Address | Approximately 319 East Fourth Street
Additional Notes | Unmarked. The location is private property.

The Department of the Ohio headquarters was located here from August 28, 1862, until January 12, 1864. The building was abuzz with activity during the Siege of Cincinnati in September 1862 and Confederate brigadier general John Hunt Morgan's ride around Cincinnati on the night of July 13–14, 1863. In 1864, the building served as the headquarters for the local Veteran Reserve Corps.[142]

DISTRICT OF CINCINNATI HEADQUARTERS SITE (39.101262°, -84.506100°)
Address | East side of Broadway, between Fourth and Fifth Streets
Additional Notes | Unmarked. The location is private property.

In this vicinity was the headquarters for the Military District of Cincinnati from September 1862 to February 1864. The city's military headquarters was reestablished on July 21, 1864, in the District of Ohio's headquarters building (39.100309°, -84.503752°), where it remained until July 8, 1865.[143]

FEDERAL HEADQUARTERS SITE (39.100303°, -84.505773°)
Address | Southeast corner of Broadway and Arch Street
Additional Notes | Unmarked. The location is private property.

A four-story brick building that stood at this site during the Civil War served as the local Union army headquarters from 1861 and as headquarters for the Military District of Ohio from May 1863 until July 18, 1864, when it was moved to the southeast corner of East Third and Lawrence Streets (39.100309°, -84.503752°). Both edifices were razed in the twentieth century. A marker on the corner wall of the present-day structure indicates that this was also the site of Fort Washington's powder magazine.[144]

FIFTH STREET MARKET HOUSE SITE (39.101249°, -84.512181°)
Address | North side of East Fifth Street, along the southeast boundary of Fountain Square
Additional Notes | Unmarked. The location is accessible to the public.

Federal headquarters for the District of Ohio, 108 Broadway at Arch Street, Cincinnati, circa mid-1864. This building served as the office of the military district commandant from 1861 to 1864. *Courtesy of the National Archives.*

The Fifth Street Market House, which was built in 1829 and torn down in 1870 to make way for the Tyler-Davidson Fountain, played a key role in the Civil War. It was here that patriotic Cincinnati residents fed and entertained visiting Union regiments before they moved on to their planned destinations. During the September 1862 crisis, the "Squirrel Hunter" regiments ate here. Also, the Great Western Sanitary Fair of 1864 occurred in the Fifth Street Market (39.101508°, -84.510554°), now today's Government Square, where Lincoln had spoken in September 1859.[145]

GIBSON HOUSE HOTEL SITE (39.100775°, -84.511539°)
Address | 425 Walnut Street
Additional Notes | Unmarked. The location is private property.

The three-hundred-room Gibson House, opened in 1849, was a well-frequented hotel in Cincinnati during the Civil War. The proprietor was a staunch Unionist, and his hotel was the first business in the city to raise the U.S. flag over its establishment after the firing on Fort Sumter. The Gibson House often hosted local political meetings and fed Union soldiers a complimentary meal before they left the city. The building no longer exists.[146]

JAMES PRESLEY BALL'S PHOTOGRAPHIC GALLERY SITE (39.100373°, -84.510512°)
Address | 128 East Fourth Street
Additional Notes | Unmarked. The location is private property.

James P. Ball was a world-renowned African American photographer and abolitionist who photographed many notable persons such as Charles Dickens, Queen Victoria, Jenny Lind and Frederick Douglass. Ball maintained a photography studio and gallery at this site throughout the Civil War, during which period he created daguerreotype photos for hundreds of civilians, politicians, soldiers and officers.

NATIONAL THEATER SITE (39.100226°, -84.507500°)
Address | Northeast corner of Hammond Street and Sycamore Street
Additional Notes | Unmarked. The location is private property.

The sizable National Theater opened to patrons on July 3, 1837. Cincinnatians favored this playhouse, which hosted many notable entertainers, such as Jenny Lind, Edwin Forrest and Junius Booth Jr. The building was razed in 1940.[147]

PIKE'S OPERA HOUSE SITE (39.099909°, -84.511967°) AND HOME GUARD HEADQUARTERS (39.100026°, -84.511292°)
Address | 3 East Fourth Street and 43–53 East Fourth Street
Additional Notes | Unmarked. The locations are private property.

Lucrative liquor dealer Samuel Pike built an ornate five-story building here in 1859. The maximum seating capacity of the theater's auditorium was three thousand. The three main entrances and marble-laden lobby welcomed customers to a vast array of performances, such as operas, concerts, lectures and dramas. Special events were held here, too, including public salutes to visiting hero-generals Phil Sheridan and Ulysses S. Grant. It was here that James E. Murdoch presented the first public reading of

Soldiers march along Fourth Street past Pike's Opera House (*left center, with eagle on roof*) in April 1861. The post office and customhouse is on the far right. *Courtesy of Public Library of Cincinnati and Hamilton County.*

Thomas Buchanan Read's poem "Sheridan's Ride," only a few hours after it had been completed. Actor Junius Booth Jr. was performing at Pike's when his brother John Wilkes Booth shot President Lincoln in Washington. The building burned down twice after the Civil War. The second blaze in 1903 ended its run.

Nearby at numbers 43–53 is the site of the Carlisle Building, which held the Cincinnati Home Guard headquarters in 1861.[148]

SAINT PAUL'S EPISCOPAL CHURCH SITE (39.100201°, -84.510579°)
Address | 111 East Fourth Street
Additional Notes | Unmarked. The location is private property.

Saint Paul's Church, which stood here from 1853 to 1883, served as a parish for many leading citizens of Cincinnati, including Salmon P. Chase, who was the superintendent of the Sunday school here.[149]

SALMON P. CHASE HISTORICAL MARKER (39.099073°, -84.508937°)
Address | Southeast corner of East Third Street and Main Street
Additional Notes | The marker is accessible to the public. The location is private property.

Salmon Portland Chase established his first law practice and residence in Cincinnati in 1830 in a building that sat at the northeast corner of this intersection. The current sandstone building replaced the original structure. Salmon Chase earned national fame from this law office as the "Attorney General for Runaway Negroes," a sobriquet he received for his tireless work in defending escaped slaves and Underground Railroad conductors.

His subsequent political career led him to become one of the founders of the Republican Party, which he represented as governor of Ohio and a U.S. senator. President Abraham Lincoln selected him in 1861 to be his secretary of the treasury, in which position Chase performed with great ingenuity and skill. After a scandal involving his potential bid for the U.S. presidency, Chase resigned in 1864, but Lincoln appointed Chase to the seat of chief justice of the United States Supreme Court, a place where his pro–African American sentiments played an important role in bringing America's emancipated slaves closer to equality during the Reconstruction era.

At the time of the Civil War, Chase's former workplace served as the District of Ohio headquarters from July 1862 to April 28, 1863, and as the office for the U.S. Commissary Department until October 1, 1864.[150]

"SHERIDAN'S RIDE" MARKER (39.104502°, -84.512707°)
Address | 21 East Eighth Street
Additional Notes | The marker is accessible to the public. The location is private property.

Thomas Buchanan Read, a poet and painter, lived in a brick house at this site during the Civil War. Here on October 31, 1864, he penned his most famous poem, "Sheridan's Ride," which commemorates Union major general Phil Sheridan's October 9 journey on horseback to the battlefield at Cedar Creek, Virginia, an act that eventually turned the tide of the battle in the Union army's favor. The resulting popularity of "Sheridan's Ride" made General Sheridan and Thomas Read household names of their day.[151]

SOLDIERS' HOME SITE (39.099484°, -84.505113°)
Address | Approximately 411 East Third Street on the south side of the street, directly opposite the halfway point of the garage
Additional Notes | Unmarked. The location is private property.

Today's interstate highway bridge located across Third Street from the Western–Southern Life garage marks the site of the Soldiers' Home that the Cincinnati Branch of the U.S. Sanitary Commission opened on May 15, 1862. The building had originally housed Trollope's Bazaar and the Ohio Mechanics Institute. Colonel G.W.D. Andrews was the home's superintendent. The establishment reported that from its inception up through April 1865, it had served 112,163 soldiers. The home provided 656,704 meals and lodged 45,400 men by the time it closed on October 8, 1865.

About seventy yards east of the home stood the U.S. Quartermaster Department office in 1863.[152]

WOOD'S THEATER SITE (39.102292°, -84.513003°)
Address | Southeast corner of Sixth Street and Vine Street
Additional Notes | Unmarked. The location is private property.

George Wood built his theater at this site in 1856 following the destruction of the People's Theater here. Wood's establishment entertained Cincinnatians for two decades with drama of all kinds. During the Civil War, actors John Wilkes Booth and Edwin Booth performed here.[153]

Eden Park

GRAND ARMY OF THE REPUBLIC FLAGSTAFF (39.117721°, -84.489317°)
Address | Eden Park, at the southeast corner of St. Paul Drive and Alpine Place
Additional Notes | The location is accessible to the public.

The Daughters of Union Veterans dedicated this memorial flagpole on the first day of the Sixty-Fourth National Encampment of the Grand Army of the Republic, which was held in Cincinnati, August 24–28, 1930. The ceremony was broadcast on radio nationwide.[154]

Lytle Park

ABRAHAM LINCOLN STATUE (39.101144°, -84.504308°)
Address | Lytle Park, at the southeast corner of East Fourth Street and Ludlow Street
Additional Notes | The location is accessible to the public.

Sponsored by Charles Phelps Taft, half brother of U.S. president William Howard Taft, and sculpted by George Grey Barnard, this statue of a beardless Lincoln was dedicated by former President Taft on March 31, 1917.[155]

BRIGADIER GENERAL WILLIAM HAINES LYTLE'S HOUSE SITE (39.101038°, -84.503870°)
Address | Lytle Park, at the southeast corner of East Fourth Street and Ludlow Street, east of the Lincoln statue
Additional Notes | The location is accessible to the public. A map on the nearby wall of markers *(see separate listing)* shows the spot.

Brigadier General William H. Lytle, the "Poet-Warrior," had earned national acclaim as a poet of antebellum America. His most famous poem was "Antony and Cleopatra," which many Civil War soldiers could recite from memory. At the start of the Civil War, Lytle commanded Camp Harrison in Cincinnati, but then he chose to serve as colonel of the Tenth Ohio Infantry. He was later promoted for gallantry in battle but was mortally wounded at the Battle of Chickamauga, Georgia, on September 20, 1863. Lytle lived in a house erected at this site in 1809, and he left for the Civil War from here. Even though his family donated the house and land to the city as a park, the city demolished the brick mansion in 1908.[156]

FORT WASHINGTON MONUMENT (39.100927°, -84.504861°)
Address | Southwest corner of East Fourth Street and Ludlow Street
Additional Notes | The location is accessible to the public.

On Ludlow Street is a monument marking the location of Fort Washington, which was built in 1789 to protect Cincinnati from hostile Native Americans. Newport Barracks forced the abandonment of the fort in 1804.[157]

LITERARY CLUB OF CINCINNATI BUILDING (39.101426°, -84.504682°)
Address | 500 East Fourth Street
Additional Notes | Unmarked. The location is private property.

Founded in 1849, the Literary Club represented the elite of the city. Among the members were Civil War notables Salmon P. Chase, George B. McClellan, Rutherford B. Hayes, August Willich, Edward F. Noyes, Andrew Hickenlooper, William Dickson, Israel Garrard, John Pope, Manning Force, Thomas Ewing Jr., Alphonso Taft and Thomas Buchanan Read. In 1861, a group of Literary Club patrons, including Hayes, formed their own military company called the Burnet Rifles. Most of them later served in the field. The current Fourth Street building (circa 1820) became home to the Literary Club in 1930.[158]

Lytle Park Historic Markers Wall (39.100545°, -84.504005°)
Address | Southeast corner of East Fourth Street and Ludlow Street, south of the Lytle house site
Additional Notes | The location is accessible to the public.

Lytle Park was named after the prominent Cincinnati founding family from which Civil War general William H. Lytle descended. Markers attached to a wall in the south section of the park tell of the rich history of the surrounding neighborhood.[159]

Stephen Foster's Boardinghouse Marker (39.100735°, -84.505305°)
Address | At the main door to Guilford School, southwest corner of East Fourth Street and Ludlow Street
Additional Notes | The marker is accessible to the public. The location is private property.

Stephen C. Foster, the writer of many famous folk songs that were sung during the Civil War, lived in Jane Griffin's boardinghouse at this site between 1846 and 1850. Here, while working as a bookkeeper in his brother's steamboat agency in Cincinnati, Foster composed the folk songs "Oh! Susanna," "Nelly Was a Lady," "Away Down South" and "Stay Summer Breath." Also among the twenty-eight songs he wrote or published during his time in Cincinnati were "Old Uncle Ned," "Camptown Races" and "Nelly Bly."[160]

Taft Museum of Art (39.102082°, -84.502850°) and George McClellan's house site (39.101326°, -84.503056°)
Address | 316 Pike Street
Additional Notes | The museum is accessible to the public, but the other locations are private property.

The historic Baum-Longworth home displays a fine collection of artwork acquired by the Taft family. Built in 1820 by wealthy businessman Martin Baum, the house served as the residence of millionaire land speculator and grape-grower Nicholas Longworth Sr. from 1830 until his death in 1863. Abraham Lincoln came here during his visit to Cincinnati in September 1855. Longworth's family continued to live here until 1871. Charles P. Taft bought the house in 1873; his half brother William Howard Taft received the Republican nomination for president on the portico steps of this house.

At the nearby northwest corner of Pike and East Third Streets stood a rental house in which Major General George B. McClellan and his wife, Mary Ellen, lived while he was the Ohio & Mississippi Railroad superintendent at the outbreak of the Civil War. His neighbor and friend Larz Anderson lived in a large house at the northeast corner (39.101655°, -84.502548°). Generals William T. Sherman, George H. Thomas and Robert Anderson met at Anderson's on September 1–2, 1861, to discuss Union military strategy in Kentucky. General William "Bull" Nelson stayed here while he recovered from his wound received at the Battle of Richmond, Kentucky. Both structures are gone.[161]

Mount Adams

CINCINNATI ASTRONOMICAL OBSERVATORY SITE (39.107675°, -84.499062°)
Address | 1055 St. Paul Place
Additional Notes | Unmarked. The location is private property.

The former Holy Cross Monastery stands on the site of the Cincinnati Astronomical Observatory, whose cornerstone former U.S president John Quincy Adams dedicated on November 9, 1843. The event led to the changing of the name of the hill from "Mount Ida" to "Mount Adams" in honor of the president. Astronomer, mathematician, railroad builder and brigadier general Ormsby MacKnight Mitchel had been instrumental in raising the funds necessary to buy an eleven-inch Merz telescope lens in Germany and to build a structure to house the telescope. Both ventures were successful. The Cincinnati Observatory began operation on April 14, 1845, boasting the largest refractor telescope in the Western Hemisphere.

As the first director of the observatory, Mitchel wrote the first astronomical journal in the United States. His successor, Cleveland Abbe, published the first weather forecasts in the nation. For these reasons, the site of the Cincinnati Observatory is considered the Birthplace of American Astronomy and the U.S. Weather Bureau. The Observatory was moved in 1873 to the Mt. Lookout suburb of Cincinnati to escape the blinding

October 1861 Frank Leslie sketch of the Newport Ferry crossing the Ohio River from Cincinnati. Mount Adams, its Church of the Immaculata and the Mount Adams Battery immediately right of the church (*center*) stand over the Little Miami Railroad passenger station (*above the ferry smokestacks*) and the waterworks to its right. *Courtesy of New York Public Library Digital Collections.*

smog of downtown; soon afterward, the building on Mount Adams was razed. However, the original 1842 telescope remains in use today at the Mt. Lookout facility.[162]

IMMACULATA CATHOLIC CHURCH (39.107108°, -84.496454°)
Address | 30 Guido Street
Additional Notes | The location is accessible to the public.

This Catholic church was built in 1859 under the direction of Archbishop John B. Purcell. It stood watch over the Mount Adams Battery, which was constructed in 1861 across from the church on Pavilion Street. As it did in the Civil War, the building remains a well-known landmark that stands out against the city's skyline.[163]

Appendix C

Over-the-Rhine

AUGUST WILLICH HOUSE (39.111895°, -84.512518°)
Address | 1419–21 Main Street
Additional Notes | Unmarked. The location is private property.

Brigadier General August Willich lived in this house. He was an influential leader in German American society who became colonel of the Thirty-Second Indiana Infantry during the Civil War.[164]

EAGLE IRON WORKS SITE (39.107895°, -84.512576°)
Address | Northeast corner of Walnut Street and East Central Parkway
Additional Notes | Unmarked. The location is private property.

Industrialist and inventor Miles Greenwood established the Eagle Iron Works at this site. The factory produced astounding numbers of rifles, cannon, tools, military vehicles and metal plates for ironclad gunboats throughout the Civil War. In 1862, his foundry produced America's first Gatling rapid-fire guns. The facility made such a positive impact on the Union war effort that Confederate sympathizers tried to destroy the building multiple times but failed in their attempts. In 1911, the present structure replaced the original and became the new home to the Ohio Mechanics Institute, of which Greenwood had served as president and benefactor.[165]

FINDLAY MARKET (39.115315°, -84.519069°) AND LAFAYETTE HALL (39.116369°, -84.518185°)
Address | 1801 Race Street and 1826–28 Race Street
Additional Notes | The market is accessible to the public, but the hall is private property.

This structure dating to 1852 is the oldest continuously operated public market in Ohio. It is the last one standing of nine public market houses that once served Cincinnati. During the Siege of Cincinnati in September 1862, the Findlay Market was the headquarters for the Twelfth Regiment of Cincinnati Militia. Nearby, at 1826, is the circa 1857 brick Lafayette Hall, a popular meeting place for German Americans during the Civil War. Some German American military companies formed here, including the Lafayette Guards.[166]

GUSTAV TAFEL HOUSE (39.111292°, -84.513716°) AND SITE OF TURNER HALL (39.111415°, -84.514359°)
Address | Northeast corner of East Fourteenth and Walnut Streets and 1407 Walnut Street
Additional Notes | Unmarked. The locations are private property.

Lieutenant Gustav Tafel of the Ninth Ohio Infantry, and later lieutenant colonel of the 106th Ohio Infantry, lived in this house from 1848 to 1870. Turner Hall, the center for all German American military activities in Cincinnati during the Civil War, stood at 1407 Walnut Street until it was razed in 1972.[167]

Pendleton

GEORGE HUNT PENDLETON HOUSE (39.112037°, -84.504466°)
Address | 559 Liberty Hill
Additional Notes | Unmarked. The location is private property.

The U.S. congressman and Peace Democrat from Cincinnati built this house for himself in 1870.

PENDLETON BARRACKS (TENEMENT HOUSE) (39.109384°, -84.508423°)
Address | 1121–23 Broadway
Additional Notes | Unmarked. The locations are private property.

This large brick building of Pendleton Barracks dates to prior to the Civil War. It witnessed scenes related to the war activities that took place around it, such as soldiers' fights and riots. Behind the tenement building stood a tavern where officers stayed while stationed in Cincinnati. Across Broadway from the tenement building was a vacant lot where soldiers from the barracks practiced shooting their rifles. Legend has it that Confederate spies were executed on the lot.

Two blocks east of here is the site of the Kelton Barracks. A block west, at the southwest corner of Sycamore Street and Michael Bany Way, is the site of the Sycamore Street Barracks (39.108750°, -84.510385°), a military prison that opened in the old county jail on August 15, 1862. Farther west, at 1150 Main Street, stands Jefferson Hall (39.109139°, -84.511388°), where the Turner Regiment briefly quartered during their preparation for war in April 1861.[168]

WOODWARD POST HOSPITAL SITE (39.110780°, -84.508869°)
Address | Northeast corner of Woodward High School grounds
Additional Notes | Unmarked. The location is accessible to the public.

The grassy area along Broadway near the northeast corner of the school was the site of the three-story Woodward Post Hospital from February 11, 1863, to August 21, 1865. Previously, it was the private boarding school that Harriet Beecher Stowe had attended, and then in 1842, it was converted into the St. John's Hotel for Invalids. In late 1865, it became St. Luke's Hospital. The facility contained twenty-eight rooms that could treat a maximum capacity of 120 sick and wounded soldiers.

Next door is Woodward High School. The present structure dates to 1910, but a school has sat at that location since 1831. It was the first free high school west of the Alleghenies. William Holmes McGuffey, of *McGuffey Readers* fame, taught here. The institution contributed to the Union and Confederacy one major general, fifteen brigadier generals, twenty colonels, nine lieutenant colonels, three adjutants, eleven majors, thirty-five captains, twenty-one lieutenants, seven corporals, three sergeants, seven quartermasters, three judge advocates, five chaplains, twelve surgeons and eight navy officers.[169]

Sawyer Point Park

LITTLE MIAMI RAILROAD STATION SITE (39.102101°, -84.496614°)
Address | Along the upper walkway, next to the playground
Additional Notes | Unmarked. The location is accessible to the public.

Located a short distance southwest of the Cincinnati Water Works, this southern terminus station of the Little Miami & Xenia Railroad hosted politicians, Union officers and tens of thousands of Federal soldiers traveling between the eastern and western theaters of the Civil War. The station was also the departure point where wounded men would be loaded onto trains to be sent to the Camp Dennison General Hospital sixteen miles away. Abraham Lincoln boarded a train here at 9:00 a.m. on February 13, 1861, on his journey to his inauguration as president of the United States.[170]

SITES OF THE NILES IRON WORKS (39.101361°, -84.498187°) AND SWIFT & NILES BOATYARD (39.101151°, -84.497837°)
Address | In front of the Sawyer Point Park stage

Additional Notes | Unmarked. The location is accessible to the public.

The Niles Iron Works and the boatyard located across from it on Front Street produced iron plating and two ironclad monitor gunboats for the U.S. Navy. The Miami & Erie Canal terminated at the Ohio River just behind the boatyard. Now the sites lie unmarked in the grassy area fronting the Sawyer Point Park stage.[171]

SULTANA AND BLACK BRIGADE HISTORICAL MARKERS (39.100080°, -84.498556°)
Address | Along the riverside walkway, just east of the L & N Pedestrian "Purple People" Bridge
Additional Notes | The location is accessible to the public.

The *Sultana* was a government-rented Union transport and supply steamboat that was built at Cincinnati's John Litherbury boatyard in January 1863. On April 25, 1865, only a few days after President Abraham Lincoln's assassination, the *Sultana* departed from Vicksburg, Mississippi, with a load of nearly 2,300 passengers and crew, over six times the boat's legal capacity. Between 1,800 and 2,200 of them were Union soldiers who had recently been

The Cincinnati-built USS *Sultana* lies docked at Helena, Arkansas, April 26, 1865. The photo was taken only hours before the steamboat's boilers exploded above Memphis, Tennessee, resulting in the worst maritime disaster in American history. *Courtesy of the Library of Congress.*

released from the Confederate prisoner-of-war camps at Cahaba, Alabama, and Andersonville, Georgia. About 2:00 a.m. on April 27, as the steamboat chugged up the Mississippi River just north of Memphis, Tennessee, three of its four high-pressure boilers exploded. The boat sank in a fiery instant. It is estimated that between 1,547 and 1,900 passengers died, more than the number lost on the *Titanic*, making the *Sultana* accident the worst in U.S. maritime history. Among the dead were 791 soldiers from Ohio, including 50 from Cincinnati.[172]

The Black Brigade was a military unit of about one thousand African Americans who volunteered to defend Cincinnati in September 1862. Initially, Cincinnati police rounded up the Black men of the city at gunpoint to force them to work on the entrenchments being built in Northern Kentucky. Enraged by the mistreatment of these men, Union major general Lew Wallace tasked local judge William M. Dickson with recruiting and taking command as colonel of an African American volunteer unit that would become known as the "Black Brigade."

Amazingly, all four hundred of the original forced-labor men plus three hundred additional African Americans enlisted for duty on September 5. Another three hundred men would enlist over the next three weeks. The result was the Union army's first mustered Black unit to engage in military service in the Civil War. On September 20, after performing admirable service for their country, the men of the Black Brigade marched through the streets of Cincinnati with their banner flying proudly before them and crowds cheering them. The brigade was formally mustered out, paid and dismissed that day at Fifth Street and Broadway. The men presented a ceremonial sword to Judge Dickson in appreciation for the fair opportunity that he had given them.[173]

Smale Park

BLACK BRIGADE MONUMENT (39.095537°, -84.508738°) AND U.S. NAVAL RENDEZVOUS SITE (39.096595°, -84.507926°)
Address | South end of Joe Nuxhall Way
Additional Notes | The locations, except for the Naval Rendezvous, are accessible to the public.

This fitting monument to the Black Brigade, the Civil War's first mustered African American Union military unit that saw service at the front, was dedicated on September 8, 2012, exactly 150 years after these soldiers had served their country. The monument wall is shaped like a redan, which recalls the earthworks they built in defense of Cincinnati. The memorial overlooks the site of the northern end of the pontoon bridge (39.094902°, -84.509699°) that the brigade used to enter Northern Kentucky. On the wall are plaques, etchings and relief sculptures that detail the history of the Black Brigade and a list of 706 enrolled names from its thousand-man roster. Also, a bronze sculpture depicts Private Marshall P.H. Jones handing the ceremonial sword to Colonel William M. Dickson. Among the members of the Black Brigade was Powhatan Beaty, who would be awarded the Congressional Medal of Honor for his bravery in action in 1864.

Northwest of the memorial, on West Mehring Way, were the approximate wartime sites (39.095997°, -84.509676°) of a government hay warehouse and an adjacent military tent factory. Northeast of the intersection of Mehring Way and Joe Nuxhall Way was the site of the Cincinnati U.S. Naval Rendezvous, where 4,757 men were recruited for service in the U.S. Navy from August 1862 through May 1865.[174]

Yeatman's Cove Park

MOORE & RICHARDSON COMPANY SITE (39.099528°, -84.501614°)
Address | Along the park's primary city-side walkway, near the center of the park
Additional Notes | Unmarked. The location is accessible to the public.

The building stood at the northwest corner of Front Street (the park's main east–west walkway) and Pike Street. During the war, the company manufactured steamboat boilers and engines, including those used on the ill-fated *Sultana*.

PUBLIC BOAT LANDING (39.096439°, -84.505332°) AND THE NATIONAL STEAMBOAT MONUMENT (39.096589°, -84.505070°)
Address | East Mehring Way at Broadway, at the west end of Yeatman's Cove Park
Additional Notes | The locations are accessible to the public.

From the time the first settlers landed here until the end of the steamboat era, the Public Boat Landing was a bustling scene of people and products loading and unloading on and off rivercraft. During the Civil War, the landing was especially busy with the boarding of thousands of Union soldiers onto steamer transports for their journeys to the South, or the daily movement of war material onto supply boats heading toward the front, or the unloading of wounded soldiers to the Greater Cincinnati hospitals. Most of the brick-covered landing has been built over; it encompassed the area bounded by the river, Broadway, the ballpark and Joe Nuxhall Way. However, in the remaining remnant located here, one can still see the large iron rings embedded into the pavement that were used to moor the steamboats that often waited in line for hours to get their turn at the landing.[175]

The adjoining National Steamboat Monument is a hand-activated structure that recalls the heyday of the steamboats that helped make Cincinnati one of the largest and most important cities in the United States. Rising high above the memorial is a sixty-ton replica of the paddle wheel from the steamboat *American Queen*, one of the largest steamboats in the world. Photographs and histories of various steamboats that plied the waters of the Ohio River are placed around the monument.

SPENCER HOUSE HOTEL SITE (39.097174°, -84.505534°)
Address | Northwest corner of East Mehring Way and Broadway
Additional Notes | Unmarked. The location is private property.

The hotel that stood here became one of the elite hotels in the city when it opened its doors in 1853 to serve steamboat travelers. During the Civil War, it was among Cincinnati's most popular hotels for visiting Union officers and former Confederate officers alike. Dozens of Union dignitaries and generals such as William T. Sherman and Ulysses S. Grant stayed here. In 1866, a large reception was thrown here for President Andrew Johnson. The event counted among its guests Secretary of State William Seward, Admiral David Farragut and Generals Ulysses Grant and George Custer. The hotel was razed in 1935. Now it is the location of the professional baseball stadium.

Throughout the nineteenth century, the riverfront areas along Front Street (today's Mehring Way and the main east–west walkway through Yeatman's Cove Park) were known as Rat Row and Sausage Row. They were a haven for thieves, prostitutes and low-class citizens who spent their wages at the many saloons and brothels that thrived along the wharves.[176]

Western Cincinnati, Ohio
(west of Interstate 75)

Carthage

Camp Monroe Site (39.202682°, -84.473255°)
Address | 7801 Anthony Wayne Avenue
Additional Notes | Unmarked. The location is private property.

The Hamilton County Fairgrounds served as Camp Monroe, a training facility for Union soldiers in the early part of the Civil War. Henry W. Burdsall's Independent Company Ohio Cavalry, also known as the First Independent Company Ohio Cavalry, camped here for most of June 1861. The regiment occupied the grounds until June 24. Captain Harry Getty's Battery C, Fourth U.S. Artillery, and Colonel Jeptha Garrard's Sixth Independent Company Ohio Cavalry also spent time here. From September 9, 1862, to the end of the war, the U.S. quartermaster rented the fairgrounds for use as one of the largest mule and horse yards in the United States. Tens of thousands of horses and mules were corralled here before they were sent to the Union armies.[177]

Cumminsville

Camp Gurley / Camp Capture Site (39.161293°, -84.551270°)
Address | Beckman Street (U.S. 27), between Colerain Avenue and Interstate 74
Additional Notes | Unmarked. The location is private property.

From August 5 to November 18, 1861, the Fourth Ohio Cavalry used this hilltop as a training camp. It was named for Congressman John A. Gurley. The camp's site is bounded today by Colerain Avenue on the north, West Fork Mill Creek on the east, Hoffner Street on the south and Herron Avenue on the west. Large numbers of civilians from Cincinnati often visited the camp. After the Fourth Cavalry left for war, the camp was abandoned until early 1864, when the U.S. Quartermaster Department established a large horse yard here dubbed Camp Capture, which closed in 1866.[178]

Wesleyan Cemetery (39.159179°, -84.545091°)
Address | 4003 Colerain Avenue
Additional Notes | The location is accessible to the public.

Near the entrance to the cemetery is a ten-foot obelisk that the Grand Army of the Republic erected in 1954 to honor over six hundred Civil War veterans buried here. Corporal William Steinmetz (1847–1903) of Company G, Eighty-Third Indiana Infantry, is among them. He was awarded the Congressional Medal of Honor for his extraordinary heroism in the May 22, 1863 assault on the Confederate earthworks at Vicksburg, Mississippi. [Sec. S, Range 10, Grave 22]. Also interred here is Colonel John Halliday Patrick (1818–1864) of the Fifth Ohio Infantry. Patrick was killed leading his regiment at the Battle of New Hope Church, Georgia, on May 25, 1864. [Sec. B, Lot 72, Grave 3].

Wesleyan Cemetery was the first integrated cemetery in Greater Cincinnati. In antebellum times, runaway slaves hid in a safehouse in the cemetery. Prominent abolitionists John Van Zandt (1791–1847) [Sec. E, Lot 71], Zebulon Strong (1788–1875) [Sec. Q, Lot 51] and Reverend Henry Hathaway (1804–1871) [Sec. F, Lot 61] are buried here.[179]

Fairmount

FAIRMOUNT OFFICERS' GENERAL HOSPITAL SITE (39.130176°, -84.548720°)
Address | St. Clair Heights Park, Fairmount Avenue and Iroquois Street
Additional Notes | The location is accessible to the public.

The Officers' General Hospital, commanded by U.S. Army surgeon Dr. William H. Gobrecht, opened on August 6, 1864, in the main Baptist Theological Seminary building. The hospital treated convalescing and sick officers until it closed on June 13, 1865.

Price Hill

ST. JOSEPH CEMETERY (39.106328°, -84.576899°)
Address | West Eighth Street and Seton Avenue
Additional Notes | The location is accessible to the public.

The cemetery contains the grave of Corporal Henry (Heinrich) Hoffman (1836–1894), Company M, Second Ohio Cavalry, who received the Congressional Medal of Honor for his actions in capturing an enemy flag at the Battle of Sailor's Creek, Virginia, on April 6, 1865. [Old Block 18, Lot 7][180]

UNION BAPTIST CEMETERY (39.118417°, -84.602433°)
Address | 4933 Cleves-Warsaw Road
Additional Notes | The location is accessible to the public.

Established in 1864, it is the final resting place of many Black Civil War veterans, Underground Railroad conductors and former enslaved persons, including Edith Hern Fossett (1787–1854), who was President Thomas Jefferson's head cook, and her husband, Joseph (1780–1858), who was Jefferson's blacksmith [Sec. B-West].[181] A monument to the cemetery's 120 Civil War dead stands beside the office. Alongside the main cemetery lane lies the grave of Sergeant Powhatan Beaty (1837–1916), who received the Congressional Medal of Honor as a member of Company G, Fifth U.S. Colored Infantry, for his heroic actions at the Battle of Chaffin's Farm, Virginia. He was also a veteran of the Black Brigade of Cincinnati. [Sec. A, Lot 4, Grave 8] A historical marker near the office remembers Beaty.

WILLIAM S. ROSECRANS HOUSE (39.114716°, -84.559415°)
Address | 2935 Lehman Road
Additional Notes | Unmarked. The location is private property.

Union major general William S. Rosecrans lived at this three-story house when he commanded the military in the Cincinnati area during the Civil War.[182]

Saint Bernard

CAMP HARRISON SITE (39.178475°, -84.498448°)
Address | 5401 Spring Grove Avenue
Additional Notes | Unmarked. The location is private property.

The area bounded by the railroad to the west, June Street to the south, Spring Grove Avenue to the east and Murray Road to the north was the site of the Cincinnati Trotting Park, which the camp occupied. Camp Harrison served as the main training facility for the three-months' Cincinnati regiments from April 19 to May 18, 1861, after which time the camp held new recruits until it was abandoned around June 6. It was named after U.S. president William Henry Harrison, a Greater Cincinnati resident and War of 1812 hero. Men of the Fifth Ohio Infantry, Sixth Ohio Infantry, Ninth Ohio Infantry and

Tenth Ohio Infantry learned the art of war here. In September 1862, the U.S. Quartermaster's Department used the Trotting Park to stable horses and mules.[183]

SPRING GROVE CEMETERY (39.164707°, -84.523108°)
Address | 4521 Spring Grove Avenue
Additional Notes | The location is accessible to the public.

See the appendix on Spring Grove Cemetery and Arboretum for more details.

EASTERN CINCINNATI, OHIO (EAST OF INTERSTATE 75)

Avondale

LINCOLN AND LIBERTY MONUMENT (39.144257°, -84.491247°)
Address | Southwest corner of Reading Road and Forest Avenue
Additional Notes | The location is accessible to the public.

A Civil War veteran donated this monument to the Cincinnati Public Schools to honor the sixteenth president of the United States. Erected in 1902, the monument features Abraham Lincoln with a reclining figure of Liberty at the base.[184]

Columbia-Tusculum

STEPHEN FOSTER MONUMENT (39.112266°, -84.429606°)
Address | Alms Park, 710 Tusculum Avenue
Additional Notes | The location is accessible to the public.

This monument to the famous American folk song composer Stephen Foster was unveiled in 1937. Foster lived in Cincinnati for four years, during which time he wrote several of his best-known songs sung around many a Civil War soldier's campfire. Foster's monument faces southward toward Kentucky, the state that most inspired his music.[185]

Appendix C

Evanston

WALNUT HILLS UNITED JEWISH CEMETERY (39.140309°, -84.473051°)
Address | 3400 Montgomery Road
Additional Notes | The location is accessible to the public.

The Jewish Civil War Memorial obelisk (39.140032°, -84.472503°) stands in this cemetery. The monument was completed in 1868. It originally honored Lieutenant Louis Reiter, a Cincinnatian who was killed in battle in 1862. The graves of several Jewish Civil War veterans rest beside the monument. Also buried here is Congressional Medal of Honor recipient Corporal David Urbansky (Orbansky) (1843–1897) of Company B, Fifty-Eighth Ohio Infantry, one of only six Jewish soldiers of the Civil War honored with the medal. He received the medal for his gallantry at the battles of Shiloh, Tennessee, and Vicksburg, Mississippi. [Sec. 4, Lot 146, Grave 3][186]

Hyde Park

CAMP CLAY / CAMP DICK CORWINE SITE (39.121688°, -84.454526°)
Address | South of the intersection of Riverside Drive and St. Andrews Street
Additional Notes | Unmarked. The location is private property.

When the Kentucky governor declared neutrality at the beginning of the Civil War, Kentuckians traveled to neighboring states to join either Union or Confederate units. Camp Clay, named after Kentucky statesman Henry Clay, served as a rendezvous and training ground for the First Kentucky (U.S.) Infantry and the Second Kentucky (U.S.) Infantry from April to July 1861. Even though these were Kentucky units, Ohioans (mostly Cincinnatians) filled the majority of their ranks. The Forty-Seventh Ohio Infantry also camped here between June 15 and July 29, 1861. In August of that year, the recruits of the Fifth Ohio Cavalry rendezvoused at the site and renamed it Camp Dick Corwine, after Major Richard M. Corwine. When the cavalrymen left on November 5, 1861, the camp was permanently abandoned.

Camp Clay was located at the west end of the town of Pendleton, Ohio, on property owned by George H. Pendleton. The site of the campground is delineated by present-day Riverside Drive on the north, Corbin Street on the east, the Ohio River on the south and Gotham Place on the west.[187]

APPENDIX C

Mount Auburn

EDWARD F. NOYES OUSE (39.117534°, -84.507996°)
Address | 1940 Bigelow Street
Additional Notes | Unmarked. The location is private property.

Cincinnatian Edward F. Noyes was the colonel of the Thirty-Ninth Ohio Infantry, a Civil War brigadier general, a governor of Ohio and a U.S. ambassador to France. Noyes and his family lived here for many years.[188]

JACOB D. COX HOUSE (39.121674°, -84.506643°)
Address | 241 Gilman Avenue
Additional Notes | Unmarked. The location is private property.

The Civil War major general and Ohio governor lived in this house from 1883 until 1897. During this period he performed the duties of president of the University of Cincinnati and dean of the Cincinnati Law School.[189]

WILLIAM HOWARD TAFT NATIONAL HISTORIC SITE (39.119491°, -84.508317°)
Address | 2038 Auburn Avenue
Additional Notes | The location is accessible to the public.

This was the home of the well-known Cincinnati lawyer and early Republican Party supporter Alphonso Taft and his family from 1851 to 1889. The twenty-seventh president of the United States, William Howard Taft, was born here on September 15, 1857, to Alphonso and Louise. William lived here until he left for Yale College in 1874.[190]

Theodore M. Berry International Friendship Park

JOHNSON, MORTON & COMPANY BOATYARD SITE (39.107098°, -84.492067°)
Address | 1135 Riverside Drive
Additional Notes | Unmarked. The location is accessible to the public.

The *Mirrored Reflections* sculpture stands on the site of the Johnson, Morton & Company Boatyard, which built steamboats and refitted navy boats for the Union war effort.[191]

Appendix C

Walnut Hills

HARRIET BEECHER STOWE HOUSE (39.133164°, -84.487427°)
Address | 2950 Gilbert Avenue
Additional Notes | The location is accessible to the public.

Harriet Beecher Stowe, the famous antislavery advocate and author of the world-renowned novel *Uncle Tom's Cabin* (1852), lived in this house with her parents from 1832 to 1836. Her father was Dr. Lyman Beecher, co-founder and leader of the American Temperance Society. Dr. Beecher moved his family from Connecticut to Cincinnati when he accepted the presidency of Lane Theological Seminary, located nearby.

During this period of her life in Cincinnati, Harriet immersed herself in the antislavery movement. She often took trips to Kentucky, where she witnessed slavery firsthand and listened to the stories of enslaved persons. Prominent abolitionists often visited the Beecher house, and several of them lived in the neighborhood, such as Levi Coffin at former 3131 Wehrman Avenue (39.135824°, -84.492400°). Reports of escaped slaves and trials of Underground Railroad conductors filled the local newspapers. The Lane Seminary Debates of 1834 brought national attention to the issue of slavery in America. All these events from Harriet's years in Cincinnati formed the material for her famous novel.

On January 6, 1836, Harriet married Calvin Stowe, a Lane Seminary professor and an ardent antislavery supporter. In the fall of 1839, Calvin and Harriet moved to their own home at 2622 Gilbert Avenue (no longer standing; 39.128193°, -84.488768°). They lived there until 1850, when they moved to Maine.[192]

JOHN LITHERBURY'S BOATYARD SITE (39.116991°, -84.482486°)
Address | 1727 Riverside Drive
Additional Notes | Unmarked. The location is private property.

On this site was the John Litherbury boatyard. During the Civil War, it built and refitted steamboats and gunboats for the U.S. Navy. The USS *Lexington* was refitted here in June 1861. However, the boatyard's most famous creation was the SS *Sultana*.[193]

Lane Theological Seminary, circa 1846, in the Walnut Hills neighborhood of Cincinnati. The college hosted the Lane Seminary Debates that shifted many American intellectuals toward abolitionist ideals. *From* Historical Collections of Ohio *(1907)*.

LANE THEOLOGICAL SEMINARY HISTORICAL MARKER AND SITE (39.130189°, -84.488289°)

Address | 2820 Gilbert Avenue

Additional Notes | The marker is accessible to the public. The location is private property.

The Lane Theological Seminary was chartered on February 11, 1829. Dr. Lyman Beecher served as its first president for eighteen years. In February 1834, former slave James Bradley and other students organized an eighteen-night series of debates over colonization of enslaved persons versus abolition of slavery in America. Moderated by Theodore Dwight Weld, the highly publicized debates ended with nearly all the students converted into abolitionists. They became known as the "Lane Rebels." These men went on to make Oberlin Collegiate Institute in Oberlin, Ohio, the first integrated and co-educational college in the United States, and they spread the abolitionist movement across the nation. The Lane Seminary closed in 1932 and was demolished in 1956. The parking lot behind the modern car dealership building lies on the site of the campus.[194]

MARINE RAILWAY AND DRY DOCK SITE (39.118799°, -84.479480°)
Address | 1841 Riverside Drive
Additional Notes | Unmarked. The location is private property.

During the Civil War, the Marine Railway boatyard sat at the location of the modern building and its surrounding lot. The boatyard refitted for the U.S. Navy at least forty-six civilian steamboats into tinclad gunboats that were highly successful in bringing Confederate waters under Union control. The dry dock also converted one of the most famous Union navy gunboats to ply the western rivers: the timberclad USS *Tyler*. In addition, the company manufactured pontoon bridge components for the Union army.[195]

S.T. HAMBLETON'S BOATYARD SITE (39.120245°, -84.476334°)
Address | 2021 Riverside Drive
Additional Notes | Unmarked. The location is private property.

The Hambleton boatyard stood where a modern structure now resides. Samuel T. Hambleton's firm built and refitted several Union gunboats during the Civil War at this location, including the timberclad USS *Conestoga* and the ironclad monitors USS *Klamath* and USS *Yuma*.[196]

WESTERN HAMILTON COUNTY, OHIO
(WEST OF INTERSTATE 75)

Bevis

CAMP COLERAIN SITE AND JOHN HUNT MORGAN HERITAGE TRAIL INTERPRETIVE PANEL NO. 2 (39.248920°, -84.596050°)
Address | South side of Springdale Road, just east of Colerain Avenue
Additional Notes | The location is accessible to the public.

The panel describes the village of Bevis, a well-known rest stop on the Colerain Turnpike, as the rendezvous point that Morgan selected to bring together his various Confederate cavalry detachments in the gathering darkness of July 13, 1863. Colonel Adam Johnson met two spies here that he had sent into downtown Cincinnati to assess the Union military response.

The shopping area behind the marker was the site of Camp Colerain. The campsite is roughly delineated by present-day Springdale Road and Coleen Drive on the north, Colerain Avenue on the west, Statewood Drive on the south and Loralinda Drive on the east. Prior to the Civil War, the Methodist congregations of Greater Cincinnati used this plot of land for their annual meeting ground. After the firing on Fort Sumter in April 1861, several Union regiments commandeered the Methodist Meeting Grounds for their recruiting and rendezvous camp. Units that came here included the Forty-Eighth Ohio Infantry and portions of the Twenty-Eighth Ohio Infantry, Thirty-Ninth Ohio Infantry, First Kentucky (U.S.) Infantry and Second Kentucky (U.S.) Infantry. By August 1861, after these troops had left for the front, the military had abandoned the camp permanently.[197]

College Hill

SAMUEL AND SALLY WILSON HOUSE (39.192031°, -84.544288°) AND FARMER'S COLLEGE SITE (39.191729°, -84.548328°)
Address | 1502 Aster Place
Additional Notes | Unmarked. The location is private property.

The Wilsons were Presbyterian educators who moved to College Hill because of the town's predominate antislavery sentiment. Samuel and Sally built this house in 1849 and made it their home. Their four adult children, three grandchildren and aunt lived with them. Three of the Wilson children were noted abolitionists. The house doubly served as a way station on the Underground Railroad from 1849 to 1852. Escaped slaves stopped here for food, clothing and shelter before proceeding north.

Farmers' College was a well-known abolitionist institution that gave College Hill its name. Future U.S. president Benjamin Harrison was a student there.[198]

ZEBULON STRONG HOUSE (39.185980°, -84.544383°)
Address | 5350 Hamilton Avenue
Additional Notes | Unmarked. The location is private property.

Well-known abolitionist Zebulon Strong owned this circa 1850 house and used it as an Underground Railroad station along the Hamilton Turnpike, the "Road to Freedom." The wooded ravine east of the house, in present-day

Laboiteaux Woods Park, provided shelter and comfort for runaway slaves as they moved north. The park contains several worn paths that escaped slaves blazed during America's antebellum years.[199]

Glendale

Benjamin R. Stevens House (39.270779°, -84.449251°)
Address | Southwest corner of East Sharon Road and Glen Meadow Court
Additional Notes | Unmarked. The location is private property.

Benjamin Stevens, whose Cincinnati carriage factory made Union army ambulances, owned this house during the Civil War; it dates to 1860. The house witnessed Morgan's Confederate raiders pass by on the morning of July 14, 1863. One of the raiders stole Stevens's prized stallion, Sir Henry Bacchus, which was worth $4,000 at the time. Stevens offered a $250 reward for its return. Amazingly, Captain A.C. Stockton of the Eighth Michigan Cavalry, who was present at Morgan's surrender near West Point, Ohio, recognized the stallion and brought the horse back to Stevens. Stockton received the reward as promised.[200]

C.H. Allen house, "The Pillars" (39.267167°, -84.468556°)
Address | 780 Congress Avenue
Additional Notes | Unmarked. The location is private property.

The Charles Henry Allen house, which was built in 1856, was a station on the Underground Railroad. Tunnels connected the house and adjacent gazebo to other homes and buildings nearby. Supposedly, the Allen family hid their horses in these tunnels before Morgan's troops arrived.[201]

C.W. Moulton house (39.270221°, -84.461079°)
Address | 175 East Fountain Avenue
Additional Notes | Unmarked. The location is private property.

Colonel Charles W. Moulton and his wife, Frances Beecher Sherman Moulton, lived in this house, built in 1855. "Fanny" Sherman was Major General William T. Sherman's little sister.[202]

Appendix C

"ELIZA" HOUSE MARKER (39.262080°, -84.450630°)
Address | Southeast corner of Oak Road and Chester Road.
Additional Notes | The location is accessible to the public. The site of the house is private property.

Some 780 yards southeast of the marker (300 yards east, as stated on the sign, is incorrect) stood abolitionist John Van Zandt's brick house (39.260352°, -84.442700°), a major Underground Railroad station that figured into the story of *Uncle Tom's Cabin* as John Van Trompe's house, where the character Eliza Harris hides during her escape to Canada. The Van Zandt home no longer exists.[203]

JOHN HUNT MORGAN HERITAGE TRAIL INTERPRETIVE PANEL NO. 3 AND GLENDALE HERITAGE PRESERVATION MUSEUM (39.271290°, -84.459345°)
Address | Center of the Glendale village square
Additional Notes | The locations are accessible to the public.

Incorporated in 1855, Glendale was the first planned railroad commuter town in the United States. John H. Morgan's Confederate scouts arrived here around 2:00 a.m. on July 14, 1863, expecting to find Union soldiers protecting the Cincinnati, Hamilton & Dayton Railroad. However, they found none. Morgan's ruses had tricked Union major general Ambrose Burnside into thinking Morgan was heading to Hamilton, Ohio. George "Lightning" Ellsworth, Morgan's talented telegrapher, took control of the telegraph in the railroad depot and sent inaccurate dispatches to Union headquarters—a pioneering form of electronic warfare. Morgan's raiders foraged from the town's citizens and tore up some of the railroad tracks before they left. When Hobson's Union cavalrymen arrived later that day, Glendale's women and children lined the streets and handed the soldiers food and drink as they rode by.[204]

The adjacent postwar railroad station stands on the site of the Civil War–era structure where George Ellsworth performed his extraordinary work. The former depot houses the Glendale Heritage Preservation Museum, which contains an exhibit on Morgan's Raiders.

JOHN R. WRIGHT HOUSE (39.270087°, -84.462992°)
Address | 140 Fountain Avenue
Additional Notes | Unmarked. The locations are private property.

Mrs. Wright took pity on two young Confederate cavalrymen of Morgan's raiders who were hidden in her brick carriage house, still standing at 930 Laurel Avenue (39.270684°, -84.463271°). She gave them food and drink before they went on their way.[205]

ROBERTS HOUSE (39.268118°, -84.467393°)
Address | 50 East Fountain Avenue
Additional Notes | Unmarked. The location is private property.

Built in 1855 by Britton Roberts, the house served as an Underground Railroad station until the end of the Civil War.[206]

Harrison

AMERICAN HOUSE HOTEL (39.261936°, -84.818849°)
Address | 130–34 Harrison Avenue
Additional Notes | Unmarked. The location is private property.

Confederate brigadier general John Hunt Morgan's two thousand Confederate cavalrymen entered Ohio at Clinker Run Lane and State Street, south of town, about noon on July 13, 1863. Morgan set up his headquarters on the third floor of this former hotel. When facing its façade, the third and fourth windows from the left identify his room. Here, he discussed his strategy of circumventing Cincinnati with his brigade commanders, Colonel Basil Duke and Colonel Adam R. Johnson. After Morgan's troopers had departed, Brigadier General Edward Hobson's Union Provisional Division occupied Harrison and encamped in its streets on the night of July 13. General Hobson bedded down that evening in the American House.[207]

JOHN HUNT MORGAN HERITAGE TRAIL INTERPRETIVE PANEL NO. 1 (39.261948°, -84.818266°)
Address | Southeast corner of Harrison Avenue and South Walnut Street
Additional Notes | The location is accessible to the public.

This interpretive panel is the first of fifty-six that relates the history of Confederate brigadier general John Hunt Morgan's raid through Ohio in July 1863. Known as the John Hunt Morgan Heritage Trail of Ohio, a series of road signs maintained by the Ohio History Connection mark Morgan's

557-mile path through the state. Kentucky and Indiana have similar driving trails. Morgan's raid was the only major Civil War action to occur in Ohio. The panel here gives a brief summary of the Indiana-Ohio (or "Great") Raid as well as some stories about what happened in Harrison during Morgan's five-hour visit.

Miamitown

MORGAN'S FIRST SKIRMISH IN OHIO HISTORICAL MARKER (39.216179°, -84.703922°)
Address | Northwest end of the Harrison Avenue bridge over the Great Miami River
Additional Notes | The location is accessible to the public.

On the opposite side of the bridge from here, just after 6:00 p.m. on July 13, 1863, twenty-three Union militiamen and scouts under Major Bill Raney attacked a detachment of five hundred Confederate troopers from Morgan's division. Although the fight lasted only a few minutes, the skirmish resulted in two killed and three wounded among the Confederates and one captured Union scout. Under orders not to engage the enemy, the Confederate troopers quickly vanished down the roads to New Baltimore and Bevis, where they would meet the main column that had crossed the river several miles to the north.[208]

Monfort Heights

GERMAN HERITAGE MUSEUM (39.192696°, -84.619884°)
Address | 4764 West Fork Road
Additional Notes | The location is accessible to the public.

This museum is dedicated to recalling the history of the German Americans who settled in Greater Cincinnati and helped win the Civil War for the Union.

Appendix C

Mount Healthy

Benjamin A. Hunt house (39.227042°, -84.547486°)
Address | 1575 St. Clair Avenue
Additional Notes | Unmarked. The location is private property.

The Benjamin Hunt house was reportedly a station on the Underground Railroad. Benjamin A. Hunt served on the board of directors of Farmers' College in College Hill.

Mount Healthy Historical Society Museum / Free Meeting House (39.233451°, -84.545108°)
Address | 1546 McMakin Avenue
Additional Notes | The location is accessible to the public.

During antebellum times, Mount Pleasant (now called Mount Healthy) was a hotbed of abolitionism and a major stop on the Underground Railroad. This circa 1825 Free Meeting House, originally located at the northeast corner of Compton Road and Perry Street, hosted many antislavery, Liberty Party and Republican Party conventions. It is now the home of the Mount Healthy Historical Society museum.

Rev. John Scott house (39.232685°, -84.548308°)
Address | Northwest corner of Hamilton Avenue and Compton Road
Additional Notes | The marker is accessible to the public. The location is private property.

This store was formerly a house that the antislavery minister and professor John W. Scott owned. Benjamin Harrison, a Civil War officer and future president of the United States, married the reverend's daughter, Caroline. Benjamin often visited here to court Caroline. Prior to the Civil War, Professor Scott used the house as an Underground Railroad station. A marker attached to the outside wall denotes this fact.[209]

Mount St. Joseph

Mount St. Joseph Cemetery (39.099229°, -84.648065°)
Address | 5900 Delhi Pike
Additional Notes | The location is accessible to the public.

The cemetery for the nunnery contains the grave of Sister Mary (Anthony) O'Connell (1814–1897), known by Civil War soldiers as the "Angel of the Battlefield." A government tombstone marks her grave. For many years after her death, Civil War veterans visited her tomb every Independence Day to remember her tireless work as a war nurse with the Sisters of Charity. [Sec. A, Grave 3]

New Baltimore

GREAT MIAMI RIVER COVERED BRIDGE SITE (39.263705°, -84.667575°)
Address | South end of Locust Street
Additional Notes | The location is accessible to the public.

The bridge abutments are all that remain of a 410-foot covered bridge that Morgan's men burned in the twilight hours of July 13, 1863. The flames from the fire lit up the night sky for miles around; the reflection off the clouds could be seen as far away as downtown Cincinnati. Hobson's main column entered the town on the morning of July 14 and forced two suspected Copperhead citizens to point out a nearby ford over the river. The Union cavalrymen made the two Confederate sympathizers walk the ford several times to prove its location.[210]

Springdale

MORGAN'S RAID THROUGH SPRINGDALE HISTORICAL MARKER (39.286772°, -84.485020°)
Address | Southeast corner of Springdale Road and Springfield Pike
Additional Notes | The location is accessible to the public.

During their arduous nonstop ride around Cincinnati on the night of July 13–14, 1863, Morgan's Confederate troopers entered the town of Springfield (Springdale Post Office) here around midnight. General John Morgan and his brother, Colonel Dick Morgan, threatened to burn down the town butcher's house if he did not start a fire to cook them a meal. The butcher obliged.[211]

OLD ST. MARY'S CEMETERY HISTORICAL MARKER (39.280822°, -84.484892°)
Address | Northwest corner of Springfield Pike and Cameron Road
Additional Notes | The location is accessible to the public.

Two exhausted Confederate cavalrymen fell asleep among the tombstones of this cemetery on the night of July 13–14, 1863. Local Union home guards awoke them the next morning and took them prisoner.[212]

Wyoming

CAMP JOHN MCLEAN MEMORIAL PARK (39.242410°, -84.473548°)
Address | Northwest corner of Bonham Road and Harmon Drive
Additional Notes | The location is accessible to the public.

A monument stands at the site of Camp John McLean, where the Seventy-Fifth Ohio Infantry trained from November 1861 to January 27, 1862. The camp was dismantled when the Seventy-Fifth finished its instruction. The facility was named in honor of former U.S. Supreme Court justice John McLean.

EASTERN HAMILTON COUNTY, OHIO
(EAST OF INTERSTATE 75)

Blue Ash

BLUE ASH BICENTENNIAL VETERANS MEMORIAL (39.230075°, -84.375462°)
Address | Southwest corner of Hunt Road and Cooper Road
Additional Notes | The location is accessible to the public.

The memorial park was established in 1991. It contains a circular plaza ringed with statues of soldiers representing all of America's wars, including one of a Union infantryman that honors those in the region who served during the Civil War. The nearby American Heritage Bell Tower presents brief biographies of important Americans such as Harriet Tubman and Abraham Lincoln.[213]

JOHN C. HUNT HOUSE AND JOHN HUNT MORGAN HERITAGE TRAIL
INTERPRETIVE PANEL NO. 6 (39.229562°, -84.390795°)
Address | 4364 Hunt Road
Additional Notes | The locations are accessible to the public.

Wealthy farmer and horse breeder John C. Hunt completed this house
in 1861. The City of Blue Ash maintains it as a museum that is publicly
accessible by appointment. John Hunt and his family lost six horses to
Confederate troopers on July 14, 1863, as Morgan's men scoured the
countryside in eastern Hamilton County to replace their worn-out steeds.
Like most of the citizens living along the raid path who had lost property to
Confederate and Union soldiers, Hunt filed damage claims against the State
of Ohio for four of the six horses. After the war, the state paid him money
for the horses, but only at fair-market value.[214]

Camp Dennison

CAMP DENNISON LAYOUT SITES

The following sites, all unmarked, give a general sense of the size and layout
of Camp Dennison. It encompassed over seven hundred acres of rented
land that stretched south from the Little Miami River at Miamiville, Ohio,
to just south of Reservoir Hill, to the ridge on the west overlooking the
river bottoms. The list starts at the Waldschmidt House Museum and goes
clockwise around the present-day town of Camp Dennison.

CHRISTIAN WALDSCHMIDT HOMESTEAD MUSEUM (39.191632°, -84.290243°)
Address | 7567 Glendale-Milford Road
Additional Notes | The location is accessible to the public.

Christian Waldschmidt, a Revolutionary War veteran, constructed this large
stone house in 1804. John Kugler, who was Christian's grandson-in-law,
owned the house during the Civil War. On April 27, 1861, John and other
residents of the village of Germany leased their properties to the State of
Ohio for use as a military campsite. The U.S. government paid the leases
from June 1861 to June 1866.

On April 29, 1861, Major General George B. McClellan ordered Ohio's
Union recruits to be transferred to Camp Dennison. McClellan occupied

A bird's-eye view of Camp Dennison as it would have looked in 1865. The line of hospital and Veteran Reserve Corps barracks are on the left; the soldiers' barracks are at the top tight. *Courtesy of the Library of Congress.*

the Waldschmidt-Kugler house for his headquarters when he inspected the troops at the campground. On May 17, the commander of the troops from Camp Harrison, Brigadier General Joshua Bates, arrived and took over the house for use as the post headquarters. However, the house was not written into the original lease; therefore, Bates needed to find a new location. The house served as the post headquarters of Camp Dennison from May through June 1861, after which time the headquarters moved to its permanent location on Lincoln Road next to the railroad depot.

The Waldschmidt house contains period furnishings and exhibits. Behind the house is the welcome center and museum, which displays several artifacts, including President James Garfield's personal surrey.[215]

CAMP DENNISON CIVIL WAR MUSEUM (39.190775°, -84.290338°)
Address | 7567 Glendale-Milford Road
Additional Notes | The location is accessible to the public.

The museum is maintained in a small fieldstone house built in 1804 that was used as a guardhouse for Camp Dennison during the period that the Waldschmidt-Kugler home served as the post headquarters.[216] The museum contains exhibits on the history of the Civil War camp as well as period artifacts found in the area. One must access the Civil War museum through the Christian Waldschmidt Homestead Museum.

SECREST MONUMENT AND JOHN HUNT MORGAN HERITAGE TRAIL
INTERPRETIVE PANEL NO. 8 (39.189352°, -84.292028°)
Address | Intersection of Kugler Mill Road and Glendale-Milford Road
Additional Notes | The location is accessible to the public.

The Secrest Monument is named after Jacob Secrest, a commander of the Department of Ohio of the Grand Army of the Republic who raised funds for the monument. It was dedicated on October 2, 1932, to honor the military units that were formed at Camp Dennison over the course of the Civil War. A bronze plaque on the monument lists those units. Hundreds of other units from various states and for various reasons stopped or passed through Camp Dennison. It is estimated that between fifty and seventy-five thousand men entered the camp during the war.[217]

The small park surrounding the monument hosts interpretive signs, a flagpole and a cannon. The John Hunt Morgan Heritage Trail Interpretive Panel gives more information about Camp Dennison and the Skirmish at the Crossroads. The cannon is a relic from the Spanish-American War.

Reservoir Hill (39.189024°, -84.289588°)
Address | The hill located across Glendale-Milford Road from the Secrest Monument
Additional Notes | Unmarked. The location is private property.

At the top of the hill lay a deep forty-three-foot-diameter reservoir containing water that was pumped from the Kugler millrace off the Little Miami River and then distributed to the camp's hospital wards through metal pipes. Fires heated one of the main outlet pipes to deliver hot water to the soldiers. The reservoir bricks are gone, but a depression in the ground still exists.

Hospital Barn site (39.189601°, -84.292856°) and early Parade Ground (39.189433°, -84.293176°)
Address | Kugler Mill Soccer Fields, northeast corner of Kugler Mill Road and Camp Road
Additional Notes | Unmarked. The location is accessible to the public.

About thirty yards east of the road entrance to the soccer fields, on the north side of Kugler Mill Road, sat the Twelfth Division Hospital, a large two-story barn converted into a hospital when the camp first opened in April 1861. John Kugler owned the barn before the war, but the government commandeered the structure and modified it for large-scale use. It could accommodate 340 patients. Even after the hospital barracks were built, the barn remained an active hospital for the rest of the war.

Surrounding the parking lot for the soccer fields is the camp parade ground on which most of the Cincinnati Brigade drilled. Other regiments trained here, too, throughout the war.

Camp Road and the line of Hospital Barracks and Veteran Reserve Corps Barracks site (39.190566°, -84.295385°)
Address | Camp Road, from Kugler Mill Road to Cunningham Road
Additional Notes | Unmarked. The locations are accessible to the public only at the soccer fields.

A single line of sixty-seven wooden barracks stood in a mile-long row that paralleled the west side of present-day Camp Road. The military constructed Camp Road for the purpose of north–south navigation through the extensive military base, and after the camp was dismantled from November 8, 1865, to June 1, 1866, locals continued to use the road.

Of the sixty-seven barracks, fifty large barracks originally housed recruits, but after the Battle of Shiloh, these barracks were converted into hospital wards. Seventeen small barracks lay at the north end of the row and were utilized as follows: six quartered the Veteran Reserve Corps soldiers, one housed the camp band members, nine sheltered the convalescent soldiers and one contained wares. Fifty-nine of the barracks had behind them a kitchen house (most were used as storerooms or workshops), an attendants' quarters and a sink. Other buildings behind the hospital wards served general purposes.

Inserted in May 1861 within the row of barracks was a small chapel building (39.193034°, -84.295182°) that sat on the creek that flows under Camp Road about a quarter of a mile north of Kugler Mill Road. On July 20, 1863, carpenters completed an expansion to the chapel to allow five hundred men to attend services; it reopened on August 13. A steam laundry (39.188638°, -84.296532°) was built on the south side of Kugler Mill Road about 130 yards southwest of Camp Road.

OFFICERS' QUARTERS SITE (39.197476°, -84.296317°)
Address | West side of Daniel Avenue, between Jackson Street and Washington Avenue
Additional Notes | Unmarked. The location is private property.

On the hillside above the modern houses lays the site of seven officers' quarters that overlooked the camp.

SOLDIERS' BARRACKS SITE (39.200178°, -84.285031°)
Address | Grand Valley Preserve, 8270 Glendale-Milford Road
Additional Notes | Unmarked. The location is private property.

A line of thirty soldiers' barracks stretched from Ulrich Street north-northeast into the present-day quarry lake in Grand Valley Preserve Park. Behind the north end of the barracks was a parallel row of six cavalry stables constructed in December 1861. The parade grounds occupied the plain lying between the barracks and the Veteran Reserve Corps barracks at the base of the hill to the west. The artillery training grounds were located north of the soldiers' barracks near the eastern end of present-day Fletcher Lane. The young artillerymen would practice firing their cannons by aiming into the steep river bluff called Devil's Backbone (39.214236°, -84.285413°). Long after the war had ended, residents found spent cannonballs and shells in the river at the bottom of the bluff.

POST HEADQUARTERS, DEPOT AND QUARTERMASTER BUILDINGS (39.195312°, -84.291324°)
Address | Lincoln Road at the Little Miami Scenic Bike Trail
Additional Notes | Unmarked. The locations are private property.

The Little Miami Scenic Bike Trail lies on the bed of the Little Miami & Xenia Railroad, which split the camp in two halves—east and west.

At the southeast corner of Lincoln Road and the Bike Trail stands a one-story wooden house that was once the post headquarters for Camp Dennison. It was from here that Lieutenant Colonel George W. Neff directed the defense of the camp during Morgan's Raid in July 1863. The railroad depot stood along the Bike Trail on the southwest side of the house, and southeast of it sat the camp prison building. Across the street on Lincoln Road is an old brick house; this did not exist until after the camp was dismantled in 1865.

On each side of the railroad tracks (now the Bike Trail) between Lincoln and Cunningham Roads were buildings that served the whole camp. On the east side stood a post office, telegraph office, carpenter shop and forage houses. On the west side were the post quartermaster, post commissary, clerks' mess and warehouses.

On Lincoln Road, between here and Glendale-Milford Road, stood the provost marshal's office, a reading room, a photography gallery, a jewelry store, a bowling alley and a sutler's store for the soldiers to entertain themselves and buy gifts. To the west, on Lincoln Road near its intersection with Camp Road, the soldiers built a continuously flowing decorative fountain.

CAMP DENNISON (WALDSCHMIDT) CEMETERY (39.194466°, -84.287811°)
Address | 7792 Glendale-Milford Road
Additional Notes | The location is accessible to the public.

The Waldschmidt Cemetery served both the civilian community and the military during the Civil War. Deceased soldiers, both Union and Confederate, were buried in the cemetery's central section, which is currently surrounded by a circular driveway. The government removed the soldiers' bodies from here in 1866. The Confederate dead were reinterred at Camp Chase Confederate Cemetery in Columbus, Ohio, while the Union dead were reburied in the mounds at Spring Grove Cemetery in Cincinnati.

Two government stables stood in the field across from the cemetery gate on Glendale-Milford Road. Larger stables were located along the west side and the north end of present-day Singleton Alley.[218]

METHODIST CHURCH SITE (39.192975°, -84.288661°)
Address | East side of Glendale-Milford Road, opposite No. 7685
Additional Notes | Unmarked. The location is accessible to the public.

About fifteen yards from the edge of Glendale-Milford Road is the first site of Germany village's Methodist church. It was built here in 1845 next to the town well. After Camp Dennison was established on April 27, 1861, the first soldiers began to arrive within days. Those men who became sick were brought to the Kugler barn for treatment. When a measles epidemic broke out, the Sisters of Charity from Cincinnati came to the camp to tend to the sick and dying soldiers. To avoid the long trips back and forth to Cincinnati, the Sisters commandeered the Methodist church for their quarters while they stayed at Camp Dennison. Their nursing here marked the beginning of the work that the Sisters of Charity performed throughout the Civil War in manning hospitals to help sick and wounded soldiers.[219]

Deer Park

JOHN SCHENCK HOUSE AND JOHN HUNT MORGAN HERITAGE TRAIL INTERPRETIVE PANEL NO. 7 (39.206028°, -84.396275°)
Address | 4208 Schenck Avenue
Additional Notes | The marker is accessible to the public. The location is private property.

Built in 1806, this house is among the oldest in Hamilton County. John and Amelia Schenck and their family of eleven children lived here on a 175-acre farm when Brigadier General John Hunt Morgan's Confederate scouts appeared about 5:00 a.m. on July 14, 1863. One of the scouts knocked at the door, and one of the Schenck women in nurse's garb answered. The soldier politely asked the woman for food and for directions to where the Schencks' horses were kept. She pointed to the barn where only useless old workhorses were stabled, and then she told them to wait outside the house while she brought them food and drink, because inside the house was a child sick with smallpox. Sheets on the door and windows of the parlor indicated quarantine. The soldiers obeyed, and the woman fed them.

Meanwhile, General Morgan and his staff rode up to the house and requested food. The Schenck women served the general and his men outside on the porch and lawn. In about thirty minutes, Morgan and his troopers rode away. They never realized that inside the parlor covered with hay were four escaped slaves (John Henry and Clara Jane Thompson and their two children) and two expensive Spanish horses that the Thompsons kept hushed.[220]

Evendale

GEORGE BROWN FARM (GORMAN HERITAGE FARM) AND JOHN HUNT MORGAN HERITAGE TRAIL INTERPRETIVE PANEL NO. 5 (39.245181°, -84.425045°)
Address | 10052 Reading Road
Additional Notes | The location is accessible to the public.

George Brown owned this farm during the Civil War. The house, banked barn and outbuildings were built around 1835. Brown lost two horses to Morgan's troopers on the morning of July 14, 1863. The Confederate soldiers took a drink from Brown's lower springhouse (39.243587°, -84.423325°) and then led the farmer's horses from the banked barn (39.242843°, -84.423729°). It owns the unique distinction of being the only original barn among the thousands from which Morgan's men foraged along the raid path that visitors can explore today. The Gorman Heritage Farm is an outdoor museum that allows the general public to see how a farm works.[221]

Indian Hill

SKIRMISH AT THE CROSSROADS SITE (39.200988°, -84.339149°)
Address | Intersection (the "Crossroads") of Loveland-Madeira Road, Kugler Mill Road and Camargo Road
Additional Notes | Unmarked. The location is private property.

A skirmish occurred here from 6:00 a.m. to 6:30 a.m. on July 14, 1863, between the pickets of Colonel Adam R. Johnson's Confederate brigade and about 350 Union militiamen, civilians and convalescent soldiers from Camp Dennison. General Morgan, who accompanied Johnson, intended to damage or capture Camp Dennison. However, prior to the Confederate vanguard's arrival at the crossroads, Union lieutenant colonel George Neff had ordered a contingent of men with axes and shovels to fell trees at the crossroads and dig rifle pits on the hill immediately east of the intersection.

The Union soldiers sought shelter behind the rifle pits during the skirmish. Morgan ordered Captain Byrne's artillery to fire a few rounds to dislodge the stubborn defenders, but the line held. Not wanting to get into a general engagement, Morgan ordered the brigade to retreat to Montgomery to meet Duke's brigade there. No casualties were reported on either side.[222]

Miamiville

JOHN H. ANDERSON GRAVE (39.211660°, -84.310366°) AND MADISONVILLE TURNPIKE BRIDGE SKIRMISH SITE (39.210829°, -84.312138°)
Address | Evergreen Cemetery, 234 Center Street
Additional Notes | The location is accessible to the public.

At the first lane on the left from the cemetery entrance are the graves of John H. Anderson and his wife, Katherine Deerwester Anderson. Confederate private John H. Anderson of the Second Kentucky Cavalry met Katherine when he came to forage food and horses from the Deerwester farm near Goshen, Ohio, during Morgan's Great Raid. They fell in love at first sight, and John promised he would come back for Katherine after the war ended. He honored his commitment; in 1866, he returned to Ohio and married Katherine. They are buried together here.[223]

Interred next to the Andersons is Charlie Rich, the man who dealt the first "Dead Man's Hand" in poker to a doomed Civil War veteran named "Wild Bill" Hickok in Deadwood, South Dakota. A large, colorful marker adorns Rich's grave, and a historical marker at the cemetery entrance tells more about him.

Across the road from the cemetery, at the bend in the highway, lie the remains of the Madisonville Turnpike bridge over the Little Miami River. About 7:45 a.m. on July 14, 1863, Confederate scouts from Brigadier General John Hunt Morgan's division surprised and dispersed the pickets of the Eleventh Ohio Cavalry as they were playing cards on the Madisonville Pike Bridge. The bridge floor is gone, but its shore abutments and center pier still exist.[224]

LITTLE MIAMI RAILROAD BRIDGE SKIRMISH SITE (39.210655°, -84.293647°), TRAIN DERAILMENT SITE (39.220468°, -84.312755°), AND JOHN HUNT MORGAN HERITAGE TRAIL INTERPRETIVE PANELS NO. 9 AND NO. 10 (39.212936°, -84.296010°)

Address | Southeast corner of Glendale-Milford Road and the Little Miami Scenic Bike Trail
Additional Notes | The locations are accessible to the public. The derailment site is unmarked.

On July 14, 1863, about two hundred Union militiamen and a small detachment from the Eleventh Ohio Cavalry successfully held off dismounted skirmishers and artillery from Confederate colonel Basil Duke's brigade. The three-hour skirmish ended when Lieutenant Colonel George W. Neff, the commander of Camp Dennison, led a squad of convalescent troops in a bayonet charge over the railroad bridge. Duke's brigade retreated hastily to the village of Ward's Corner north of here to meet up with the rest of Brigadier General John Hunt Morgan's raiders. One can freely visit the location of the Little Miami Railroad Bridge where the skirmish occurred; the modern Bike Trail bridge over the river stands on the site.

Around 7:15 a.m. on July 14, 1863, less than an hour before the skirmish at the Little Miami Railroad Bridge, a group of Morgan's scouts from the

BRIDGE OVER LITTLE MIAMI, AT MIAMIVILLE.

Little Miami Railroad Bridge, where Lieutenant Colonel George Neff's soldiers fought a three-hour skirmish with Morgan's raiders on July 14, 1863. Neff emerged victorious. *From Edward Mansfield's* The Ohio Railroad Guide, Illustrated *(1854).*

Fourteenth Kentucky Cavalry placed a barricade onto the tracks of the Little Miami & Xenia Railroad, just over a mile northwest of Miamiville. A passenger train headed toward Camp Dennison hit the barricade at full speed, derailing the locomotive "Kilgour" and its tender. The fireman was killed, and the engineer was severely injured in the crash. However, the passenger cars, which were filled with civilians and 115 raw militiamen from Clark County, miraculously stayed on the tracks. Morgan's troopers captured the militiamen without a shot and burned the cars. One can hike along the Little Miami Scenic Bike Trail to reach the spot of the derailment.

John Hunt Morgan Heritage Trail markers no. 9 and no. 10 provide maps and more details about the skirmish and the train derailment incident. The panels stand in the area where Neff's convalescents fought hand-to-hand with some of the dismounted raiders of Duke's brigade.[225]

Montgomery

PORTER'S (HAMILTON'S) MILL FORD (39.223505°, -84.319825°)
Address | Behind the Camp Livingston Lodge, 9350 Given Road
Additional Notes | The lodge grounds are accessible to the public, but the house, mill site and ford are private property.

Located behind the Camp Livingston Lodge is the Porter's Mill ford, also known as Hamilton's Mill ford. Here the majority of Confederate brigadier general John H. Morgan's men, along with their artillery and wagon train, crossed the Little Miami River between 7:00 a.m. and 9:00 a.m. on July 14, 1863. Remnants of the mill and millrace are located on private property. The Elliott-Hamilton house, built in 1802, stands in front of the ford. The house is presently a private residence.[226]

SAGE TAVERN (39.227004°, -84.354497°)
Address | 9410 Montgomery Road
Additional Notes | Unmarked. The location is private property.

The Sage Tavern was three times longer than the present-day remaining structure when the log building was erected in 1818–19. Modern siding has covered the logs. The owner at the time of the Civil War, John W. Sage, lost to Morgan's Raiders his horse worth one hundred dollars and his entire stock of liquor, valued at ten dollars. The state reimbursed Sage's claim for the horse, but the government did not honor the loss of his liquor. The State of Ohio never reimbursed liquor claims.

Brigadier General John Hunt Morgan chose Montgomery to be the place of rendezvous for his scattered columns who had foraged over a three-mile-wide swath of northeastern Hamilton County throughout the morning of July 14, 1863. Colonel Basil Duke's First Brigade entered the town from the northwest on Zig Zag Road, then General Morgan and Colonel Adam Rankin Johnson's Second Brigade rode into town on Montgomery Road from the south, after they had fought a thirty-minute duel with Union infantry sent from Camp Dennison. Brigadier General Edward Hobson's pursuing column of 2,500 Union cavalry and artillery passed through Montgomery on the evening of July 14.

Montgomery contains many other period houses and buildings that have Civil War–related histories, including the house at 9433 Montgomery Road, which was the home of Dr. John Naylor, a surgeon at Camp Dennison. The Universalist church (circa 1837) at the southwest corner of Montgomery and Remington Roads served as the backdrop for artist Mort Kunstler's painting *Morgan's Ohio Raid*.[227]

Sharonville

TWELVE-MILE HOUSE AND JOHN HUNT MORGAN HERITAGE TRAIL
INTERPRETIVE PANEL NO. 4 (39.268462°, -84.412900°)
Address | Northeast corner of East Sharon Road and Reading Road
Additional Notes | The markers are accessible to the public. The location is private property.

At the time of the Civil War, the circa 1842 Twelve-Mile House tavern and saloon were managed by Christopher Myer, a known Copperhead (Peace Democrat). When Brigadier General John Hunt Morgan's Confederate cavalrymen arrived in Sharon (Sharonville Post Office) around 3:00 a.m. on July 14, 1863, Morgan and his officers entered the saloon to rest and to discuss plans for their movements eastward to the Little Miami River.

Myer brought out his best bottle of brandy to give to the officers, alerting Morgan that the tavernkeeper was a Confederate sympathizer. Morgan and his men despised the Copperheads for their treasonous thoughts and for their refusal to fight for the Confederacy. In response to the Copperhead's unusual kindness, Morgan and his officers drank down the bottle of liquor and then stole four boxes of cigars and a horse from Myer. No one cursed Morgan more after that day than Myer.[228]

There are two markers here. One is affixed to the wall near the door of the former tavern. The other is the John Hunt Morgan Heritage Trail panel that stands along the sidewalk at the side of the building.

DOWNTOWN COVINGTON, KENTUCKY

AMOS SHINKLE TOWNHOUSE (39.089479°, -84.506929°)
Address | 215 Garrard Street
Additional Notes | The location is private property.

Amos Shinkle, a successful Covington steamboat businessman, was influential in funding the construction of the Roebling Suspension Bridge. He worked with the Covington and Cincinnati Bridge Company from 1856 to 1866. Although the bridge's construction slowed during the Civil War, he pushed to complete the project quickly after the war ended. Shinkle served as a colonel in the Kentucky Home Guards, who helped defend Cincinnati in September 1862. This townhouse, where he lived until 1869, dates to 1854.[229]

CARNEAL (GANO-SOUTHGATE) HOUSE AND MARKER (39.090270°, -84.504826°)
Address | 405 East Second Street
Additional Notes | The location is private property.

Built in 1815, it is the oldest brick house in Covington. It was used as an Underground Railroad station prior to the Civil War. A tunnel leads from the basement of the house to the bank of the Licking River nearby. Famous visitors to the house included the Marquis de Lafayette, Daniel Webster, Henry Clay and Andrew Jackson.[230]

FIRST CITY HALL MARKER (39.088861°, -84.508205°)
Address | Northwest corner of Greenup Street and East Third Street
Additional Notes | The location is accessible to the public.

The Covington City Hall originally stood nearby, where the current war memorial sits today at the north end of Court Avenue. The building witnessed many antislavery meetings and pro-Union political and military activities during the Civil War.

Garner Slave Escape Historical Marker (39.084170°, -84.517353°)
Address | West Sixth Street at Main Street
Additional Notes | The locations are accessible to the public.

The marker summarizes the story of the attempted escape of enslaved persons Margaret Garner; her husband, Robert; their four children; and Robert's parents on the snowy night of January 27, 1856. When she and her family were captured the next morning in Elijah Kite's cabin (39.101936°, -84.546857°) near Cincinnati, Margaret killed her two-year-old daughter rather than allow her to return to slavery. This highly publicized event kindled a national debate on states' rights versus federal rights regarding the issues of slavery and the Fugitive Slave Act.

The Covington Sixth Street Market House (39.084207°, -84.517859°) stood between Main and Bakewell Streets. Converted in November 1862 into a barracks to shelter four hundred soldiers, the structure acted as a military convalescent hospital for less than a month during the Civil War.[231]

Government Quartermaster Warehouse and Office (39.082426°, -84.509578°)
Address | 740 Madison Avenue
Additional Notes | Unmarked. The location is private property.

Now used as a reception hall, this brick structure served as the U.S. quartermaster's office and warehouse for Covington during the Civil War. Based on government records, this is Greater Cincinnati's only remaining quartermaster building from the war. The government rented the three-story building from James C. Blick beginning on September 29, 1863. Inside was an office for the Covington post quartermaster and 116,368 cubic feet of space for storing clothing, camp and garrison equipment and other goods. Captain George P. Webster, the assistant quartermaster, commanded the building at the time. For a brief period in 1862, the building was used as a temporary hospital for sick and wounded soldiers. On the Eighth Street side of the building, one can still see the now bricked-up arched main entrance and adjoining window of the Civil War–era warehouse.[232]

Henry Bruce Jr. House No. 1 (39.084474°, -84.505888°)
Address | 622 Sanford Street
Additional Notes | Unmarked. The location is private property.

Henry Bruce Jr. was a wealthy merchant who served on the board of directors of the Covington and Cincinnati Bridge Company from 1856 to 1858 before becoming its president in 1859. John A. Roebling, the chief engineer of the Cincinnati-Covington (Roebling) Suspension Bridge, stayed in the Bruce house from 1856 to 1857.[233]

Henry Bruce Jr. House No. 2 (39.084223°, -84.505908°)
Address | 630 Sanford Street
Additional Notes | Unmarked. The location is private property.

Henry Bruce Jr. constructed this house in 1860, and it was here that Bruce and his family lived during the Civil War. Bruce fled to Canada in December 1863 when he learned that Union authorities were going to arrest him for supposedly supplying Confederate brigadier general John Hunt Morgan with funds he used to escape from the Ohio State Penitentiary.[234]

James Bradley Monument (39.091415°, -84.505574°)
Address | Riverside Drive at Kennedy Street
Additional Notes | The location is accessible to the public.

The monument displays a bronze sculpture of a pensive James Bradley seated on a bench overlooking the Ohio River. Bradley was a freed slave and a well-educated, influential abolitionist who participated in the nationally recognized Lane Seminary Debates on slavery.[235]

Jesse and Hannah Grant House and Marker (39.085871°, -84.507169°)
Address | 520 Greenup Street
Additional Notes | The locations are private property.

From 1859 to 1873, this was the home of Jesse and Hannah Simpson Grant, the parents of Ulysses S. Grant, lieutenant general and president of the United States. Jesse Grant worked as the postmaster of Covington from 1866 to 1872. General Grant visited the house often. His wife, Julia, and their four children came to live here in January 1862. During the war, Ulysses's and

Julia's son Frederick attended a private school in the Clay-Bullock house at 528 Greenup Street (39.085425°, -84.507015°).

Civil War notables William T. Sherman, John Rawlins and George Stoneman also spent time at the Jesse Grant house. On July 7, 1863, Jesse spoke from its front entrance to a large crowd that had assembled outside to celebrate his son's capture of Vicksburg, Mississippi.[236]

MURALS ON THE COVINGTON FLOODWALL (39.090666°, -84.510185°)
Address | Riverside Drive west of Riverside Place
Additional Notes | The location is accessible to the public.

Robert Dafford painted these beautiful murals from 2002 to 2008. They depict important moments in the history of Covington. The murals related to the antebellum and Civil War period are titled *Flight of the Garner Family* (the enslaved Garner family crossing the ice-choked Ohio River in January 1856), *Pontoon Bridge* (Union troops crossing the Ohio River pontoon bridge in early September 1862), *Jacob Price* (a tireless advocate of education for African Americans after the war) and *Vision and Ingenuity* (the opening of the Roebling Suspension Bridge in 1867).[237]

NEWPORT-COVINGTON SUSPENSION BRIDGE SITE (39.088118°, -84.504416°)
Address | East Fourth Street at the Licking River
Additional Notes | The location is accessible to the public.

The current Fourth Street Bridge stands on the site of the Newport-Covington Suspension Bridge that was opened on December 28, 1853. During the Civil War, Union troops and supply trains frequently crossed the bridge to move between the cities. From September 24 to 29, 1862, soldiers built a temporary pontoon bridge (39.088537°, -84.504372°) over the Licking River to detour traffic while the suspension bridge remained closed for repairs for several months. After the war, Washington Roebling, John Roebling's son, strengthened the cabling system with metal castings manufactured at the Eagle Iron Works in Cincinnati. The bridge was demolished in 1886; the present structure dates to 1936. A marker at the Newport end of the bridge relates its history.[238]

ODD FELLOWS HALL (39.086110°, -84.510533°)
Address | 434 Madison Avenue
Additional Notes | Unmarked. The location is private property.

Built in 1856, the building served the city as a political and social center during the Civil War. It boasted a large ballroom for hosting extravagant events, such as theatrical shows and charity balls for soldiers and their families. Locals honored General Ulysses Grant with a banquet here soon after the close of the war. Citizens established a temporary hospital here in 1862, and the building occasionally held Confederate prisoners of war and Union deserters from 1862 to 1863. The prisoners left graffiti on the interior walls that were destroyed when the building suffered a fire in 2002.

PHILLIPS & SON'S LICKING IRON WORKS SITE (39.079459°, -84.501486°)
Address | East end of Bush Street
Additional Notes | Unmarked. The location is private property.

Where a modern subdivision now stands once was the site of the Licking Iron Works. The foundry played an important role in producing iron for U.S. Navy gunboats and transport vessels.[239]

ROEBLING SUSPENSION BRIDGE, ROEBLING STATUE AND HISTORICAL MARKERS (39.090947°, -84.508469°)
Address | Riverside Drive at Riverside Place
Additional Notes | The locations are accessible to the public.

The bronze statue of German American chief engineer John A. Roebling was dedicated in 1988. An adjoining historical marker tells about Roebling and his bridge. Roebling's creation, the famous Roebling Suspension Bridge (39.093000°, -84.509873°), is best viewed from here. Work on the Roebling Bridge started in 1856, but with the advent of the Civil War, construction came to a halt, leaving only the bridge towers in a partially completed state. In the spring of 1863, building resumed, and finally the bridge opened on January 1, 1867, when it claimed the title of the world's longest bridge. This engineering wonder became the second permanent bridge built over the Ohio River (the first was completed by Charles Ellet for the National Road at Wheeling, West Virginia). The Cincinnati-Covington Suspension Bridge served as the prototype for one of Roebling's other famous projects—the Brooklyn Bridge in New York City.[240]

A short distance east on Riverside Drive is the Civil War fortifications historical marker (39.091018°, -84.508235°). It discusses the pontoon bridge that was laid September 2–3, 1862, on the river from Riverside Place on the Kentucky bank to Walnut Street on the Ohio bank. Tens of thousands of Union troops with cannons, horses, wagons and equipment crossed the bridge day and night during the crisis known as the "Siege of Cincinnati." Designed to be twenty-five feet wide, the pontoon bridge was a marvel of engineering at the time, because no other bridge had existed before then at Cincinnati. It was dismantled November 7–8, 1862.

At the southwest corner of Riverside Place and Riverside Drive stood the former Bridge Hotel (39.090731°, -84.508762°), which the government leased as the fifty-three-bed Greenup Street Military Hospital from September 4, 1862, to May 7, 1863.[241]

DOWNTOWN NEWPORT, KENTUCKY

ALEXANDER SWIFT & COMPANY IRON WORKS SITE (39.083241°, -84.500850°)
Address | Northwest corner of Lowell Street and West Ninth Street
Additional Notes | Unmarked. The location is private property.

The large ironworks foundry that once stood here produced iron plating for gunboats during the Civil War. The company also received contracts for the construction of two ironclad monitors for the U.S. Navy.[242]

GENERAL JAMES TAYLOR MANSION AND MARKER (39.096440°, -84.492241°)
Address | 335 East Third Street, opposite Overton Street
Additional Notes | The marker is accessible to the public. The location is private property.

Built in 1837 and called Bellevue, the mansion was the home of General James Taylor, the founder of Newport, Kentucky, and the builder of the Newport Barracks. Taylor owned slaves who slept in the basement of the house.[243]

NEWPORT BARRACKS MONUMENT AND HISTORICAL MARKERS (39.092417°, -84.502351°)
Address | Riverboat Row west of Columbia Street
Additional Notes | The location is accessible to the public.

Realizing the need to replace the obsolete Fort Washington in Cincinnati, the U.S. Army paid General James Taylor to build the Newport Barracks arsenal at the mouth of the Licking River. Completed in 1804, Newport Barracks accepted its first U.S. soldiers in 1806. The military installation's boundaries are roughly defined by today's West Third Street on the south, the Licking River on the west, the Ohio River on the north and Central Avenue on the east, with the center of the parade ground (39.091785°, -84.501905°) located just east of the twentieth-century Newport levee. Nearly five thousand soldiers under General Isaac Shelby occupied the barracks during the War of 1812, and British prisoners were incarcerated here.

Throughout the Civil War, the Newport Barracks housed a steady guard of U.S. regulars as well as Union troops being moved to the front. The installation also recruited volunteers for Union regiments, and it held Confederate and political prisoners, such as Copperhead leader Clement Vallandigham. More buildings were constructed during the Civil War because of the added demand for military housing.

However, continual flooding and overcrowding plagued the facility. U.S. Army general-in-chief Phil Sheridan approved in 1887 that the post be moved to a new military reservation at Fort Thomas, Kentucky, named in honor of Civil War major general George H. Thomas, "The Rock of Chickamauga." The last personnel abandoned Newport Barracks on November 29, 1894.[244]

Today, in General James Taylor Park, a monument and flagpole erected in memory of the Newport Barracks stands at what was once the northwest corner of the installation. It overlooks the confluence of the Licking and Ohio Rivers. Surrounding the monument are historical markers that describe the history of this important spot that had a profound impact on the settlement of the American West.

NORTHERN KENTON COUNTY, KENTUCKY

Eastside

CAMP COVINGTON / COVINGTON BARRACKS / GREENUP STREET BARRACKS / WEBSTER BARRACKS SITE (39.074178°, -84.504363°)
Address | Intersection of East Fifteenth Street and Greenup Street
Additional Notes | Unmarked. The location is private property.

The area currently delineated by Madison Avenue (known as the Banklick Pike during the Civil War), Pleasant Street, the Licking River and East

Seventeenth Street was the site of Camp Covington, which was established on September 3, 1862. Federal quartermaster records from August 1864 indicate that the camp stood between one mile and one and a quarter miles south of the Ohio River on the east side of the Banklick Pike.

By October 28, 1862, the expansive facility had grown to be a significant government quartermaster depot. In 1865, it contained nearly fifty structures, including officers' quarters, offices, horse and mule stables, a hospital, a military prison, storehouses, mechanic shops and ten large wooden barracks to house hundreds of troops. A separate barracks building was constructed to shelter African American soldiers and refugees. Many Union regiments, such as the 162nd Ohio Infantry, 2nd Ohio Heavy Artillery, 72nd U.S. Colored Infantry and 117th U.S. Colored Infantry, were stationed here. The Covington Barracks closed on December 13, 1865, and its buildings were sold to the public. However, a small number of the barracks structures, referred to as Webster Barracks, remained standing through December 1866 to house African American soldiers.[245]

Fort Mitchell

CONFEDERATE THRUST HISTORICAL MARKER (39.056028°, -84.554201°)
Address | Fort Mitchell Avenue at Edgewood Road
Additional Notes | The location is accessible to the public.

The marker tells of the advance on Cincinnati by a Confederate force under Brigadier General Henry Heth from September 6–12, 1862. The text indicates that the objective of the movement was to hold Federal forces long enough to prevent them from fighting Confederate general Braxton Bragg's army in Kentucky.

FORT MITCHEL HISTORICAL MARKER (39.057124°, -84.544196°)
Address | 1911 Dixie Highway
Additional Notes | The marker is accessible to the public. The locations are private property.

The marker describes the bastioned fort that served as the keystone to the defensive line that protected Covington and the vital Lexington Turnpike (now Dixie Highway) from possible Confederate attack. The fort sat at the top of the hill across the highway from the marker. About 120 yards east of the marker, a private driveway (39.058491°, -84.543205°) follows the original military roadbed leading from the turnpike up to the fort.[246] The City of Fort Mitchell, although spelled differently, derived its name from the fort.

Fort Mitchel Skirmish Site (39.048456°, -84.554323°)
Address | Beechwood Road west of Dixie Highway
Additional Notes | Unmarked. The location is private property.

On September 10–11, 1862, during Henry Heth's "Siege of Cincinnati," Confederate and Union pickets clashed west and southwest of the Hubbel G. Buckner house, which stood near Highland Cemetery's main gate along the Dixie Highway. The skirmish occurred in the area now bounded by Woodlawn Avenue, Dixie Highway/US 25, Interstate 75/71, and Seville Court. After a whole day of desultory shooting, mostly concentrated in the region between present-day Beechwood High School and Dixie Highway, the Confederates disengaged from the fight. The 104th Ohio Infantry lost one man killed and four wounded in the skirmish. One Confederate, a Texan, was mortally wounded.[247]

Highland Cemetery (39.047537°, -84.551720°)
Address | 2167 Dixie Highway
Additional Notes | The location is accessible to the public.

The cemetery contains the following Civil War notables:

- Eli Metcalfe Bruce (1828–1866), a Confederate congressman who greatly assisted in the supply of the Confederacy during the war. [Sec. 2, Lot 142, Grave 3]
- Archibald Kincaid Gaines (1808–1871), the owner of enslaved persons Margaret Garner and her family, who were recaptured near Cincinnati during their attempted escape to Canada in 1856. Gaines is a character in the Toni Morrison novel (1987) and movie (1998) titled *Beloved*. [Sec. 3, Lot 21, Grave 4]
- Henry Thomas Harrison (1832–1923), a Confederate spy best known for supplying Lieutenant General James Longstreet with valuable intelligence on Union army movements on June 28, 1863, that ultimately led the Confederate army to the Battle of Gettysburg, Pennsylvania. Harrison is featured as a character in Michael Shaara's *The Killer Angels* (1974). [Sec. 18, Grave 207]

- James Morrison Hawes (1824–1889), a Confederate brigadier general. [Sec. 4, Lot 21, Grave 1]
- Calvary Morris Young (1840–1909), a recipient of the Congressional Medal of Honor for capturing Confederate general William Cabell at Osage, Kansas, on October 25, 1864. Young served as a sergeant in Company L, Third Iowa Cavalry, during the Civil War. [Sec. 12, Lot 43, Grave 3][248]

Fort Wright

FORT WRIGHT HISTORICAL MARKER (39.051826°, -84.536015°)
Address | 409 Kyles Lane, in front of the City of Fort Wright Administration building
Additional Notes | The marker is accessible to the public. The location is private property.

The marker tells about the Civil War fort that gave the city its name.

JAMES A. RAMAGE CIVIL WAR MUSEUM (39.055567°, -84.527236°)
Address | 1402 Highland Avenue
Additional Notes | The location is accessible to the public.

The museum focuses on the history of the Union's defense of Northern Kentucky during the Civil War. The postwar house contains displays and relics related to the batteries and forts of the region, and it tells the stories of the Black Brigade and other soldiers who defended Cincinnati against the September 1862 advance of Confederate forces. Exhibits pertaining to the history of the Fort Wright community are also shown. The museum grounds preserve the remnants of Battery Hooper, one of Northern Kentucky's Civil War earthworks.

Latonia

CAMP KING / CAMP FINNELL SITE (39.054204°, -84.501006°)
Address | Eastern end of East Thirty-First Street
Additional Notes | Unmarked. The location is private property.

Established in September 1861 and named after U.S. major John Haskell King at Newport Barracks, the camp served as a rendezvous and training facility for the Twentieth Ohio Infantry, Tenth Kentucky (U.S.) Infantry, and Twenty-Third Kentucky (U.S.) Infantry. The Second Ohio Infantry briefly stayed here in September 1861. Near the end of the war, liberated slaves used the grounds as a refugee camp. Cole's Licking Gardens (39.054426°, -84.499576°), a favorite entertainment and picnic spot for Greater Cincinnati citizens, lay within the southeast side of the camp, where the oil company stands today. Cole's Garden operated as a military convalescent hospital, opening on August 24, 1863. Camp King centered on the militarily important Kentucky Central Railroad, whose tracks lay today beside the end of East Thirty-First Street. The campgrounds were bounded by present-day East Thirty-Second Street on the south, Decoursey Avenue on the west, East Twenty-Ninth Street on the north and the Licking River on the east.[249]

In the immediate vicinity of Camp King sat Camp Finnell. The camp was established at the old Queen City racecourse along the Kentucky Central Railroad in November 1861 and was named in honor of John W. Finnell, Kentucky's Union adjutant general. The campground was abandoned later that year.[250]

Park Hills

BATTERY BATES (39.0735206°, -84.5448764°)
Address | Devou Park, Sleepy Hollow Road
Additional Notes | The location is accessible to the public.

To obtain a trail map, go online or visit the Behringer-Crawford Museum. Metal-detecting and digging are strictly prohibited. From where the Bates-Coombs Way Trail dead-ends into the Bates-Coombs Loop Trail at Loop Trail marker 313BC11 (39.0737247°, -84.5459459°), turn northeast and walk about 50 yards along the Bates-Coombs Loop Trail to a location (39.0739206°, -84.5456757°) northwest of the battery. Face southeast, move into the undergrowth and head uphill along a remnant of the Civil War military road. Climb about 100 yards; the battery lies at the top of the hill. If one approaches from the south side of the battery on the Bates-Coombs Way Trail (accessed from near 484 Glengarry Way, Fort Wright, Kentucky), one should go to a spot (39.0725237°, -84.5462339°) directly below the battery where an old road, identified by a deep depression,

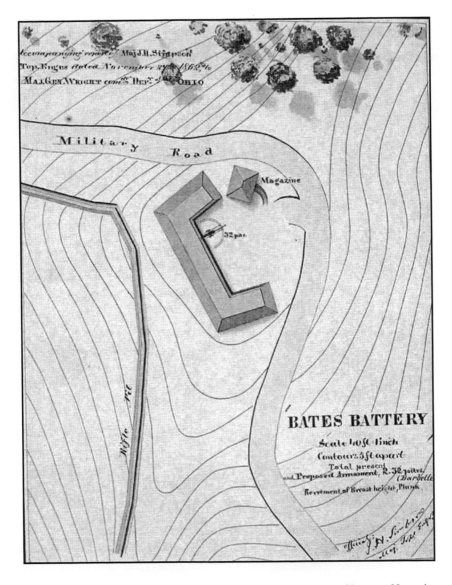

Plan of Battery Bates that accompanied the report of Major James H. Simpson, November 27, 1862. *Courtesy of the National Archives.*

intersects the trail. Head uphill 190 yards northeast along the overgrown road; it will wind its way to the right and then left to go up the hill. The battery stands at the top of the rise.

The battery survives mostly intact. The powder magazine remains as an oval-shaped depression at the back right end of the battery's walls, and the rifle trenches lie below the crest of the hill in front of the main earthworks. The Civil War military road passes behind the battery.

Battery Coombs (39.0786004°, -84.5515983°)
Address | Devou Park, Sleepy Hollow Road
Additional Notes | The location is accessible to the public.

To obtain a trail map, go online or visit the Behringer-Crawford Museum. Metal-detecting and digging are strictly prohibited. Take the Bates-Coombs Loop Trail to its intersection with the Trail of Devou-tion, at marker 313BC25 (39.0788795, -84.5516758). Face in the opposite direction of the Trail of Devou-tion and head southeast toward the top of the hill along the yellow-blazed southern extension trail. After you climb thirty-five yards, the trail crosses a shallow hump below the hillcrest; here one enters the site of Battery Coombs. The hump is likely the remains of the northern end of the northwest rampart.

The few traces of this sunken battery are heavily overgrown and faint. A shallow circular depression forms part of the interior of the battery's west wall (39.0786004°, -84.5515983°), and a sunken section of the original military road (39.0781562°, -84.5510434°) defines a portion of the southern extension to the Trail of Devou-tion. The extension is marked by yellow blazes. Other remnants of the three-sided main redan wall can be seen when the foliage is sparse. The Bates-Coombs Loop Trail surrounding the battery on its west and south sides follows the outer rifle trenches, and the trail's intersection with the Pig's Tail Trail at marker 313BC18 (39.0780713°, -84.5520466°) denotes the apex of the rifle trenches.

Behringer-Crawford Museum (39.081185°, -84.538697°)
Address | Devour Park, 1600 Montague Road
Additional Notes | The location is accessible to the public.

The museum contains Civil War memorabilia, military artifacts found in the region and exhibits on local history. One can obtain from here a map of the Devou Park trails that allow access to Battery Bates and Battery Coombs.

APPENDIX C

Villa Hills

CAMP LEW WALLACE SITE (39.067190°, -84.590654°)
Address | On the grounds of Villa Madonna Academy and Madonna
Manor Nursing Home, Madonna Manor Drive
Additional Notes | Unmarked. The location is private property.

Union soldiers defending the hills of Northern Kentucky during the
September 1862 invasion assembled here. Among the regiments stationed
here were the Ninety-Ninth Ohio Infantry, Eighteenth Michigan Infantry
and Twenty-Second Michigan Infantry. The camp site is bounded by
present-day Villa Drive, Villa Madonna Drive, Madonna Manor Drive and
Amsterdam Road.[251]

Westside

LINDEN GROVE CEMETERY & ARBORETUM (39.073834°, -84.513456°)
Address | 401 West Thirteenth Street
Additional Notes | The location is accessible to the public.

The Western Baptist Theological Institute established this cemetery in 1843.
It contains the graves of Confederate and Union veterans. The following is
a list of particularly interesting sites within the cemetery:

- The Grand Army of the Republic Memorial, erected in
  1929, was the second GAR monument raised in Kentucky. Its
  sarcophagus shape is the only one of its kind among Civil War
  monuments in the state.[252] (39.073490°, -84.514705°)
- The War Between the States Veterans Memorial is an unusual
  monument because it recognizes both Union and Confederate
  dead. Veterans of both sides dedicated the memorial in 1933.
  The graves of Confederate and Union soldiers surround the cut-
  limestone monument.[253] (39.073295°, -84.514505°)
- John William Finnell (1821–1888), Kentucky's Union adjutant
  general during the Civil War. His rank was brigadier general of
  Kentucky (U.S.) State Troops. (39.074695°, -84.514459°)
- John William Menzies (1819–1897), a U.S. Representative from
  Covington, Kentucky, from 1861 to 1863. (Range X, Lot 47)

Northern Campbell County, Kentucky

Southgate

Evergreen Cemetery (39.069607°, -84.468861°)
Address | 25 Alexandria Pike
Additional Notes | The location is accessible to the public.

This cemetery contains Battery Shaler and a line of Civil War field trenches (see separate listings). It also contains the graves of several Civil War personages, including:

- Charles John Helm Sr. (1817–1868), the Confederacy's consul general to Cuba. [Sec. 17, Lot 73]
- George Baird Hodge (1828–1892), a Confederate brigadier general [Sec. 6, Lot 14]
- William H. Horsfall (1847–1922), a Congressional Medal of Honor recipient who served as a drummer boy in Company G, First Kentucky (U.S.) Infantry during the Civil War. He dragged a wounded officer from between the lines to safety on May 21, 1862, in the midst of heavy fighting at Corinth, Mississippi. Horsfall is among the youngest persons to ever receive the medal. A historical marker and interpretive panel stand near the grave. [Civil War Soldiers Section (15), Row 5]
- Robert Lewis Kimberly (1836–1913), a Union brevet brigadier general [Soldiers' Lot, Sec. 25/31, Row 4]
- General James Taylor (1769–1848), founder of Newport, Kentucky, and builder of Newport Barracks. [Sec. 16, Lot 66-A][254]

Battery Shaler (39.065493°, -84.472967°)
Address | Evergreen Cemetery, 25 Alexandria Pike
Additional Notes | The location is accessible to the public.

Metal-detecting and digging are strictly prohibited. From the main cemetery entrance, follow the cemetery lane that is marked with yellow center lines. About halfway through the cemetery, one will see the bandstand on a hilltop to the left.

Soldiers of the Black Brigade worked at Battery Shaler in September 1862, when Camp Shaler was temporarily established in the cemetery. Battery

Shaler's earthworks were reconstructed in the early twentieth century. The bandstand, which serves as a war memorial, lies on the site of the battery's magazine.[255]

FIELD TRENCHES (39.063227°, -84.478106°)
Address | Evergreen Cemetery, 25 Alexandria Pike
Additional Notes | The location is accessible to the public.

Metal-detecting and digging are strictly prohibited. From the main cemetery entrance, follow the cemetery lane that is marked with yellow center lines. The line of trenches lies along the eastern crest of the ridge in the woods about 150 yards south-southwest of the cemetery's Garden Mausoleum building.

    This line of rifle trenches offers an excellent example of the semipermanent infantry defenses built during the Civil War in the Greater Cincinnati region. They were likely the handiwork of the Black Brigade, which was assigned to this sector during the Siege of Cincinnati.[256]

Wilder

BATTERY HOLT (39.055489°, -84.483935°)
Address | Vista Pointe Apartments, Vista Point Drive
Additional Notes | The location is private property.

Metal-detecting and digging are strictly prohibited. Ask permission from the apartment manager to access the battery, which is located directly behind the apartment complex's clubhouse.

    The circular plan of the battery's main wall is unusual. The rampart, the two barbettes and the sunken magazine at the northeast corner are intact but heavily overgrown with underbrush.

Appendix D

Spring Grove Cemetery and Arboretum

A History of Spring Grove Cemetery

Thousands of deaths from the cholera epidemics of the 1830s and 1840s exposed the lack of properly maintained cemeteries in Cincinnati. Residents looked for a better way to honor their dead. The Cincinnati Horticultural Society formed a cemetery association to acquire land for a large, rural, park-like cemetery near the city. Before selecting a location, the association's members traveled across the United States and Europe to observe the best designed cemeteries in the world at that time. The study concluded when the association purchased 220 wooded acres along present-day Spring Grove Avenue. With attorney Salmon P. Chase's assistance, the association incorporated Spring Grove Cemetery in 1845 as a nonprofit, nondenominational cemetery. It was dedicated on August 28, 1845, and the first burial occurred four days later.[257]

In 1855, a world-renowned Prussian landscape architect, Adolph Strauch, introduced the radical idea of creating a "Landscape Lawn Plan of Design" for Spring Grove Cemetery. As superintendent of the cemetery, Strauch put the plan into effect, resulting in over half of the grounds being left undeveloped. Strauch transformed these pristine areas into gardens, woods and lakes. Today, Spring Grove hosts fifteen lakes, the most in any cemetery in the nation. It also contains 20 state champion trees and over 1,200 different species of plants, shrubs and trees from around the world. Spring Grove has maintained the park-like atmosphere its original founders had intended.[258]

After Strauch's innovative initiative took hold, Spring Grove Cemetery quickly became Cincinnati's preferred burial place as well as a tourist destination. Illinois lawyer Abraham Lincoln joined William M. Dickson on a tour of Spring Grove Cemetery on September 24, 1855. It was one of several stops that Dickson wanted to show his friend on his first visit to the city. When war hero Lieutenant General Ulysses S. Grant and his family visited Cincinnati on September 23, 1865, they toured the cemetery with their guide, Adolph Strauch.[259]

The large size of Spring Grove Cemetery and its many wooded ravines provided cover for runaway slaves prior to the Civil War. Enslaved African Americans frequently navigated the large ravine that follows the western boundary of the cemetery. This ravine led north to College Hill, a well-known abolitionist and Underground Railroad stronghold.[260]

As the Civil War's casualty lists mounted in early 1862, Cincinnati's hospitals received soldiers who had been sent from the western theater battlefields. The soldiers who died needed a proper burial location. Cincinnati city officials thought first of Spring Grove. On March 7, 1862, the U.S. Sanitary Commission convinced the cemetery's trustees to donate a one-hundred-foot-diameter circular lot that could accept at least three hundred interments. The space quickly filled following the bloody Battle of Shiloh, Tennessee. On June 5, 1862, the trustees lobbied the Ohio state legislature to buy two additional circular lots adjacent to the first to handle the increasing demand for soldiers' graves. The state voted to pay the cemetery $3,000 for the two lots. The three circles were located toward the front of the cemetery near a lake Adolph Strauch's workmen had recently created.[261]

The quartermaster and surgeon in charge of Cincinnati's general hospital recorded the names, ages and units of the dead so "that relatives, friends, and strangers may know in all time to come, that we for whom their lives were given were not unmindful of the sacrifice they made."[262] The U.S. government transported soldiers' bodies to Spring Grove from primarily the western theater battlefields and hospitals, but many of the dead came from the eastern theater as well.

Over the course of the war, 655 soldiers were buried in the three lots identified as A, B and C. Each lot was designed to be a gradually inclined knoll that had room for about 340 graves. Before four-inch marble markers were installed in 1872, each grave was identified by a wooden peg inscribed with a unique number that corresponded to records in the cemetery office.

An officer's grave and a vertically mounted thirty-two-pounder cannon barrel crowned each mound. The design symbolized that the officers led the men in this world and, hence, would lead them in the next. Brigadier General Thomas J. Williams was one of the three officers chosen to be buried at the top of one of the three mounds. Colonel Frederick C. Jones of the Twenty-Fourth Ohio Infantry and Brigadier General Robert L. McCook occupied the other two places of honor, although McCook's body was later reinterred into his family's plot located elsewhere in the cemetery.[263]

In 1866, D.W. Tolford of the Ohio State Soldiers' Home wrote a report to Governor Jacob D. Cox in which he recommended the removal of 339 soldiers' graves from Camp Dennison Cemetery to Spring Grove. Tolford reasoned that the nine-dollar-per-grave reinterment cost "would be less expensive than to keep up a separate cemetery at Camp Dennison and erect a suitable monument." Furthermore, the beauty of the Spring Grove Cemetery layout impressed Tolford.

Tolford also found Cincinnati's newly installed soldiers' monument, named *The Sentinel*, to be appropriate for memorialization of the dead in the nearby mounds. The monument had cost donors $15,000 in gold valued at $25,000 cash. Citizens had raised the money between 1863 and 1864, and the commissioned sculptor, Randolph Rogers, completed his work in Rome, Italy, by the end of that period. In 1865, Ferdinand von Miller's Royal Foundry in Bavaria, Germany, cast the monument. It was the same foundry that later cast the iconic Tyler-Davidson Fountain of Cincinnati's Fountain Square. *The Sentinel* earned the distinction of being one of the first subscription Civil War monuments in America. Tolford wrote, "As a symbol of the great idea which has been upon the American mind for the last four years, and as a monument erected to the memory of the brave men who have fallen in the nation's late struggle, it is significant and appropriate; and as an evidence of the patriotism and noble generosity of the citizens of Cincinnati, it is beyond praise."[264]

However, Tolford expressed concern because *The Sentinel* lacked a list of the names of the dead. "It is not *inscriptive*," he surmised, "and therefore no more commemorative of individual officers and soldiers buried at Spring Grove, than of those buried elsewhere." The superintendent of the cemetery offered a proposal to build a second "noble monument" in the cemetery at an estimated purchase price of $30,000, to be raised by the cemetery trustees if the state government appropriated $10,000 toward the cost. In the end, the state voted to pay $3,000 for the transfer of the Camp Dennison graves to Spring Grove, but upon Tolford's recommendation, the government rejected the proposal to finance a second monument at the cemetery.[265]

In 1867, after *The Sentinel* had existed for nearly a year, the *Cincinnati Commercial* printed an article that agreed with Tolford's sentiment about the lack of inscription. Major General Joseph Hooker added his opinions in 1870 when he complained about the vertical cannons being "uncouth looking objects" that were "out of place entirely in a beautiful cemetery." The Spring Grove superintendent responded to these criticisms in the same way he had done with Tolford's comments—the issues could be rectified if the public funded a new, more suitable monument. This idea never materialized, and thus *The Sentinel* and the standing gun barrels remain today.[266]

A report from the inspector of national cemeteries dated June 17, 1870, indicated that 966 identified soldiers (including 2 African Americans) and 28 unidentified (all White soldiers) were buried within the soldiers' lots. The numbers matched Tolford's total of 994 graves. The majority of the bodies had originated from Greater Cincinnati's military hospitals.[267]

Greater Cincinnatians commemorated the first Decoration Day at Spring Grove on May 30, 1868. Nearly twenty thousand veterans and other citizens attended the ceremony. H.L. Burnet delivered the keynote address, and Reverend B. L. Chidlaw gave the blessing. From that day to the present, the Decoration Day (now called "Memorial Day") event sponsored by the Grand Army of the Republic has recurred annually at Spring Grove. The GAR's successors, the Sons of Union Veterans, have maintained the tradition.[268]

The present-day cemetery contains 733 acres with nearly 230,000 interments and over forty-four miles of winding roadways. It is the second-largest private cemetery in the United States and one of the largest in the world. It was designated a National Historic Landmark in April 2007.[269]

BURIALS OF UNION GENERALS OF THE CIVIL WAR

In addition to the three soldiers' lots, families interred their soldier sons, fathers and husbands into private lots scattered throughout the cemetery. From the Civil War period into the early twentieth century, the beauty and notoriety of Spring Grove attracted the families of deceased officers, as well as the living officers, to choose the cemetery for their final resting places.

An estimated 5,300 Civil War veterans are buried in Spring Grove, among whom are 40 Union generals of brevet brigadier rank or higher.

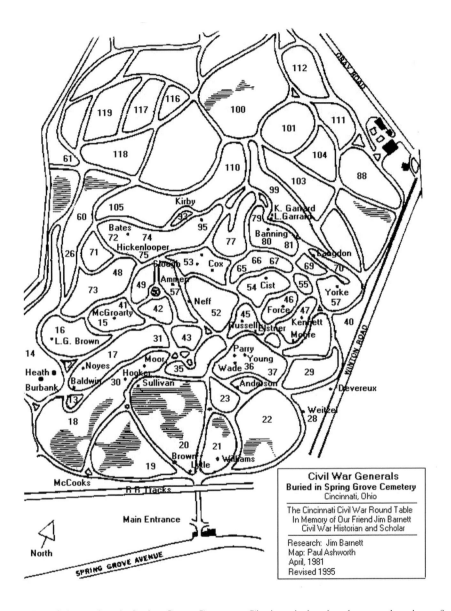

Map of the sections in Spring Grove Cemetery, Cincinnati, showing the grave locations of the forty Union generals. *Courtesy of Cincinnati Civil War Round Table.*

That count places Spring Grove Cemetery fourth in the United States in the number of Civil War Union generals interred within its grounds. Arlington National Cemetery in Virginia, Green-Wood Cemetery in Brooklyn and West Point Post Cemetery in New York State, in that order, are the only ones with more.[270]

In 1972, James Barnett, a historian and member of the Cincinnati Civil War Round Table, compiled a list of the Civil War's Union generals of brevet brigadier rank or higher who were buried in Spring Grove. His work is shared here as a table containing each general's name, birth date, death date and grave location.[271]

Table 5

Union Generals Buried in Spring Grove of Brevet Brigadier General or Higher Rank				
General's Name	Year of Birth	Year of Death	Section	Lot
Ammen, Jacob	1806	1894	51	84
Anderson, Nicholas Longworth*	1838	1892	24	2
Baldwin, William Henry*	1832	1898	17	91
Banning, Henry Blackstone*	1836	1881	80	43
Bates, Joshua H.	1817	1908	74	60
Brown, Charles Elwood*	1834	1904	20	H
Brown, Lewis Gove*	1841	1889	16	280
Burbank, Sidney*	1807	1882	14	58
Cist, Henry Martyn	1839	1902	54	116
Cox, Jacob Dolson	1828	1900	53	91
Devereux, Arthur F.*	1838	1906	28	109G
Elstner, George Ruter*	1842	1864	45	25
Force, Manning Ferguson (Medal of Honor)	1824	1899	46	99
Garrard, Jeptha*	1836	1915	99	2
Garrard, Kenner	1827	1879	99	2

General's Name	Year of Birth	Year of Death	Section	Lot
Heath, Thomas Tinsley*	1835	1925	14	99
Hickenlooper, Andrew*	1837	1904	53	167
Hooker, Joseph	1814	1879	30	A
Kennett, Henry Gassaway*	1835	1895	47	77
Kirby, Byron*	1829	1881	95	85
Langdon, Elisha Bassett*	1827	1867	70	13
Lytle, William Haines	1826	1863	20	1
McCook, Alexander McDowell	1831	1903	10	1
McCook, Jr., Daniel	1834	1864	10	1
McCook, Edwin Stanton*	1837	1873	10	1
McCook, Robert Latimer	1827	1862	10	1
McGroarty, Stephen Joseph*	1830	1870	15	116
Moor, Augustus*	1814	1883	30	91
Moore, Frederick William*	1840	1905	47	5
Neff, George Washington*	1833	1892	52	152
Noyes, Edward Follansbee*	1832	1890	17	227
Parry, Augustus Commodore*	1828	1866	36	69
Russell, Charles Sawyer*	1831	1866	45	12
Slough, John Potts	1829	1867	53	105
Sullivan, Peter John*	1821	1883	20	V
Wade, Melancthon Smith	1802	1868	36	55
Weitzel, Godfrey	1835	1884	28	3
Williams, Thomas J.*	1837	1866	21	C
Yorke, Louis Eugene*	1832	1873	57	62
Young, Thomas Lowry*	1832	1888	36	76

*Brevet rank (An honorary commission given to an individual for gallantry in action, meritorious service or prerequisite to serve in a particular staff position.)

Appendix D

Burials of Other Civil War Notables

Interred at Spring Grove are many other persons who had a significant effect on the United States shortly before the Civil War, during the war or soon after its conclusion. Phil Nuxhall, the historian of the Spring Grove Heritage Foundation, prepared several lists presenting these individuals and brief descriptions of their contributions to society.

The following is an inventory of Spring Grove's Cincinnatians who are particularly representative of the city in the Civil War era. The list is by no means comprehensive. Rather, it is meant to show how Cincinnati's citizens not only affected the outcome of the Civil War but also made great changes to their communities and their nation.[272]

Table 6

Notable Civil War Era Cincinnati Citizens and Soldiers Buried in Spring Grove Cemetery				
Person's Name	Year of Birth	Year of Death	Section	Lot
Alms, Frederick H.	1839	1898	20	U
Baldwin, Dwight Hamilton	1821	1899	86	137
Boyd, Henry	1802	1886	52	77
Breed, William	1835	1908	30	181
Brown, John H. (Medal of Honor)	1842	1898	110	390
Cameron, Wesley M.	1813	1895	39	45
Chase, Salmon Portland	1808	1873	30	10
Coffin, Levi	1798	1877	101	343
Dickson, William Martin	1827	1889	30	164
Doepke, William Frederick	1838	1908	18	30
Dorman, John Henry (Medal of Honor)	1843	1921	106	57
Foster, Seth Cutter	1823	1914	22	50

Person's Name	Year of Birth	Year of Death	Section	Lot
Gamble, James	1803	1891	13	6
Gamble, James Norris	1836	1932	13	2
Gibson, Robert George	1816	1885	16	315
Goshorn, Sir Alfred Traber	1833	1902	103	22
Gould, Charles Harvey	1846	1917	67	54
Grant, Hannah Simpson	1798	1883	29	46
Grant, Jesse Root	1794	1873	29	46
Greenwood, Miles	1807	1885	22	76
Groesbeck, William Slocum	1815	1897	22	54
Gurley, John Addison	1813	1863	36	28
Harris, Leonard A.	1824	1890	103	160
Hassaurek, Frederick	1832	1885	103	4
Hauck, John	1829	1896	21	H
Hoel, William Ryan	1824	1879	35	184
Key, Thomas Marshall	1819	1869	24	10
Latta, Alexander Bonner	1821	1865	77	14
Long, Alexander	1816	1886	27	22
Longworth, Nicholas, Sr.	1783	1863	24	1
Loyd, George A. (Medal of Honor)	1844	1917	121	1345
Luckett, Philip Noland	1824	1869	36	57
Matthews, (Thomas) Stanley	1824	1889	36	106
McAlpin, George Washington	1827	1890	20	3
McCook, Daniel, Sr.	1798	1863	10	1
McGuffey, Alexander Hamilton	1816	1896	77	82
McIlvaine, Bishop Charles Pettit	1799	1873	35	38
McLaughlin, James W.	1834	1923	54	50
McLaughlin, Mary Louise	1847	1939	54	50
Merrell, William Stanley	1798	1880	42	18A
Mitchell, Robert	1811	1899	19	M

PERSON'S NAME	YEAR OF BIRTH	YEAR OF DEATH	SECTION	LOT
Moerlein, Christian	1818	1897	37	24
Moore, Robert M., Sr.	1816	1880	22	53
Muhlhauser, Gottlieb	1836	1905	21	E
Murdoch, James Edward	1811	1893	51	109
Murphy, John P. (Medal of Honor)	1844	1911	103	110
Pendleton, George Hunt	1825	1889	36	40
Pogue, Henry	1829	1903	19	L
Proctor, William	1801	1884	47	76
Rammelsburg, Frederick	1814	1863	36	16
Robinson, John, Sr.	1807	1888	19	P
Shillito, John	1809	1879	20	E
Sprague, Katherine "Kate" Jane (Chase)	1840	1899	30	11
Stanbery, Henry	1803	1881	36	65
Stearns, George S., Sr.	1816	1889	22	49
Strauch, Adolph	1822	1883	20	S
Strobridge, Hines	1823	1909	103	168
Tafel, Gustav	1830	1908	110	254
Taft, Alphonso	1810	1891	52	114
Thatcher, Agnes Lake	1826	1907	17	2
Warder, John Aston, Jr.	1812	1883	65	1
Way, William B.	1836	1882	31-A	293
Webber, Charles T.	1825	1911	110	150
Wurlitzer, Rudolph	1831	1914	80	24

OTHER CIVIL WAR SITES IN SPRING GROVE CEMETERY	INFORMATION	SECTION	LOT
The Sentinel (or, *The Soldier of the Line*) Cincinnati's Civil War Soldiers' Monument	Commissioned in March 1863; cast in 1865; erected in 1866	20, 21, 23	intersection of the sections
5th Ohio Volunteer Infantry Regiment Monument	Dedicated in 1895; patterned after the 5th Ohio's monument at Gettysburg, PA	111	25
Three Civil War burial mounds containing 994 Union and Confederate soldiers, both known and unknown. Mounds are topped by thirty-two-pounder cannons.	Soldiers interred 1862–66	21	A, B, C

- FREDERICK H. ALMS—A Civil War veteran of Company D, Sixth Ohio Infantry, and the U.S. Signal Corps, he co-founded in 1865 the Alms & Doepke Department Store, the largest dry goods retailer in Cincinnati during the late 1800s. One of the co-founders was Frederick's brother and Sixth Ohio Reserve Militia veteran WILLIAM H. ALMS (1842–1920), who is buried in Section 8, Lot 1.[273]

- DWIGHT HAMILTON BALDWIN—A former music teacher, he founded the world-renowned Baldwin Piano Company in 1862 in Cincinnati. It became the largest manufacturer of keyboard instruments in the United States.[274]

- HENRY BOYD—Employing his talents as a carpenter, this furniture maker bought his freedom from slavery and eventually started his own workshop in Cincinnati. He invented and mass-produced the revolutionary Boyd Bedstead from 1833 to 1862, and he established one of the first racially integrated factories in the city at the northwest corner of Eighth Street and Broadway. Variations of Boyd's corded bed design are still used in the furniture industry today. Boyd also served as an Underground Railroad conductor.[275]

- WILLIAM J. BREED—In 1860, he joined his father, Abel, in managing the Crane, Breed & Company factory in Cincinnati. It manufactured caskets, including the one that held the body of President Abraham Lincoln. The company went on to build the world's first automobile hearse.[276]

- JOHN H. BROWN—As a sergeant in Company A, Forty-Seventh Ohio Infantry, he received the Congressional Medal of Honor for carrying vital information to Brigadier General Hugh Ewing through a hail of gunfire during Grant's first assault against Vicksburg, Mississippi, on May 19, 1863.[277]

- WESLEY M. CAMERON—A Cincinnati architect by trade, he persuaded Major General Lew Wallace to allow him to design and build a pontoon bridge over the Ohio River to carry men and supplies from Cincinnati to Covington during the September 1862 crisis. Miraculously, Cameron finished Cincinnati's first bridge over the Ohio River in just thirty hours—a major engineering feat.[278]

- SALMON PORTLAND CHASE—He gained national fame as a lawyer who defended runaway slaves and Underground Railroad conductors in Cincinnati. Chase later became Ohio's first Republican governor and a U.S. senator. President Abraham Lincoln selected Chase for secretary of the treasury, in which position he created a standardized national paper currency and founded the Internal Revenue Service to help fund the Civil War. He also served as chief justice of the U.S. Supreme Court from 1864 to 1873. Chase's portrait appears on the $10,000 bill.[279]

- LEVI COFFIN—At his store in Cincinnati, he began one of the first "Fair Trade" retail establishments in the United States, selling only goods made by free citizens. As Underground Railroad conductors, he and his wife, Catherine, reportedly aided over three thousand runaway slaves, for which service Levi earned the sobriquet "President of the Underground Railroad."[280]

- WILLIAM MARTIN DICKSON—He married the first cousin of Mary Todd Lincoln. In April 1854, he formed a prestigious Cincinnati law firm with Alphonso Taft and Thomas Marshall Key. Abraham Lincoln stayed a week with Dickson and his wife in September 1855 when Lincoln came to Cincinnati to work on the McCormick-Manny lawsuit. Dickson was a well-respected Common Pleas Court judge who organized and led the Black Brigade of Cincinnati, the nation's first mustered African American unit to see service during the Civil War. Because of Dickson's support for emancipation and his close associations with Abraham Lincoln, Edwin Stanton and Salmon Chase, historians believe that Dickson influenced the framing of the Emancipation Proclamation.[281]

- WILLIAM FREDERICK DOEPKE—A veteran of Company D, Sixth Ohio Infantry, and the U.S. Signal Corps, he co-founded the hugely successful Cincinnati-based department store of Alms & Doepke with cousins and fellow comrades-in-arms Frederick Alms and William Alms.[282]

- JOHN HENRY DORMAN—As a seaman of the U.S. Navy aboard the USS *Carondelet*, he courageously worked his post, even when seriously wounded. He received the Congressional Medal of Honor for his actions.[283]

- SETH CUTTER FOSTER—He co-founded a business in Cincinnati in 1846 that made cotton goods for carriage upholstery and hotel mattresses. Foster's factory was the first cotton bunting mass-producer in the United States. The business expanded to become the Stearns & Foster mattress company.[284]

- JAMES GAMBLE—He was the co-founder of Proctor & Gamble Company, which manufactured soap and candles for the Union army during the Civil War. The Cincinnati company evolved into a global manufacturer of soap, laundry and other personal care products.

- JAMES NORRIS GAMBLE—He was the son of soap entrepreneur James Gamble. In Cincinnati, James Norris Gamble joined the Squirrel Hunters as a captain in 1862. During the war, he worked as a chemist for the Proctor & Gamble Company. In 1863, he invented the formula for White Soap, which floated on water. The product was renamed Ivory Soap and was first sold in 1879. "The Soap that Floats" quickly became a household item around the world. Gamble eventually rose to vice president of the P&G corporation.[285]

- ROBERT GEORGE GIBSON—He was the co-founder of Gibson & Company Lithographers in 1850. This Cincinnati firm produced Civil War prints as well as bonds, certificates, business cards and checks. Gibson was among several lithographic design companies that made the Queen City the largest producer of wartime prints in the West. In the late 1870s, Gibson's company oversaw production of America's first Christmas, New Year's and Valentines' Day cards, and in the early 1880s, it started its own line of cards. Thus was born Gibson Greeting Cards.[286]

- SIR ALFRED TRABER GOSHORN—This Cincinnatian was a lieutenant in Company B, Pearl Street Rifles, and a captain of Company F, 137th Ohio Infantry, during the Civil War. Goshorn became the first president of the Cincinnati Base Ball Club (later the Cincinnati Reds) in 1866 and the first director of the Cincinnati Art Museum in 1882. He served as the director-general of the 1876 Centennial Exposition held in Philadelphia, Pennsylvania. It was the first world's fair in the United States, and it was highly successful. To honor Goshorn's outstanding work in arranging America's first world's fair, Queen Victoria of Great Britain knighted him.

- CHARLES HARVEY GOULD—As a member of the 1869 Cincinnati Red Stockings, America's first professional baseball team, he played at first base. Gould served as the manager of the Cincinnati Red Stockings during the inaugural year of the National League in 1876.[287]

- HANNAH SIMPSON GRANT—She was the mother of Union lieutenant general and U.S. president Ulysses Simpson Grant. Hannah lived with her husband, Jesse, and her family in Covington, Kentucky, during the Civil War. Ulysses and Julia Grant brought their children to reside with Hanna and Jesse during the war in the hopes that Covington would be a safe place for them to live.

- JESSE ROOT GRANT—He was the father and most outspoken Unionist supporter of Ulysses S. Grant. As a child, Jesse Grant had lived near Cleveland, Ohio, in a household with the famous abolitionist and martyr John Brown. Jesse served as the postmaster for the City of Covington, Kentucky, during the Civil War. He often used his political influence to promote Ulysses's public appeal, but his efforts mostly caused Ulysses frustration and embarrassment. For example, Jesse's unethical Southern cotton speculation with Cincinnati's Jewish-owned clothing manufacturers is believed to have encouraged his son to issue the notorious General Orders Number 11, which expelled Jewish families from Grant's military department—an order that President Lincoln quickly overturned.[288]

- MILES GREENWOOD JR.—He owned the innovative Eagle Iron Works foundry in Cincinnati that produced weaponry for the Union army and navy. Before the war, Greenwood manufactured the world's first practical steam fire engine. Cincinnati bought the first fire engine and thus became the first city in the world to use one. Greenwood subsequently served as Cincinnati's first fire chief of the first professional fire department in the United States.[289]

- WILLIAM SLOCUM GROESBECK—He was a lawyer who began his career in Cincinnati with Salmon P. Chase. Groesbeck served as a U.S. representative (Democrat) from 1857 to 1859 and as an Ohio state senator from 1862 to 1864. After the war, he counseled U.S. president Andrew Johnson during his impeachment trial.[290]

- JOHN ADDISON GURLEY—As a Cincinnatian, he served as a U.S. representative (Republican) from 1859 to 1863 and as a colonel and aide-de-camp to Major General John C. Frémont during the periods when Congress was not in session. President Lincoln appointed Gurley to be governor of the Arizona Territory, but he died before he could take office.[291]

- Leonard A. Harris—As the leader of the Harris Guards at the outbreak of the Civil War, he was commissioned captain of Company I, Second Ohio Infantry, in April 1861 and distinguished himself at the First Battle of Bull Run, Virginia. He was promoted to colonel in August 1861 and led a brigade at the Battle of Perryville, Kentucky, on October 8, 1862. Harris was elected mayor of Cincinnati in 1863 and 1865. While serving as mayor, he organized and commanded the 137th Ohio Infantry.[292]

- Frederick Hassaurek—A veteran of the Prussian Revolution of 1848, he campaigned for Abraham Lincoln's bid for the U.S. presidency in 1860. President Lincoln appointed Hassaurek to the position of U.S. minister to Ecuador, in which post he served from 1861 to 1865. In 1865, he became the editor of the popular German American newspaper *Cincinnati Volksblatt*.[293]

- John Hauck—He was a famous Cincinnati brewer during the Civil War, opening his first brewery in 1863 in the West End district. Hauck took ownership of the Cincinnati Red Stockings baseball team in 1885.[294]

- William Ryan Hoel—During the Civil War, he served as a naval first master on the USS *Cincinnati* and as a pilot of the USS *Lexington* and USS *Carondelet*. Hoel was wounded in action at the Battle of Fort Henry, Tennessee, and he showed exceptional leadership and skill at the Battle of Island Number Ten, Tennessee. In October 1862, he took command of the USS *Pittsburg*, aboard which he displayed great courage in the naval actions around Vicksburg, Mississippi, in 1863. For his outstanding service at Grand Gulf, Mississippi, he earned the rank of acting volunteer lieutenant commander, the first volunteer in U.S. Navy history to receive that honor. In March 1865, he accepted command of the USS *Vindicator*. Three navy destroyers were named in Hoel's honor.[295]

- THOMAS MARSHALL KEY—He was a law partner of Cincinnatians William Dickson and Alphonso Taft before the war and was elected to the Ohio State Senate as a Democrat in 1858. After the firing on Fort Sumter in April 1861, Key obtained the position of judge advocate and colonel on Major General George B. McClellan's staff, from which role he emerged as McClellan's friend and closest confidant. Key's political connections helped make McClellan commander of the Army of the Potomac, and Key advised McClellan to run against President Abraham Lincoln in the election of 1864. Key also drafted the bill in 1862 to abolish slavery in the District of Columbia.[296]

- ALEXANDER BONNER LATTA—This Cincinnati inventor is best known for designing the world's first practical steam fire engine in 1852. Miles Greenwood manufactured Latta's device at Cincinnati's Eagle Iron Works, and the City of Cincinnati purchased it in 1853. In 1845, at the Anthony Harkness engine works, Latta directed the construction of the first railroad locomotive west of the Alleghenies.[297]

- ALEXANDER LONG—This lawyer was one of Cincinnati's representatives in the Ohio House from 1848 to 1850 and in the U.S. House from 1863 to 1865 before losing his seat to Republican Rutherford B. Hayes of Cincinnati. Long was best known as a staunch Peace Democrat ("Copperhead") leader during the Civil War. Congress censured him in April 1864 for his views against the government. He promoted Salmon Chase in his bid for the U.S. presidency in 1868.

- NICHOLAS LONGWORTH SR.—He became Cincinnati's first millionaire from buying and selling property in the city. He also grew Catawba grapes on Cincinnati's hills and turned them into sparkling wine. The wine was so sweet and desirable that it was the preferred alcohol at weddings throughout the United States. Prior to the Civil War, Longworth had been the greatest philanthropist of the arts and sciences in Cincinnati. His promotion of culture made Cincinnati a world-class city in the antebellum period. Hiram Powers, an artist that Longworth had patronized, designed Longworth's tomb.[298]

- GEORGE A. LOYD—He served as a private in Company A, 122nd Ohio Infantry. He earned the Congressional Medal of Honor when he captured Confederate major general Henry Heth's division flag during the Union assault on Petersburg, Virginia, on April 2, 1865.[299]

- PHILIP NOLAND LUCKETT—He served as a Texas brevet brigadier general in the Confederate army in the Trans-Mississippi department. In 1861, as a colonel, he received the surrender of Texas's federal garrisons from Brevet Major General David E. Twiggs. During the war, Luckett fought in the Red River Campaign and Camden Expedition. In 1869, he moved from New Orleans to Cincinnati to be with family; he died soon after.[300]

- STANLEY MATTHEWS—He was a Cincinnati lawyer and an Ohio state senator (Democrat) before the Civil War. He helped found the city's Literary Club in 1849. During the war, he served as a lieutenant colonel of the Twenty-Third Ohio Infantry and as a colonel of the Fifty-First Ohio Infantry. He resigned from the army in 1863 to become a superior court judge in Cincinnati. However, Matthews commanded the Cincinnati militia during Morgan's July 1863 Great Raid. U.S. presidents Rutherford B. Hayes (Matthew's former superior officer in the war) and James Garfield nominated Matthews for the seat of U.S. Supreme Court justice, which the Senate confirmed in May 1881 after the closest vote ever cast for a U.S. Supreme Court nominee.[301]

- GEORGE WASHINGTON McALPIN—In downtown Cincinnati in 1852, he co-founded the Ellis, McAlpin & Company wholesale dry goods store, which served the Union army during the war. The store grew into the large McAlpin's retail department store chain that lasted for 146 years. McAlpin served on Cincinnati's city council for 15 years and as director of Spring Grove Cemetery from 1879 to 1890.[302]

- DANIEL McCOOK SR.—He was the law partner of President Lincoln's secretary of war Edwin Stanton and the patriarch of the "Tribe of Dan" of the famous Fighting McCooks of the Civil War. Dan's sons included Union generals Robert L. McCook, Alexander McCook, Edwin Stanton McCook, George Wythe McCook and Daniel McCook Jr. At the outbreak of the war, the sixty-three-year-old Daniel Sr. was commissioned volunteer paymaster in Cincinnati with the rank of major. During Confederate John Hunt Morgan's Great Raid through Ohio, Major McCook accompanied Union brigadier general Henry Judah's brigade to eastern Ohio to hunt down a Rebel cavalryman in Morgan's division who supposedly had murdered Robert McCook in Alabama. At the Battle of Buffington Island, Ohio, on July 19, 1863, Dan McCook Sr. was mortally wounded in the opening salvo of the fight. He died en route back to Cincinnati on July 21—in the same week that his sons Charles and Daniel Jr. died in different years of the war.[303]

- ALEXANDER HAMILTON MCGUFFEY—As a Cincinnati author and educator, he helped compile *McGuffey's Eclectic Spelling Book* and co-wrote the multivolume series of the *McGuffey Eclectic Reader* with his brother William. The books taught young Americans of the Civil War era the basics of spelling, reading, literature and civics using moral and ethical examples. After the war ended, schools in thirty-seven states taught their students with McGuffey Readers, and by 1920, nearly 122 million copies had been sold. The books revolutionized and standardized American curriculum.[304]

- BISHOP CHARLES PETIT MCILVAINE—He was an influential Episcopal bishop and author from Ohio who lived in Clifton, Cincinnati, during the Civil War. Because of McIlvaine's international acclaim, President Lincoln sent the bishop overseas to persuade the British government to not recognize the Confederacy as a sovereign entity. McIlvaine often visited with influential British politicians and educators to convince them to support the Union's cause. After he died in 1873, his body lay in state at Westminster Abbey in London, the only U.S. citizen to have received this honor.[305]

- JAMES W. MCLAUGHLIN—As a Cincinnatian, he served as a lieutenant in Company C of the Benton Cadets, Missouri

Infantry, during the Civil War. He also made sketches in the field for *Frank Leslie's Illustrated Newspaper*. After the war, he returned to his architectural firm in Cincinnati. Among his famous designs in Cincinnati were the Shillito's Department Store, the McAlpin's Department Store, the Cincinnati Art Museum, the Cincinnati Zoo structures, the Art Academy of Cincinnati and the Hamilton County Courthouse.[306]

• MARY LOUISE McLAUGHLIN—She was the daughter of a wealthy Cincinnati dry goods company owner and a sister of James W. McLaughlin. Mary is best known for being a pioneer of ceramic painting in the United States. She wrote a book on the subject titled *China Painting: A Practical Manual for the Use of Amateurs in the Decoration of Hard Porcelain* (1894). She and her competitor, fellow Cincinnatian Maria Longworth Nichols Storer, led the advancements in art pottery in America.[307]

• WILLIAM STANLEY MERRELL—During the Civil War, he owned a wholesale drug business in Cincinnati that his sons expanded in 1880 into the William S. Merrell Chemical Company, the forerunner of today's Merrell-Dow Pharmaceuticals.[308]

• ROBERT MITCHELL—He co-founded the furniture-making firm of Mitchell & Rammelsberg in 1846 in Cincinnati. The company was the first Cincinnati manufacturer to use steam-driven machinery to build furniture on a large scale. The large walnut and oak forests of the South and Midwest and the populous consumers of the North and Europe made the company the largest furniture manufacturer in the nation. By the 1870s, the firm employed one thousand workers.[309]

• CHRISTIAN MOERLEIN—He was a well-known brewer during the Civil War. He established his Cincinnati-based beer brewery in the back of a blacksmith shop in 1853. Moerlein's larger complex at Elm and Henry Streets evolved to be one of the largest breweries in the United States prior to Prohibition. His name appears on a brand of beer today. Moerlein also served for a month in Company A, Eighth Ohio Reserve Militia, in September 1862.[310]

- ROBERT M. MOORE—He was a veteran of the Mexican American War and a lieutenant colonel of the Tenth Ohio Infantry during the Civil War. He was among the original group of Union veterans who organized the Grand Army of the Republic in Ohio. Moore served as a mayor of Cincinnati from 1877 to 1879. He is best known for being an influential advocate of Grand Army of the Republic commander John A. Logan's platform to establish a formal Memorial Day holiday in the United States. Moore was also among the first to lobby the U.S. Congress to provide pensions to Civil War veterans.[311]

- GOTTLIEB MUHLHAUSER—During the Civil War, his steam flouring factory supplied flour for the Union army. After the war, he co-founded the Lion Brewing Company with his brother Heinrich, who had served as a sergeant in Company A, Eighth Ohio Reserve Militia. Lion Brewing grew into the Muhlhauser-Windisch Brewing Company in 1882, one of the largest beer makers in the country. It was one of the first breweries to use ice machines in its brewing process.[312]

- JAMES EDWARD MURDOCH—He was an internationally famous actor, comedian and elocutionist who lived in Warren County, Ohio, during the Civil War. Beginning in 1861, he turned down acting work to dedicate himself to promoting the Union cause. He appeared frequently on Cincinnati's stages to recite patriotic literature and give speeches to crowds, most often to benefit soldiers' aid charities. His reading of the poem "Sheridan's Ride" on October 31, 1864, is considered one of his greatest performances. Despite his grief over the death of his son, Thomas, at the Battle of Chickamauga, Murdoch raised over $250,000 during the war. Murdoch also volunteered on the staff of General Lew Wallace during the Siege of Cincinnati.

- JOHN P. MURPHY—This Cincinnatian was a private in Company K, Fifth Ohio Infantry, on September 17, 1862, when he captured the flag of the Thirteenth Alabama Infantry at the Battle of Antietam, Maryland. For this accomplishment, he received the Congressional Medal of Honor.[313]

- GEORGE HUNT PENDLETON—He was a Cincinnati lawyer and son-in-law of Francis Scott Key, of "Star-Spangled Banner" fame. Pendleton served Cincinnati as a Democrat in the Ohio Senate and in the U.S. House of Representatives. During the Civil War, he became a leader in the Peace Democrat, or Copperhead, movement. He ran unsuccessfully for vice president of the United States with Democrat George B. McClellan in the national election of 1864. Pendleton simultaneously lost his U.S. House seat to Republican Benjamin Eggleston of Cincinnati, but Pendleton was elected to the U.S. Senate in 1879. He is best known for writing the Pendleton Civil Service Reform Act of 1883.[314]

- HENRY POGUE—He and his brothers bought out the interests of John Crawford's dry goods store in Cincinnati in 1865 and renamed it the H.&S. Pogue Dry Goods Company. The firm grew into the Pogue's department store chain that lasted until the 1980s.[315]

- WILLIAM PROCTOR—In 1837, he co-founded the Proctor & Gamble Company, which manufactured soap and candles for the Union army during the Civil War. The business later became the world's largest producer of personal care goods.[316]

- FREDERICK RAMMELSBURG—He co-founded the furniture-making firm of Mitchell & Rammelsberg Furniture Company in 1846 in Cincinnati. It became the largest mass-producer of furniture in the nation in the 1870s.[317]

- JOHN ROBINSON SR.—He started the nation's first traveling circus in 1824 and made Terrace Park near Cincinnati the home base for his circus company during the off-season. Circus animals often roamed Terrace Park's streets. Robinson was also instrumental in the establishment of a printing business in Cincinnati called Russell & Morgan Printing, which evolved into the U.S. Playing Card Company.[318]

- JOHN SHILLITO—In 1830, he and his partners started a dry goods business in Cincinnati, and by 1860, he was the sole proprietor.

During the Civil War, his company sold flags to Union regiments. The store expanded to employ over one thousand employees by the time Shillito died in 1879. It was Cincinnati's first department store and one of the largest retailers in the United States. The company lasted in name until 1986.[319]

- KATHERINE "KATE" JANE (CHASE) SPRAGUE—Born in Cincinnati, she was the daughter of Secretary of the Treasury Salmon P. Chase. Kate served as her father's hostess at personal gatherings that often involved some of the most influential persons in the United States. Her father's political ambitions and power in Washington during the Civil War allowed Kate to rise to prominence within the city's social circles. She married Rhode Island governor William Sprague on November 12, 1863. Their wedding was a major social affair in Washington, and President Lincoln attended the reception. Following Salmon's resignation from the Lincoln cabinet in 1864, Kate's social powers and fortunes declined. She ran her father's campaign for the Democratic nomination for president in 1868, but her father was not selected. Kate and William suffered from many marital problems, which led to their divorce in 1882. She became a recluse, lost her fortune and died penniless. Her body was shipped to Cincinnati to be buried next to her father, to whom she had devoted her life.[320]

- HENRY STANBERY—After serving as Ohio's first attorney general from 1846 to 1851, he came to reside in Cincinnati. President Andrew Johnson appointed Stanbery to the position of U.S. attorney general in 1866, but he resigned the post in March 1868 to defend Johnson at his impeachment trial.[321]

- GEORGE S. STEARNS—He was the co-founder (with Seth C. Foster) of the Stearns & Foster mattress company. Stearns is buried next to his former business partner.[322]

- ADOLPH STRAUCH—He was an internationally acclaimed landscape architect who devised the "Landscape Lawn Plan of Design." His designs in Cincinnati included Spring Grove Cemetery, Mount Storm Park, Eden Park, Burnet Woods and Lincoln Park. World-renowned landscape designers Frederick Law Olmsted and Édouard André, especially praised Strauch's work at Spring Grove, which is considered Strauch's masterpiece.[323]

- HINES STROBRIDGE—He was a former bookseller who partnered in the lithographic firm of Elijah Middleton of Cincinnati in 1854. During the Civil War, the Middleton, Strobridge & Company factory produced many varieties of prints that were displayed on the walls and over the mantels of American homes across the nation. In 1867, Strobridge bought out his partner's shares in the establishment and renamed it the Strobridge Lithographing Company. It stayed in business until 1960. The company is best known for producing the colorful posters of the Ringling Brothers and Barnum & Bailey circuses.[324]

- GUSTAV TAFEL—He was a German immigrant who helped found the Turnverein, a German association of gymnasts, in Cincinnati. When the Civil War erupted, he led the city's Turnverein as its president. He joined Company A of the 9th Ohio Infantry, Cincinnati's first German American unit, at the rank of sergeant. Over the course of his service with the regiment, he rose to the rank of lieutenant. In August 1862, as a lieutenant colonel, he assisted in raising the 106th Ohio Infantry, another German American regiment, and was appointed its commander. After the war, he was elected as an Ohio legislator and as a mayor of Cincinnati. Tafel authored the book *The Cincinnati Germans in the Civil War*.[325]

- ALPHONSO TAFT—After moving to Cincinnati in 1839, he started his own law practice and became a member of Cincinnati City Council. During the Civil War, his many political connections made him an influential person in Ohio. After the war, Taft served as a judge on the Superior Court of Cincinnati. President Ulysses S. Grant appointed Taft to the position of U.S. secretary of war in March 1876 and to U.S. attorney general in May of that same year. His son was President of the United States William Howard Taft.[326]

- AGNES LAKE THATCHER—As a young woman, she married a circus clown named Bill Lake Thatcher. She soon learned to walk the tightrope, tame lions and perform tricks on horses, and her acts became well known throughout the country. In 1860, she formed a partnership with circus magnate John Robinson to create the Robinson Lake Circus, which performed throughout the Civil War. Tragically, Thatcher's husband was killed in a brawl in 1869. Two years later, she met Civil War veteran and Wild West lawman "Wild Bill" Hickok in Abilene, Kansas. Finding mutual attraction, they corresponded frequently with each other, and they were married in Cheyenne, Wyoming, on March 5, 1876. Only five months later, a man shot Bill Hickok dead in Deadwood, South Dakota. Agnes was living in Cincinnati with her daughter when she heard the news. Agnes performed in the John Robison Circus until 1880, when she retired to live in Cheyenne. She later moved to New Jersey to be with family. She is buried next to her first husband in Cincinnati.[327]

- JOHN ASTON WARDER—After working as a Cincinnati doctor for two decades, he turned to his interests in horticulture, editing the *Western Horticulture Review* from 1850 to 1854 and becoming president of the Cincinnati Society of Natural History. During the Civil War, Warder dedicated his skills to the Union cause by volunteering as the brigade surgeon of the First Brigade of Ohio Militia. In September 1875, he became the founder and first president of the American Forestry Association, the nation's oldest citizen's conservation group. Often called the "Father of American Forestry," Warder is considered a pioneering leader in the fields of managed forestry and horticulture in America.[328]

- WILLIAM B. WAY—Originally a resident of Pontiac, Michigan, he served in the First Michigan Cavalry as a lieutenant and was later promoted to captain for his bravery in battle. In April 1863, he was appointed major of the Ninth Michigan Cavalry, which confronted Confederate brigadier general John H. Morgan's cavalry division in Kentucky. During Morgan's Great Raid of July 1863, Major Way's detachment of Ninth Michigan cavalrymen defeated Morgan's troopers in the action at Salineville, Ohio, on July 26, 1863, which is considered the Civil War's northernmost fight between regular troops east of the Mississippi River. Way was promoted to lieutenant colonel in November of that year. In 1865, Way again distinguished himself at the Battle of Monroe's Crossroads, North Carolina, where he bravely supported General Judson Kilpatrick's troopers. In recognition of his actions, he received a promotion to colonel. After the war, Way contracted consumption, and he died during a visit to Cincinnati in 1882.[329]

- CHARLES T. WEBBER—After moving in 1858 to Covington, Kentucky, he opened the Artists' Photographic and Picture Gallery in Cincinnati with several partners. However, the Civil War forced the closure of the gallery. Undaunted, Webber started his own portrait gallery on East Fourth Street, which flourished into the 1880s. He became an art educator and leader within the Cincinnati art scene. Over his lifetime, Webber created hundreds of paintings, the most famous being *The Underground Railroad* (1893), which exhibited at the World's Columbian Exposition of 1893. His *Portrait of a Boy* (1868) hangs in the Smithsonian American Art Museum.[330]

- RUDOLPH WURLITZER—After settling in Cincinnati in 1853, he began selling musical instruments imported directly from his family's factories in Germany. As his business boomed, he started his own musical instrument factory in 1861 in Cincinnati. During the Civil War, he primarily sold and manufactured instruments for military bands, but he also built pianos and harps. He won a contract with the U.S. Army at the beginning of the war that resulted in many Union regiments' drums, bugles and trumpets carrying the Wurlitzer stamp. In addition to supplying the army with musical instruments, Wurlitzer served with Company E, Second Ohio Reserve Militia, during the September 1862 crisis. The demands on his factory grew, and by 1890, he founded the Rudolph Wurlitzer Company, which he led as president from 1890 to 1912. Wurlitzer's organs and player pianos gained fame among America's movie theaters of the silent film era in the early 1900s. The company also developed the jukebox that is most identified with mid-twentieth-century American music culture.[331]

Appendix E

MILITARY UNITS COMPOSED OF CINCINNATI OR HAMILTON COUNTY RESIDENTS

T he impact that Cincinnatians had on the outcome of the Civil War cannot be fully appreciated until one understands Cincinnati's military presence in the field. With the city being the seventh largest in the United States in 1860, it is no wonder that the Queen City contributed a great many recruits to fill the regiments of its native state of Ohio. James F. Noble wrote to Governor William Dennison on August 31, 1861, that "recruiting officers were becoming as numerous in Cincinnati as coffee houses." Hamilton County, encompassing Cincinnati, supplied 41,960 enrolled militiamen during the war. From April 12, 1861, to October 1, 1862, the county recorded 39,966 militiamen, 14,795 volunteers and 1,175 draftees. As of July 27, 1864, county records indicated that 20,757 men from Cincinnati and 5,780 men from the remainder of Hamilton County served in the Union armed forces. However, what surprises historians and readers alike is Cincinnati's footprint within the non-Ohio military units.[332]

The "Immense Roster" published in Henry and Kate Ford's *History of Hamilton County, Ohio* (1881), pages 84–192, served as the starting point for finding the Union military units composed of residents from the city of Cincinnati and its parent political division, Hamilton County. The Fords had derived the names of resident soldiers at the time of enlistment from the adjutant general of Ohio's muster rolls, from which the authors listed the soldiers and officers by company and by unit. Unfortunately, the Fords left their work incomplete for many understandable reasons.

Following the Fords' approach for the other units in Ohio and from outside of the state, it became quickly apparent that a list of soldiers' names would fill several volumes. Thus, the table that follows captures the Union infantry and cavalry companies and the Union artillery batteries in which these men served, as well as any organized support units, such as the engineers. The sources used for this new research can be found in the bibliography under "Rosters and Unit Records."

In addition, as part of this research, the numbers of Hamilton County and Cincinnati residents in each company or battery were counted. Average unit sizes were based on Rodney C. Lackey's study "Notes on Civil War Logistics." In the Federal army, a typical company recruited an average total of 100 men and officers, and a normal artillery battery started with about 150 enlisted men and officers. On average, field and staff (identified as "FS" in the table) counted 16 men per regiment and regimental bands (marked as "RB" in the table) each contained about 14 men total.

Therefore, to determine if a company, field and staff, regimental band or artillery battery was composed mostly of soldiers from Cincinnati or Hamilton County, the average totals were divided in half. If the soldier counts exceeded the halved totals, for example, fifty-one men in a company or eight men in a regimental band, then those groups received "Cincinnati" designations, which is the asterisk (*) in the table. If at least half of the total companies in a regiment are marked with an asterisk, or more than seventy-five men and officers from Cincinnati existed in the battery, then the entire regiment or battery is designated a "Cincinnati" unit, which is the plus sign (+) in the table.

If regimental companies or batteries reorganized after their original three-year enlistment terms had expired, then they are called "Veteran Volunteer" units. The companies and batteries in the table incorporate veteran reenlistments, transfers, substitutes, draftees and late-war recruits from Hamilton County in addition to the county's enlistees at the unit's inception. However, some companies and batteries appear with the word *Veteran* after them if the veteran group recruited its majority from Cincinnati or Hamilton County citizens while the original group had not.

The nicknames of specific companies or military units are also given in the table. Many of these special titles existed before the war began, because the companies had been formed from paramilitary militia units having these names. The soldiers normally created regimental or battery nicknames during the war as a show of pride for their unit. In the table, company nicknames are listed after a dash (-) following the company letter, while regimental or battery nicknames are given in brackets ([]) under the official name of the unit. If there are multiple nicknames, they are either separated by a semicolon (for units) or by an ampersand (for companies). Furthermore, if a company or unit consisted primarily of soldiers of German or Irish birth, which was a source of nationalistic honor for them, those ethnicities appear in parentheses in the table.

STATE OR FEDERALLY ORGANIZED CIVIL WAR U.S. UNITS CONTAINING RESIDENTS FROM CINCINNATI OR HAMILTON COUNTY, OHIO

Important Notes

- FS = Field & Staff
- RB = Regimental Band
- ASTERISK (*) = Composed of Cincinnati or Hamilton County men that match one of the following counts: fifty-one or more men and officers in an infantry/cavalry company, or nine or more field and staff, or eight or more regimental band members, or seventy-six or more men and officers in a battery.
- PLUS (+) = Unit is composed of 50 percent or greater number of asterisked companies.

TABLE 7

OHIO UNITS		
UNIT	SERVICE PERIOD	COMPANIES AND COMPANY NAMES
1st Ohio Infantry	3 months	B(German) - Lafayette Jaegers, C - Dayton Light Guards
1st Ohio Infantry	3 years	FS, B, C, D - Cleveland Grays
2nd Ohio Infantry	3 months	FS, A* - Rover Guards, D* - Zouave Guards, E*(German) - Lafayette Guards, I - Covington Blues & Harris Guards

Unit	Service Period	Companies and Company Names
2nd Ohio Infantry	3 years	FS*, RB*, A, B, D*, E, F, H*, I
3rd Ohio Infantry	3 years	FS, A, G*
4th Ohio Infantry [Gibraltar Brigade]	3 years	G - Kenton Rangers
4th Ohio Battalion Infantry	3 years	A, B, C
5th Ohio Infantry+	3 months	FS*, RB*, A* - Continental Battalion, B* - Cincinnati Highland Guards, C* - Rover Guards, D* - Cincinnati Highland Guards, E* - Continental Battalion, F* - Continental Battalion, G* - Cincinnati Zouaves, H* - River Boatmen Company, I* - Printer Company & Franklin Guards, K* - Continental Battalion
5th Ohio Infantry+	3 years	FS*, RB*, A* - Continental Battalion, B* - Cincinnati Highland Guards, C* - Rover Guards, D* - Cincinnati Highland Guards, E* - Continental Battalion, F* - Continental Battalion, G* - Cincinnati Zouaves, H* - River Boatmen Company, I* - Printer Company & Franklin Guards, K* - Continental Battalion
6th Ohio Infantry+ [1st Foot Volunteers; Guthrie Greys]	3 months	FS*, RB* - Menter's Brass Band, A* - Guthrie Grey Battalion, B* - Guthrie Grey Battalion, C*, D*, E*, F*, G*, H*, I*, K*
6th Ohio Infantry+ [1st Foot Volunteers; Guthrie Greys, Guthrie's Grays]	3 years	FS*, A*, B*, C*, D*, E*, F*, G*, H*, I*, K*

Appendix E

Unit	Service Period	Companies and Company Names
7th Ohio Infantry	3 years	B - Sprague Zouave Cadets
8th Ohio Infantry [Gibraltar Brigade]	3 years	A, D, G, I
9th Ohio Infantry+(German) [Bloody Dutch; Dutch Devils; McCook's Dutchmen; Turner Regiment; 1st German Regiment]	3 months	FS*, RB*, A*, B*, C*, D*, E*, F*, G*, H*, I*, K*
9th Ohio Infantry+(German) [Bloody Dutch; Dutch Devils; McCook's Dutchmen; Turner Regiment; 1st German Regiment]	3 years	FS*, RB*, A*, B*, C*, D*, E*, F*, G*, H*, I*, K*
10th Ohio Infantry+(Irish)	3 months	FS*, RB*, A*, B*, C*, D*, E*, F*(German) - Montgomery Guards & Sarsfield Guards, G*, H*, I*, K*(Anglo-American) - California Guards
10th Ohio Infantry+(Irish) [Montgomery Regiment; Bloody Tenth; Bloody Tinth]	3 years	FS*, RB*, A*, B*(German), C*, D*, E*, F*(German), G*, H*, I*, K*(Anglo-American) - California Guards
11th Ohio Infantry	3 years	FS, A - Washington Gun Squad & Dayton Riflemen, B, D, E*(1862), F, G, H, I(1862), K* - Lane's Sappers and Miners & Union Rifles
11th Ohio Battalion Infantry	3 years	C, E*, I
12th Ohio Infantry	3 years	A, B, C - Union Guards, H, I - Union Guards, K
13th Ohio Infantry	3 months	B, C, G
13th Ohio Infantry	3 years	FS, B, D, E, F, G, H - Alliance Guards, I, K*
13th Ohio Battalion Infantry	3 years	B
14th Ohio Infantry [Maumee Muskrats]	3 years	A, B, C, E, H, I, K

Unit	Service Period	Companies and Company Names
15th Ohio Infantry	3 years	A, B, C, E, K
16th Ohio Infantry [Carrington Guards; Jefferson Guards]	3 months	E
16th Ohio Infantry	3 years	F
17th Ohio Infantry	3 years	A, B, C - Eagle Guards, E, F, G, I
18th Ohio Infantry	3 years	FS, B, C, D, E, E(Veteran)*, F, G, H, I, I(Veteran)*, K
19th Ohio Infantry	3 years	C, D, H, I
20th Ohio Infantry	3 months	A - Nichols Guards, B - University Rifles
20th Ohio Infantry	3 years	FS, B, D, E, G, H, I, K
21st Ohio Infantry	3 months	FS
21st Ohio Infantry	3 years	FS, D
22nd Ohio Infantry [13th Missouri Infantry; 3rd Missouri Rifles]	3 years	FS, A, B, C*, D, F, H, I, K
22nd Ohio Battalion Infantry	3 years	A, B
23rd Ohio Infantry [Charging Regiment]	3 years	FS, A, B, C, D, E, F, G, H, I, K
24th Ohio Infantry	3 years	FS, E - Buckeye Guards, F, I
25th Ohio Infantry [Ohio Brigade]	3 years	D - Johnson's Battery & King's Independent Infantry Company, F
26th Ohio Infantry [Groundhog Regiment]	3 years	FS, A - Butler Pioneers, B, C, D, F, I
27th Ohio Infantry [Fuller's Ohio Brigade]	3 years	FS, A, B*, C, D, E, G, H, I, K
28th Ohio Infantry+(German) [2nd German Regiment]	3 years	FS*, A*, B*, C*, D*, E*, F*, G*, H*, I*, K*

Unit	Service Period	Companies and Company Names
28th Ohio Battalion Infantry+(German)	3 years	A*, B*, C
29th Ohio Infantry	3 years	B, C, D, E, G, K
30th Ohio Infantry	3 years	FS
31st Ohio Infantry	3 years	FS, A, C, E, F, I, K
32nd Ohio Infantry	3 years	F - Potts's Battery
33rd Ohio Infantry	3 years	FS, F, H
34th Ohio Infantry [Piatt's Zouaves; 1st Regiment Zouaves]	3 years	FS, A, B, C*, D, E, F, G, H, I, K
35th Ohio Infantry [Persimmon Regiment]	3 years	FS, A, B - Anderson Grays, C, H, I
36th Ohio Infantry	3 years	FS, A, B, C, D, E, F, G, H, I, K
37th Ohio Infantry (German) [3rd German Regiment]	3 years	B, E, F, H, K
38th Ohio Infantry	3 years	A, E, F, G, K
39th Ohio Infantry [Groesbeck's Regiment; Groesbeck's Rifles; Fuller's Ohio Brigade]	3 years	FS*, A, B - Washington County Rifle Guards, C, D*, E*, F(German) - Koenig's German Rifles, G*, H - Clinton Grays, I, K - Rhoades's Railroad Guard
41st Ohio Infantry [Wetmore's Battery]	3 years	A, C, D, F, G - Geauga Zouaves, I
42nd Ohio Infantry	3 years	A, B, D, K
43rd Ohio Infantry [Martin Box Regiment; Fuller's Ohio Brigade]	3 years	A, B, C, E, F, G, H, K
45th Ohio Infantry	3 years	FS, A, H, K
46th Ohio Infantry	3 years	FS, E

Unit	Service Period	Companies and Company Names
47th Ohio Infantry+ [Wilstach Regiment]	3 years	FS, RB*, A*, B, C*(German), D, E, F, G*(German), H*(German), I, K*(German)
48th Ohio Infantry [Hawhe's Battalion Non-Veterans]	3 years	FS, A, B, F, G, H, I, K*
48th Ohio Battalion Infantry	3 years	FS, A, B, C, D
49th Ohio Infantry	3 years	F
50th Ohio Infantry	3 years	FS, A, B, D*, E, F, G, H*, I*, K
51st Ohio Infantry	3 years	FS, C
52nd Ohio Infantry [McCook's Avengers]	3 years	FS, A, B, C, D, H*, I, K*
53rd Ohio Infantry	3 years	A, F, K*
54th Ohio Infantry [2nd Regiment Zouaves]	3 years	FS, A, C, D, E, F*, G - Doty's Independent Infantry Company, H - Cornelius Neff's Independent Infantry Company, I, K
56th Ohio Infantry	1 year	D
57th Ohio Infantry	3 years	FS, B, D*, E*, F
58th Ohio Infantry (German) [Company B, Ohio Infantry Battalion]	3 years	A, B, C, G
59th Ohio Infantry	3 years	D
60th Ohio Infantry (1862)	1 year	FS, B
60th Ohio Infantry (1864)	3 years	FS, E - Quintrell's Independent Infantry Company, I, K*(1 year)
61st Ohio Infantry	3 years	FS, A, B, C, E, F, G, H, I
63rd Ohio Infantry [Fuller's Ohio Brigade]	3 years	FS, D, E, F

Unit	Service Period	Companies and Company Names
64th Ohio Infantry [Sherman's Brigade]	3 years	FS
66th Ohio Infantry	3 years	FS, A, B, F, H, I
69th Ohio Infantry	3 years	FS, A, C, D, F, G, I
70th Ohio Infantry	3 years	D*, E, F, I*
71st Ohio Infantry	3 years	FS, B, D, K*
72nd Ohio Infantry	3 years	C, E, F, G, K*
73rd Ohio Infantry [Talbott's Independent Infantry Company; Ohio Brigade]	3 years	C
74th Ohio Infantry	3 years	FS, C, D, E, H, I, K
75th Ohio Infantry [Ohio Brigade]	3 years	FS*, A*, E, F, G, H, I, K*
77th Ohio Infantry	3 years	FS, B
79th Ohio Infantry	3 years	FS, A, B, F*, K - Flegle's 1st (4th) Independent Company Sharpshooters
80th Ohio Infantry	3 years	I
81st Ohio Infantry [Morton's Independent Rifles]	3 years	F
82nd Ohio Infantry [Independent Battalion Sharpshooters; 105th Ohio Infantry; Western Reserve Regiment; Ohio Brigade]	3 years	FS, B, H, I
83rd Ohio Infantry+ [Greyhounds]	3 years	FS*, A*, B*, C*, D*, E*, F*, G, H, I, K*
84th Ohio Infantry	3 months	E, G, H
85th Ohio Infantry	3 months	FS, D, E, G
86th Ohio Infantry	3 months	A, C, E
86th Ohio Infantry	6 months	B, F, G, K
87th Ohio Infantry	3 months	D

Unit	Service Period	Companies and Company Names
88th Ohio Infantry [1st Battalion Governor's Guards]	3 years	FS, A, D, G
89th Ohio Infantry	3 years	A, D, F
91st Ohio Infantry	3 years	D
92nd Ohio Infantry	3 years	F
95th Ohio Infantry	3 years	FS, I
96th Ohio Infantry	3 years	C, K
97th Ohio Infantry	3 years	D
106th Ohio Infantry+(German) [4th German Regiment]	3 years	FS*, A*, B*, C*, D, E*, F*, G*, H*, I*(1864, 1 year) - Ruh's Independent Infantry Company, K*(1864, 1 year) - Bauman's Independent Infantry Company
107th Ohio Infantry (German) [5th German Regiment]	3 years	FS, F - Sandusky Jaegers
108th Ohio Infantry+(German) [6th German Regiment]	3 years	FS*, A*, B*, C*, D, E*, F*, G*, H*, I* - Heintz's Independent Infantry Company, K* - Haffner's Independent Infantry Company
110th Ohio Infantry	3 years	FS, A, B, E
113th Ohio Infantry	3 years	I(Irish) - Corcoran Avengers
116th Ohio Infantry	3 years	FS
121st Ohio Infantry	3 years	FS
124th Ohio Infantry	3 years	FS, C, F, G*, I*
126th Ohio Infantry	3 years	G
128th Ohio Infantry	3 years	B - Hoffman Battalion, G
131st Ohio Infantry	100 days	C
133rd Ohio Infantry [3rd and 58th Ohio National Guard]	100 days	D, F

Appendix E

Unit	Service Period	Companies and Company Names
137th Ohio Infantry+ [7th Ohio National Guard]	100 days	FS*, A*, B*, C*, D*, E*, F*, G*, H*, I*, K*
138th Ohio Infantry+ [8th Ohio National Guard]	100 days	FS*, A*, B*, C*, D*, E*, F*, G*, H*, I*, K*
139th Ohio Infantry+ [9th Ohio National Guard]	100 days	FS, A*, B*, C*, D*, E*, F*, G*
146th Ohio Infantry	100 days	D
156th Ohio Infantry [34th Ohio National Guard]	100 days	FS
165th Battalion Ohio Infantry+ (German) [10th Ohio National Guard]	100 days	FS, A*, B*, D*, E*, F*, G*, H*
173rd Ohio Infantry	1 year	H
175th Ohio Infantry	1 year	H, I
179th Ohio Infantry	1 year	C, K
181st Ohio Infantry+	1 year	FS*, A*, B*, C*, D*, E*, F*, G*, H*, I*, K*
182nd Ohio Infantry	1 year	FS, G, H*, I
183rd Ohio Infantry+	1 year	FS*, A, B*(German), C*(German), D*, E*(German), F*, H*(German), I*(German), K*
184th Ohio Infantry	1 year	A, H
186th Ohio Infantry	1 year	H*, I*, K*
187th Ohio Infantry	1 year	A, E*, F, H*, I
188th Ohio Infantry	1 year	C*, E, H*, K*
189th Ohio Infantry	1 year	B, E*, F*
191st Ohio Infantry	1 year	FS, I*, K
192nd Ohio Infantry	1 year	F*, K*
193rd Ohio Infantry	1 year	FS, F*, I, K*
194th Ohio Infantry	1 year	B, G*, I

Unit	Service Period	Companies and Company Names
195th Ohio Infantry	1 year	FS, B, F*, I, K
196th Ohio Infantry	1 year	B, F, H*, I*, K
197th Ohio Infantry	1 year	FS, D, F*, G, H, K*
198th Ohio Infantry	1 year	A, B*, C, F*, G*, H*
8th Independent Company Ohio Sharpshooters [Barton's Sharpshooters]	3 years	
Dennison Guards [Brookfield's Independent Infantry Company]	3 years	
Jones's Independent Battalion Ohio Infantry+ [Jones's Railroad Guard; Cincinnati Home Guard]	Indefinite; 3 months	Julius Ochs's Company*(German), Benjamin F. Gossin's Company*, Anthony Volters's Company*(German), Charles Stewart's Company*
Squirrel Hunters (1862)	30 days	83rd District*
Capt. Sylvester W. Bard's Independent Company Ohio Infantry (Cavalry)+ [Bard's Independent Company of Foot; Independent Guard]	30 days	
Wallace Guards+ [Worthington's Independent Company]	30 days	
2nd Ohio Reserve Militia+ [Cincinnati Reserve Militia]	1 month	FS*, A*, B*, C, D*, E*, F*, G*, H*, I*, K*
6th Ohio Reserve Militia+ (German)	1 month	FS*, A*, B*, C*, D*, E*, F*, G*, H*, I*, K*
8th Ohio Reserve Militia+ (German)	1 month	FS*, A*, B*, C*, D*, E*, F*, G*, H*, I*, K*

Unit	Service Period	Companies and Company Names
11th Ohio Reserve Militia+ (German)	1 month	FS*(Anglo-American), A*(Anglo-American), B*, C*, D*, E*(Anglo-American), F*, G*, H*, I*(Anglo-American)
1st Ohio Cavalry	3 years	FS, C* - Pope's Escort & Shields's Body Guard, D, G, H, I, K, M
2nd Ohio Cavalry [Wade and Hutchins's 1st Cavalry; Hollister's Battery]	3 years	FS, A, B, C, E, F, G, H, I*, K, M
3rd Ohio Cavalry	3 years	FS, A, B, H, I, K, L
4th Ohio Cavalry+ [Union Dragoons; Cincinnati Union Dragoons]	3 years	FS*, RB*, A*, B*, C*, D*, E*, F, G, G(Veteran)*, H, I, K*, L*, M*
5th Ohio Cavalry	3 years	FS*, RB*, A, B, C, D*, E, F, G*, H, I, K*, L, M
6th Ohio Cavalry [Wade and Hutchins's 2nd Cavalry]	3 years	B - 1st Independent Battalion Cavalry
7th Ohio Cavalry [River Regiment]	3 years	FS, A*, B*, C*, D - Stoneman's Body Guard, G - Hartsuff's Escort & Schofield's Escort, I, K, L, M
8th Ohio Cavalry [44th Ohio Infantry]	3 years	D
9th Ohio Cavalry [9th Regiment, 1st Mounted Battalion]	3 years	D - Independent Cavalry Battalion & 1st Battalion Mounted Volunteers, E, F, G - Hestler's Unterrified Crampers, H, K, L, M
10th Ohio Cavalry	3 years	C, I, K
11th Ohio Cavalry [Rocky Mountain Cavalry]	3 years	FS, E* - 3rd Independent Battalion Cavalry, F - 3rd Independent Battalion Cavalry, G, H, I, K
12th Ohio Cavalry	3 years	FS, A, D

Unit	Service Period	Companies and Company Names
13th Ohio Cavalry+ [Tod Scouts]	3 years	FS, A*, C*, D*, E*, G, H*, I*, K*, L*, M*
2nd Independent Battalion Ohio Cavalry [Buck's Battalion Cavalry]	60 days	A*
4th Independent Battalion Ohio Cavalry [Wheeler's Cavalry Battalion]	6 months	FS*, A*, B, C, D, E
3rd Independent Company Ohio Cavalry+ (German) [Capt. Philip Pfau's Cavalry Company; Frank Smith's Independent Cavalry; Cox's Body Guard; Gibson's Battalion]	3 years	
4th Independent Company Ohio Cavalry [Capt. John Foster's Company; Halleck's Escort; McPherson's Escort; King's Cavalry Company]	3 years	
5th Independent Company Ohio Cavalry+ [Fremont's Body Guard; Zagonyi's Battalion Cavalry, Company C; Capt. James Foley's Independent Company]	3 years	
6th Independent Company Ohio Cavalry+ [Capt. Jeptha Garrard's Independent Company]	3 years	
Henry W. Burdsall's Independent Company Ohio Cavalry+ [1st Independent Company Ohio Cavalry]	3 months	
McLaughlin's 1st Independent Squadron Ohio Cavalry [McFall's Squadron Cavalry; Rice's Squadron Cavalry]	3 years	A

Unit	Service Period	Companies and Company Names
1st Ohio Heavy Artillery [117th Ohio Infantry]	3 years	FS*, A, B, C, D, E, F, G, H, I, L, M
2nd Ohio Heavy Artillery	3 years	FS, A, B, C, D, E, F, G, H, I, K, L, M
1st Ohio Light Artillery, Battery B [Standardt's Battery; Standart's Ohio Battery; Baldwin's Battery]	3 years	
1st Ohio Light Artillery, Battery F [Cockerill's Battery; Pease's Battery]	3 years	
1st Ohio Light Artillery, Battery G [Barlett's Battery; Marshall's Battery]	3 years	
1st Ohio Light Artillery, Battery H [Huntington's Battery; Dorsey's Battery; Norton's Battery]	3 years	
1st Ohio Light Artillery, Battery I+ (German) [Cincinnati City Battery; Dilger's Battery; Bennett's Battery; Hyman's Battery; 12th Independent Battery; King's Battery]	3 years	
1st Ohio Light Artillery, Battery K [DeBeck's Battery; Heckman's Battery]	3 years	
1st Ohio Light Artillery, Battery M (German) [Schultz's Battery]	3 years	
1st Ohio Independent Battery [Kirtland's Battery; McMullin's Battery]	3 years	
2nd Ohio Independent Battery [Smith's Battery; Chapman's Battery; Beach's Battery; Carlin's Battery]	3 years	
3rd Ohio Independent Battery [Sullivan's Battery; Williams's Battery]	3 years	

Unit	Service Period	Companies and Company Names
4th Ohio Independent Battery+ (German) [Hoffman's Battery; Froehlich's Battery; Lademann's Detachment Missouri Veterans]	3 years	
5th Ohio Independent Battery+ [Hickenlooper's Battery; Kate's Battery]	3 years	
6th Ohio Independent Battery [Baldwin's Battery; Bradley's Battery]	3 years	
7th Ohio Independent Battery [Burnap's Battery; McNaughton's Battery]	3 years	
8th Ohio Independent Battery (German) [Markgraf's Battery; Putnam's Battery; Schmidt's Battery]	3 years	
10th Ohio Independent Battery [Crain's Battery; Seaman's Battery; White's Battery]	3 years	Veteran*
11th Ohio Independent Battery+ [Sands's Battery; Armstrong's Battery; Constable's Battery]	3 years	
12th Ohio Independent Battery [Jackson's Battery; Noecker's Battery; Johnson's Battery; King's Battery; Company D, 25th Ohio Infantry]	3 years	
15th Ohio Independent Battery [Spear's Battery; Burdick's Battery]	3 years	
16th Ohio Independent Battery [Springfield's Light Artillery; Mitchell's Battery; Twist's Battery]	3 years	
17th Ohio Independent Battery [Rice's Battery; Blount's Battery]	3 years	

Unit	Service Period	Companies and Company Names
18th Ohio Independent Battery [Aleshire's Battery]	3 years	
21st Ohio Independent Battery [Patterson's Battery; Walley's Battery]	3 years	
24th Ohio Independent Battery [Hill's Battery]	3 years	
25th Ohio Independent Battery [Stockton's Battery; Hadley's Battery; 3rd Kansas Battery]	3 years	
26th Ohio Independent Battery [Potts's Battery; Yost's Captured Battery; Company F, 32nd Ohio Infantry]	3 years	
August Paulsen's Battery+ (German) [Cincinnati Independent Artillery]	1 month	

Alabama (U.S.) Units		
1st Alabama (U.S.) Cavalry	3 years	FS

Arkansas (U.S.) Units		
4th Arkansas (U.S.) Cavalry	3 years	FS

California Units		
1st Battalion California Mountaineers	3 years	A

Connecticut Units		
5th Connecticut Infantry [Colt's Rifle Regiment]	3 years	C, D, F, H

Delaware Units		
4th Delaware Infantry	3 years	C

Unit	Service Period	Companies and Company Names
Illinois Units		
12th Illinois Infantry [1st Scotch Regiment]	3 years	FS
14th Illinois Infantry	3 years	D, E, G
14th Illinois (Reorganized) Infantry	3 years	D
14th and 15th Illinois Veteran Battalion Infantry	3 years	D
15th Illinois Infantry	3 years	D
16th Illinois Infantry	3 years	I
17th Illinois Infantry	3 years	D
18th Illinois (Reorganized) Infantry	3 years	C
19th Illinois Infantry	3 years	C
24th Illinois Infantry (German) [Lincoln Rifles; 1st Hecker Regiment; Mihalotzy Rifles; Hecker Jaeger Regiment]	3 years	A, D, E, G, K
26th Illinois Infantry	3 years	D
29th Illinois Infantry	3 years	I
37th Illinois Infantry [Fremont Rifles]	3 years	I
38th Illinois Infantry	3 years	A
39th Illinois Infantry [Yates's Phalanx]	3 years	I
42nd Illinois Infantry [Douglas Brigade, 1st Regiment]	3 years	B
43rd Illinois Infantry (German) [Koerner Regiment]	3 years	FS, I
43rd Illinois (Reorganized) Infantry (German)	3 years	F
45th Illinois Infantry [Washburne Lead Mine Regiment]	3 years	B

Unit	Service Period	Companies and Company Names
46th Illinois Infantry	3 years	A
50th Illinois Infantry [Blind Half Hundred]	3 years	E
59th Illinois Infantry [Zouaves; part of USS *Switzerland* of Mississippi Marine Brigade; 9th Missouri Infantry]	3 years	I
61st Illinois Infantry	3 years	B
65th Illinois Infantry [2nd Scotch Regiment; Cameron's Highlanders]	3 years	D
66th Illinois Infantry [Birge's Western Sharpshooters; 14th Missouri Infantry]	3 years	A
67th Illinois Infantry	3 months	I, K
68th Illinois Infantry	3 months	A
107th Illinois Infantry [Boyle's Battery; Colvin's Battery]	3 years	I
6th Illinois Cavalry [Franklin's Battery]	3 years	C
7th Illinois Cavalry	3 years	E, H
8th Illinois Cavalry	3 years	A
9th Illinois Cavalry [Brackett's Cavalry Regiment; 1st Western Cavalry]	3 years	C, D
10th Illinois Cavalry	3 years	A
12th Illinois Cavalry	3 years	B
14th Illinois Cavalry	3 years	M

Unit	Service Period	Companies and Company Names
1ˢᵗ Illinois Light Artillery, Battery D [Cooper's Battery; McAllister's Battery; Plainfield Artillery; Rogers's Battery; Madison's Battery]	3 years	
1ˢᵗ Illinois Light Artillery, Battery H [DeGress's Battery; Silversparre's Battery; Hart's Battery]	3 years	
2ⁿᵈ Illinois Light Artillery, Battery C [Flood's Battery; Springfield Artillery; Hopkins's Battery; Keith's Battery]	3 years	
2ⁿᵈ Illinois Light Artillery, Battery E [Cram's Battery; Fitch's Battery; Waterhouse's Battery; Schwartz's Missouri Battery; Gumbart's Battery; Nispel's Battery]	3 years	

Indiana Units		
12ᵗʰ Indiana Infantry	3 years	K
13ᵗʰ Indiana Infantry [Reynolds's Indiana Brigade; Reynolds's Cheat Mountain Brigade]	3 years	H, K
13ᵗʰ Indiana Infantry (Re-organized)	3 years	A, C
17ᵗʰ Indiana Infantry [Reynolds's Indiana Brigade; Reynolds's Cheat Mountain Brigade; Wilder's Lightning Brigade]	3 years	C, F, I, K
18ᵗʰ Indiana Infantry	3 years	A, D
22ⁿᵈ Indiana Infantry	3 years	A, F, I
25ᵗʰ Indiana Infantry	3 years	G
26ᵗʰ Indiana Infantry	3 years	B, F, I, K

Unit	Service Period	Companies and Company Names
27th Indiana Infantry	3 years	F
31st Indiana Infantry	3 years	D
32nd Indiana Infantry (German) [1st German Regiment]	3 years	FS, A, B, C, F*, G, I
34th Indiana Infantry [Morton Rifles]	3 years	FS, F
35th Indiana Infantry (Irish) [1st Irish Regiment]	3 years	B, C, I
37th Indiana Infantry	3 years	B, D
37th Indiana Infantry (Reorganized)	3 years	B
38th Indiana Infantry	3 years	I
40th Indiana Infantry	3 years	I
42nd Indiana Infantry	3 years	B
47th Indiana Infantry	3 years	H
49th Indiana Infantry [Hawhe's Battalion Non-Veterans]	3 years	B, C
51st Indiana Infantry	3 years	C, I
52nd Indiana Infantry [Railroad Regiment]	3 years	FS, A, D, E, F, G, H, I
52nd Indiana Infantry (Reorganized) [Railroad Regiment]	3 years	FS, H
53rd Indiana Infantry	3 years	C
57th Indiana Infantry	3 years	A
58th Indiana Infantry	3 years	F
60th Indiana Infantry	3 years	FS
65th Indiana Infantry	3 years	FS, C
68th Indiana Infantry	3 years	E, F
69th Indiana Infantry	3 years	FS
70th Indiana Infantry	3 years	K
73rd Indiana Infantry	3 years	F

Unit	Service Period	Companies and Company Names
79th Indiana Infantry	3 years	A, C
80th Indiana Infantry	3 years	C
82nd Indiana Infantry	3 years	H
83rd Indiana Infantry	3 years	C, E, H
84th Indiana Infantry	3 years	I
91st Indiana Infantry	3 years	E, G
104th Indiana Infantry [Minute Men]	10 days	H
124th Indiana Infantry	3 years	FS, D
130th Indiana Infantry	3 years	H
143rd Indiana Infantry	1 year	A, B
144th Indiana Infantry	1 year	A
146th Indiana Infantry	1 year	A, F, G, H
147th Indiana Infantry	1 year	E, F, H
1st Indiana Cavalry [28th Indiana Infantry]	3 years	B, K - Howard's Escort & Siegel's Body Guard & Fremont's Body Guard & Bracken's Company Mounted Volunteers
5th Indiana Cavalry [90th Indiana Infantry]	3 years	C, E, G, H, K
6th Indiana Cavalry [71st Indiana Infantry]	3 years	D, H
9th Indiana Cavalry [121st Indiana Infantry]	3 years	D
11th Indiana Cavalry [126th Indiana Infantry]	3 years	M
13th Indiana Cavalry [131st Indiana Infantry]	3 years	E, M
1st Indiana Heavy Artillery [21st Indiana Infantry; Jackass Regiment]	3 years	A, B, L

Unit	Service Period	Companies and Company Names
2nd Indiana Battery Light Artillery [Espey's Battery; Rabb's Battery; Whicher's Battery]	3 years	
12th Indiana Battery Light Artillery [Dunwoody's Battery; Sterling's Battery; White's Battery]	3 years	
13th Indiana Battery Light Artillery [Nicklin's Battery]	3 years	
26th Indiana Battery Light Artillery [Wilder Battery; 17th Indiana Infantry, Company A; Rigby's Battery; Thomas's Battery; 1st Indiana Independent Battery]	3 years	

Iowa Units		
1st Iowa Infantry (Colored) [60th U.S. Colored Infantry]	3 years	I
3rd Iowa Infantry	3 years	A, K
2nd & 3rd Iowa Consolidated Infantry	3 years	A
6th Iowa Infantry	3 years	D, E
8th Iowa Infantry [Union Brigade]	3 years	E
17th Iowa Infantry	3 years	F
36th Iowa Infantry	3 years	G, K
3rd Iowa Cavalry	3 years	I, K
5th Iowa Cavalry [Curtis Horse]	3 years	F(German) - 1st Missouri Western Cavalry Fremont Hussars, L(Irish) - Naughton's Irish Dragoons
5th Iowa Consolidated Cavalry	3 years	F, L
8th Iowa Cavalry	3 years	H

Unit	Service Period	Companies and Company Names
2nd Iowa Battery Light Artillery [Reed's Battery; Spoor's Battery; 4th Iowa Infantry, Artillery Company L]	3 years	
2nd Battalion, Southern Border Brigade [Iowa State Militia]	1 month	B

Kansas Units		
5th Kansas Cavalry	3 years	F, H
6th Kansas Cavalry	3 years	I - Vansickle's Scouts
7th Kansas Cavalry [Jennison's Jayhawkers]	3 years	K

Kentucky (U.S.) Units		
1st Kentucky (U.S.) Infantry+	3 months/ 3 years	FS*, A*, B*, C*, D* - Fulton Continentals, E* - Simmonds's Battery, F, G* - Kenton Rangers, H*, I*, K*(German)
2nd Kentucky (U.S.) Infantry+	3 years	FS*, RB, A*, B - Woodruff Rifles & Woodruff Guards, C*(German) - Rough and Ready Guards & Union Guards, D* - Woodward Guards, E* - Valley Guards & Woodruff Zouaves, F, G* - Doubleday Guards, H* - Zouave Guards & Zouave Cadets, I* - Union Artillery, K*(German)
4th Kentucky (U.S.) Infantry	3 years	K
5th Kentucky (U.S.) Infantry [3rd Infantry; Louisville Legion]	3 years	E
12th Kentucky (U.S.) Infantry	3 years	G, H, I

Unit	Service Period	Companies and Company Names
15th Kentucky (U.S.) Infantry	3 years	FS, G(Irish), I(German), K*
16th Kentucky (U.S.) Infantry	3 years	A, E
18th Kentucky (U.S.) Infantry	3 years	C, F, K
23rd Kentucky (U.S.) Infantry	3 years	FS, A, B, C, D, E, F, G, H, I, K
24th Kentucky (U.S.) Infantry	3 years	FS, F, I
26th Kentucky (U.S.) Infantry [Burbridge's Infantry Regiment; Riflemen]	3 years	G
27th (U.S.) Infantry	3 years	E, G
39th Kentucky (U.S.) Infantry	3 years	E, I
53rd Kentucky (U.S.) Infantry	3 years	B
54th Kentucky (U.S.) Infantry	3 years	FS
2nd Kentucky (U.S.) Cavalry [Rousseau's Cavalry]	3 years	B - Fry's Escort, I
3rd Kentucky (U.S.) Cavalry [Jackson's Scouts]	3 years	FS, E, G - Twyman's Independent Company Scouts & Ward's Independent Company Scouts
4th Kentucky (U.S.) Cavalry	3 years	FS, L
5th Kentucky (U.S.) Cavalry	3 years	A
6th Kentucky (U.S.) Cavalry [1st Battalion Kentucky Cavalry; Munday's Battalion Cavalry]	3 years	FS, A, E, H
7th Kentucky (U.S.) Cavalry [Metcalfe Cavalry]	3 years	FS, C, F, G, K, L
9th Kentucky (U.S.) Cavalry	1 year	FS, F
1st Kentucky (U.S.) Light Artillery, Battery A [Stone's Battery; 1st (3rd) Kentucky Independent Battery; Thomasson's Battery]	3 years	

UNIT	SERVICE PERIOD	COMPANIES AND COMPANY NAMES
1st Kentucky (U.S.) Light Artillery, Battery E [Hawe's Battery; Bush's Battery; 4th (5th) Kentucky Independent Battery; Miller's Battery]	3 years	
1st Kentucky (U.S.) Independent Battery+ [Simmonds's Battery; Glassie's 1st (4th) Kentucky Independent Battery; 5th Kentucky Artillery Battery; 23rd Ohio Independent Battery]	3 years	

MARYLAND (U.S.) UNITS		
3rd Maryland (U.S.) Cavalry [Bradford Dragoons]	3 years	FS

MASSACHUSETTS UNITS		
12th Massachusetts Infantry [Webster Regiment]	3 years	F
19th Massachusetts Infantry	3 years	A - 1st Battalion Rifles Militia, F
20th Massachusetts Infantry [Harvard Regiment]	3 years	B
30th Massachusetts Infantry [Eastern Bay State Regiment]	3 years	F, K
31st Massachusetts Infantry [6th Massachusetts Cavalry; Western Bay State Regiment; Hawhe's Battalion Non-Veterans]	3 years	H
32nd Massachusetts Infantry [1st Battalion, Massachusetts Infantry]	3 years	E

Unit	Service Period	Companies and Company Names
33rd Massachusetts Infantry	3 years	K - Company K of 3rd Massachusetts Cavalry & Bunker's Cavalry Company
39th Massachusetts Infantry [Davis's Regulars]	3 years	D
54th Massachusetts Infantry (Colored) [Shaw's Black Regiment]	3 years	FS, G, H, I, K
55th Massachusetts Infantry (Colored)	3 years	A, B, C, D, E, F, G, H, K
60th Massachusetts Infantry (Militia)	100 days	G - Kent's Independent Infantry Company
2nd Massachusetts Cavalry	3 years	A - California Hundred & California Cavalry Battalion, E - California Cavalry Battalion
5th Massachusetts Cavalry	3 years	A, D, E, G, I
1st Massachusetts Heavy Artillery [14th Massachusetts Infantry; Essex County Regiment]	3 years	A - Heard Guards
2nd Massachusetts Heavy Artillery [Fort Warren Battalion]	3 years	F
2nd Massachusetts Battery Light Artillery [Boston Light Artillery; Cobb's Light Battery; Marland's Battery; Nims's Battery]	3 years	
6th Massachusetts Battery Light Artillery [Carruth's Battery; Everett's Battery; Phelps's Battery; Russell's Battery]	3 years	

Unit	Service Period	Companies and Company Names
Michigan Units		
3rd Michigan Infantry	3 years	C
4th Michigan Infantry	3 years	H - Grosvenor Guard
5th Michigan Infantry	3 years	B - Mount Clemens Rifle Guard, K - Saginaw City Light Infantry
11th Michigan Infantry	3 years	C
11th Michigan Infantry (Reorganized)	3 years	C
9th Michigan Cavalry	3 years	B
1st Michigan Light Artillery, Battery E [DeVries's Battery; Dennis's Battery; 5th Michigan Independent Battery; 1st Michigan Engineers and Mechanics Artillery Company; Ely's Battery]	3 years	

Minnesota Units		
2nd Minnesota Infantry	3 years	D
8th Minnesota Infantry	3 years	H

Missouri (U.S.) Units		
10th Missouri (U.S.) Infantry	3 years	D, I - Foster's Infantry Battalion
12th Missouri (U.S.) Infantry (German) [2nd Missouri Rifles Regiment; Lademann's Detachment Veterans]	3 years	B
15th Missouri (U.S.) Infantry (German) [Lademann's Detachment Veterans; Swiss Rifles]	3 years	G

Unit	Service Period	Companies and Company Names
17th Missouri (U.S.) Infantry (German) [Western Turner Rifles; Lademann's Detachment Veterans]	3 years	A, B, D, E, F, H, I, K
18th Missouri (U.S.) Infantry [Morgan's Rangers]	3 years	I
23rd Missouri (U.S.) Infantry	3 years	F
25th Missouri (U.S.) Infantry [13th Missouri Infantry; Kansas City Battalion U.S. Reserve Corps; Peabody's U.S. Reserve Corps Infantry; Van Horn's Battalion U.S. Reserve Corps]	3 years	D
26th Missouri (U.S.) Infantry	3 years	C - Holman's Independent Battalion Sharpshooters & Brown's Company Sharpshooters
27th Missouri (U.S.) Infantry	3 years	B, E
Benton Cadets, Missouri Infantry [Fremont's Infantry Body Guard; Marshall's Regiment]	3 years	FS, A*, B, C, D*, F
1st Missouri (U.S.) Cavalry [Banzhaf's Cavalry Battalion; Herron's Escort; Hunter's Body Guard]	3 years	FS, G
2nd Missouri (U.S.) Cavalry+ [Merrill's Horse]	3 years	FS, A, B* - McNicoll's Company Ohio Cavalry, C* - Lane's Company Ohio Cavalry, D - Marshall's Independent Cavalry Company, F, G, H - Michigan Cavalry Company, K* - Ohio Cavalry Company, L - Michigan Cavalry Company, M

UNIT	SERVICE PERIOD	COMPANIES AND COMPANY NAMES
3rd Missouri (U.S.) Cavalry	3 years	H – Fremont Rangers Illinois Cavalry
4th Missouri (U.S.) Cavalry (German)	3 years	FS, E - 1st Missouri Western Cavalry Fremont Hussars, F - Sigel's Escort & Smith's Escort & Asboth's Escort & Benton Hussars & Hamilton's Escort & Quinby's Escort & Weide's Company Illinois Cavalry & 1st Missouri Western Cavalry Fremont Hussars, I - 1st Missouri Western Cavalry Fremont Hussars
10th Missouri (U.S.) Cavalry [Bowen's Independent Battalion Cavalry; 1st Battalion Missouri Cavalry; Curtis's Body Guard; Fighting 10th; 28th Missouri Infantry]	3 years	H
1st Missouri (U.S.) Light Artillery, Battery A [Schofield's Battery; Fish's Battery; Fuchs's Infantry Company; Manter's Battery]	3 years	
1st Missouri (U.S.) Light Artillery, Battery E [Cole's Battery; Atwater's Battery; Hay's Battery; Nichols's Battery; Walling's Light Battery, Mississippi Marine Brigade; Henderson's Artillery Company; Company C, Segebarth's Battalion Pennsylvania Marine Artillery]	3 years	

UNIT	SERVICE PERIOD	COMPANIES AND COMPANY NAMES
1st Missouri (U.S.) Light Artillery, Battery G [Cavender's Battery; Hescock's Battery]	3 years	
1st Missouri (U.S.) Light Artillery, Battery H [Welker's Battery; Callahan's Battery; Yates's Infantry Company]	3 years	
1st Missouri (U.S.) Light Artillery, Battery M [Tiemeyer's Battery; Fish's Battery; Marr's Battery; Powell's Battery]	3 years	
2nd Missouri (U.S.) Light Artillery, Battery H [Montgomery's Battery; Holzscheiter's Battery; Lohman's Battery]	3 years	
Merrill's Missouri (U.S.) Horse Artillery	3 years	

NEW HAMPSHIRE UNITS		
5th New Hampshire Infantry [Fighting Fifth]	3 years	B
8th New Hampshire Infantry	3 years	H

NEW JERSEY UNITS		
6th New Jersey Infantry	3 years	H

Unit	Service Period	Companies and Company Names
New York Units		
26th New York Infantry [2nd Oneida County Regiment; Central New York Battalion; Utica Regiment]	3 years	G
65th New York Infantry [1st U.S. Chasseurs; 1st Grenadier Regiment]	3 years	H, I
83rd New York Infantry [City Guard; 9th New York Militia]	3 years	I
89th New York Infantry [Dickinson Guard]	3 years	F
103rd New York Infantry (German) [Seward Infantry; Baker Rifles; 3rd German Rifles]	3 years	A
146th New York Infantry [Garrard's Tigers; Halleck Infantry; 5th Oneida County Regiment]	3 years	FS, E
1st New York Mounted Rifles [4th New York Provisional Cavalry; Dodge's Mounted Rifles]	3 years	L
1st New York Cavalry [Carbine Rangers; Lincoln Cavalry; Sabre Regiment; 1st U.S. Cavalry]	3 years	E, I
3rd New York Cavalry [Van Alen Cavalry; Mix's Cavalry; Onondaga Cavalry]	3 years	FS, C(German) - German Hussars & Sauer's Cavalry Company, H, L* - 6th Independent Company Ohio Cavalry & Garrard's Cavalry Company
21st New York Cavalry [Griswold Light Cavalry]	3 years	FS, C

Unit	Service Period	Companies and Company Names
13th New York Independent Battery [Wheeler's Battery; Baker's Brigade Battery; E.D. Baker's Brigade Light Artillery, Company A; Bundy's Battery; Dieckmann's Battery; Sturmfels's Battery]	3 years	

North Carolina (U.S.) Units		
1st North Carolina (U.S.) Cavalry	3 years	L - Graham's Cavalry Company

Pennsylvania Units		
10th Pennsylvania Infantry	3 months	D(German) - Washington Light Infantry, I, K(German)
13th Pennsylvania Infantry [Washington Infantry]	3 months	I
15th Pennsylvania Infantry	3 months	B
45th Pennsylvania Infantry	3 years	G
50th Pennsylvania Infantry	3 years	B, I
51st Pennsylvania Infantry	3 years	A
71st Pennsylvania Infantry [1st California Infantry; Baker's Brigade; California Brigade; Philadelphia Brigade]	3 years	FS
100th Pennsylvania Infantry [The Roundheads; The Round Head Regiment]	3 years	A
111th Pennsylvania Infantry	3 years	D
192nd Pennsylvania Infantry	1 year	FS, A - McLeester's Infantry Company & Thomas Guards, B, C, H, I

Unit	Service Period	Companies and Company Names
11th Pennsylvania Cavalry [Harlan's Light Cavalry; 108th Pennsylvania Volunteers]	3 years	M - Capt. Noah M. Runyan's Ohio Company
14th Pennsylvania Cavalry [Stanton Cavalry; 159th Pennsylvania Infantry]	3 years	I

Rhode Island Units		
2nd Rhode Island Infantry	3 years	G, H - Kentish Guards, K
2nd Rhode Island Cavalry	3 years	F, G
3rd Rhode Island Cavalry	3 years	A
14th Rhode Island Heavy Artillery (Colored) [8th U.S. Colored Heavy Artillery; 11th U.S. Colored Heavy Artillery]	3 years	C
1st Rhode Island Light Artillery, Battery H [Allen's Battery; Hamlen's Battery; Hazard's Battery]	3 years	

Tennessee (U.S.) Units		
2nd Tennessee (U.S.) Cavalry	3 years	FS
9th Tennessee (U.S.) Cavalry [Governor's Guard]	3 years	G
10th Tennessee (U.S.) Cavalry	3 years	H

West Virginia Units		
1st West Virginia Infantry	3 years	I
6th West Virginia Infantry	3 years	FS
9th West Virginia Infantry	3 years	A, H

Unit	Service Period	Companies and Company Names
1st West Virginia Cavalry [Shaw's Cavalry Company; Gilmore's Independent Cavalry Company Pennsylvania Dragoons]	3 years	A - Harrison's Cavalry Company & Gibson's Battalion & McGee's Company Kelley Lancers & West's Independent Company Mounted Volunteers, G - Gibson's Battalion & McGee's Company Kelley Lancers, M

Wisconsin Units		
11th Wisconsin Infantry	3 years	E - Farmer's Guards
19th Wisconsin Infantry	3 years	K
1st Wisconsin Battery [LaCrosse Artillery; Foster's Battery; Webster's Battery]	3 years	

United States Colored Troops		
4th U.S. Colored Infantry [Louisiana Native Guards (African Descent)]	3 years	D, H, K
5th U.S. Colored Infantry [127th Ohio Infantry]	3 years	A, B, C, D, E, F, G, H, I, K
11th U.S. Colored Infantry [1st Alabama (U.S.) Siege Artillery (Colored)]	3 years	B
12th U.S. Colored Infantry [2nd Alabama (U.S.) Infantry (African Descent)]	3 years	A, B, C, D, E, F, G
14th U.S. Colored Infantry	3 years	FS, A, B, D, G, I
15th U.S. Colored Infantry [5th Regiment Engineers, Corps d'Afrique; 99th U.S. Colored Infantry]	3 years	A, C, D, E, G, H, I, K

Unit	Service Period	Companies and Company Names
16th U.S. Colored Infantry	3 years	FS, A, B, C, D, E, F, G, H, I, K
17th U.S. Colored Infantry	3 years	A, B, C, D, E, G, H, I, K
22nd U.S. Colored Infantry	3 years	F
23rd U.S. Colored Infantry	3 years	A, B, D, E, F, I
27th U.S. Colored Infantry	3 years	FS, A, B, C, D, E, F, G, H, I, K
28th U.S. Colored Infantry	3 years	H
30th U.S. Colored Infantry	3 years	FS
40th U.S. Colored Infantry	3 years	FS
42nd U.S. Colored Infantry	3 years	B, G, H, I, K
44th U.S. Colored Infantry	3 years	A, F, H, K
48th U.S. Colored Infantry [10th Louisiana (U.S.) Infantry (African Descent)]	3 years	K
49th U.S. Colored Infantry [11th Louisiana (U.S.) Infantry (African Descent)]	3 years	FS, D, G
51st U.S. Colored Infantry [1st Mississippi (U.S.) Infantry (Colored)]	3 years	G
54th U.S. Colored Infantry [2nd Arkansas (U.S.) Infantry (African Descent)]	3 years	D
55th U.S. Colored Infantry [1st Alabama (U.S.) Infantry (Colored)]	3 years	F, K
60th U.S. Colored Infantry [1st Iowa Infantry (Colored)]	3 years	I
65th U.S. Colored Infantry [2nd Missouri (U.S.) Infantry (African Descent)]	3 years	A
72nd U.S. Colored Infantry	3 years	A, B, D, E

Unit	Service Period	Companies and Company Names
88th U.S. Colored Infantry [17th Regiment Infantry, Corps d'Afrique]	3 years	B, C, E, F, K
100th U.S. Colored Infantry	3 years	FS, A, B, C, D, E, F, G, H, I, K
101st U.S. Colored Infantry	3 years	A, B, E, H
102nd U.S. Colored Infantry [1st Michigan Colored Infantry]	3 years	E
111th U.S. Colored Infantry [3rd Alabama (U.S.) Infantry (African Descent)]	3 years	FS
117th U.S. Colored Infantry	3 years	FS, C, D, E, G, H, I, K
119th U.S. Colored Infantry	3 years	E
137th U.S. Colored Infantry	3 years	FS
1st U.S. Colored Cavalry	3 years	FS, A, B, C, F - Samuel White's Company A of Mounted Rangers Corps d'Afrique, G, H, I, K
5th U.S. Colored Cavalry [5th Massachusetts Cavalry (Colored)]	3 years	C, E, K
1st U.S. Colored Heavy Artillery [7th U.S. Colored Heavy Artillery; 10th U.S. Colored Heavy Artillery]	3 years	A
3rd U.S. Colored Heavy Artillery [1st and 2nd Tennessee (U.S.) Heavy Artillery (Colored)]	3 years	C, G, H, L
5th U.S. Colored Heavy Artillery [9th Louisiana (U.S.) Infantry (African Descent); 1st and 2nd Mississippi (U.S.) Heavy Artillery (African Descent)]	3 years	A, B, C, D, E, F, G, H, I, K, M
9th U.S. Colored Heavy Artillery	3 years	B, C, D, E, I

Unit	Service Period	Companies and Company Names
10th U.S. Colored Heavy Artillery [1st Louisiana (U.S.) Heavy Artillery (African Descent)]	3 years	G
12th U.S. Colored Heavy Artillery	3 years	M
13th U.S. Colored Heavy Artillery	3 years	A, D, F, K, L, M
2nd U.S. Colored Light Artillery, Battery F [Memphis Light Battery (African Descent); 1st Tennessee (U.S.) Light Artillery (African Descent); Lamberg's Battery]	3 years	

United States Regular Units		
1st U.S. Infantry	3 years	H, K
2nd U.S. Infantry	3 years	RB*, A, B, C, D, F, G, H, I, K, M
3rd U.S. Infantry	3 years	A, D, F, G, I, K
4th U.S. Infantry	3 years	A, C, D, F - 3rd Pennsylvania Heavy Artillery, G, H, I, K
5th U.S. Infantry	3 years	H
6th U.S. Infantry	3 years	A, D, E, F, G, H, I, K
7th U.S. Infantry	3 years	B, F, G
8th U.S. Infantry	3 years	D, F
9th U.S. Infantry	3 years	C, G
10th U.S. Infantry	3 years	A, B, F, G
11th U.S. Infantry	3 years	FS
(1st Battalion)		C, D, E, F, G, I
(3rd Battalion)		A
12th U.S. Infantry	3 years	
(1st Battalion)		A, E, F, H, I
(2nd Battalion)		A
13th U.S. Infantry	3 years	FS, RB

Unit	Service Period	Companies and Company Names
(1st Battalion)		A, B, C, D, E, F, G, H, I
(2nd Battalion)		C, D, H, I
(3rd Battalion)		A
14th U.S. Infantry	3 years	
(1st Battalion)		A, B, C, D, G, I, K
(2nd Battalion)		A, D, E, G, H
15th U.S. Infantry	3 years	FS*, RB
(1st Battalion)		A, B, C, D, E, F, G, H, I
(2nd Battalion)		A, B, C, D, E, F, G
(3rd Battalion)		B, C, F
16th U.S. Infantry	3 years	FS
(1st Battalion)		A, B, C, D, E, F, G, H
(2nd Battalion)		A, D
17th U.S. Infantry	3 years	FS
(1st Battalion)		E, F, H
18th U.S. Infantry	3 years	FS*
(1st Battalion)		A, B, C, D, E, F, G, H, I, K
(2nd Battalion)		A, B, C, D, E, F, G, H, I
(3rd Battalion)		A, B, G, H, I
19th U.S. Infantry	3 years	FS
(1st Battalion)		A, B, C, D, F, G, H
(2nd Battalion)		A, H
(3rd Battalion)		A, B
U.S. General Service Infantry	3 years	
1st U.S. Sharpshooters [Berdan's Sharpshooters]	3 years	I – Michigan Sharpshooters
1st U.S. Cavalry	3 years	RB, A, B, C, D, E, F, G, H, K, L, M
2nd U.S. Cavalry	3 years	A, B, C, D, E, F, G, H, I, K, L, M

Unit	Service Period	Companies and Company Names
3rd U.S. Cavalry	3 years	FS, B, C, E, F, G, H, I, K, M
4th U.S. Cavalry	3 years	FS, A, B, C, D, E, F, H, I, M
5th U.S. Cavalry	3 years	A, B, C, D, E, F, G, H, I, K, L, M
6th U.S. Cavalry	3 years	A, B, C, D, E, F, G, I, K, L, M
U.S. Mounted Rifles	3 years	
U.S. General Mounted Service	3 years	
1st U.S. Artillery, Battery A	3 years	
1st U.S. Artillery, Battery B	3 years	
1st U.S. Artillery, Battery C	3 years	
1st U.S. Artillery, Battery E	3 years	
1st U.S. Artillery, Battery G	3 years	
1st U.S. Artillery, Battery H	3 years	
1st U.S. Artillery, Battery I	3 years	
1st U.S. Artillery, Battery K	3 years	
2nd U.S. Artillery, Battery A	3 years	
2nd U.S. Artillery, Battery B	3 years	
2nd U.S. Artillery, Battery C	3 years	
2nd U.S. Artillery, Battery D	3 years	
2nd U.S. Artillery, Battery E	3 years	
2nd U.S. Artillery, Battery F	3 years	
2nd U.S. Artillery, Battery G	3 years	
2nd U.S. Artillery, Battery L	3 years	
2nd U.S. Artillery, Battery M	3 years	
3rd U.S. Artillery, Battery C	3 years	
3rd U.S. Artillery, Battery E	3 years	
3rd U.S. Artillery, Battery I	3 years	
4th U.S. Artillery, Battery A	3 years	
4th U.S. Artillery, Battery B	3 years	
4th U.S. Artillery, Battery C	3 years	

Unit	Service Period	Companies and Company Names
4ᵗʰ U.S. Artillery, Battery E	3 years	
4ᵗʰ U.S. Artillery, Battery F	3 years	
4ᵗʰ U.S. Artillery, Battery G	3 years	
4ᵗʰ U.S. Artillery, Battery H	3 years	
4ᵗʰ U.S. Artillery, Battery I	3 years	
4ᵗʰ U.S. Artillery, Battery K	3 years	
4ᵗʰ U.S. Artillery, Battery L	3 years	
4ᵗʰ U.S. Artillery, Battery M	3 years	
5ᵗʰ U.S. Artillery, Battery A	3 years	
5ᵗʰ U.S. Artillery, Battery C	3 years	
5ᵗʰ U.S. Artillery, Battery D	3 years	
5ᵗʰ U.S. Artillery, Battery F	3 years	
5ᵗʰ U.S. Artillery, Battery G	3 years	
5ᵗʰ U.S. Artillery, Battery H	3 years	
5ᵗʰ U.S. Artillery, Battery I	3 years	
5ᵗʰ U.S. Artillery, Battery M	3 years	
West Point Artillery	3 years	
1ˢᵗ U.S. Veteran Volunteer Engineers [Merrill's Engineers]	1 year	FS, A, B, C*, D, G, H*, I, K*, L*
1ˢᵗ Company U.S. Volunteer Pontoniers [1ˢᵗ Company Louisiana Pioneers; 1ˢᵗ Company Sappers, Miners, and Pontoniers; Smith's Company Pontoniers]	1 year	
U.S. Hospital Stewards	3 years	
U.S. Navy Volunteer Recruits	3 years	Regular Officers, Volunteer Officers, Firemen, Seamen, Ordinary Seamen, Landsmen
U.S. Signal Corps	3 years	

Appendix E

Unit	Service Period	Companies and Company Names
Veteran Reserve Corps Units		
1st Veteran Reserve Corps	3 years	K
2nd Veteran Reserve Corps	3 years	B
5th Veteran Reserve Corps	3 years	C
6th Veteran Reserve Corps	3 years	C, G
7th Veteran Reserve Corps	3 years	FS, D
8th Veteran Reserve Corps	3 years	FS, B
12th Veteran Reserve Corps	3 years	G, H
13th Veteran Reserve Corps	3 years	C
14th Veteran Reserve Corps	3 years	FS, C, G
15th Veteran Reserve Corps	3 years	F, I
16th Veteran Reserve Corps	3 years	I
17th Veteran Reserve Corps	3 years	D, F
19th Veteran Reserve Corps	3 years	C, D, I
20th Veteran Reserve Corps	3 years	FS, A
21st Veteran Reserve Corps	3 years	I
22nd Veteran Reserve Corps	3 years	F
23rd Veteran Reserve Corps	3 years	FS, B, D
24th Veteran Reserve Corps	3 years	FS, K
1st Battalion, Veteran Reserve Corps	3 years	42nd Company, 60th Company, 186th Company, 245th Company
2nd Battalion, Veteran Reserve Corps	3 years	11th Company, 29th Company, 43rd Company, 46th Company, 60th Company, 66th Company, 68th Company, 94th Company, 103rd Company, 124th Company, 139th Company, 154th Company

Appendix E

Unit	Service Period	Companies and Company Names
Miscellaneous Units		
Pioneer Brigade, Army of the Cumberland [1st U.S. Veteran Volunteer Engineers]	3 years	
1st Army Corps Recruits 1861–1865 [Hancock's Corps]	3 years	Recruits sent to 1st through 9th U.S. Veteran Volunteer regiments
3rd Brigade Band, 1st Division, 9th Army Corps	3 years	

NOTES

ABBREVIATIONS

CDC   *Cincinnati Daily Commercial*
CDG   *Cincinnati Daily Gazette*
CDP   *Cincinnati Daily Press*
CDT   *Cincinnati Daily Times*
CEQ   *Cincinnati Daily Enquirer*
CVF   *Cincinnati Volksfreund*
OR   *The War of the Rebellion: A Compilation of the Official Records of the Union and Confederate Armies*
ORN   *Official Records of the Union and Confederate Navies in the War of the Rebellion*

Chapter 1. The Storm of War

1. Walters, *Stephen Foster*, 43.
2. Cincinnati Historical Society, *Queen City*, 9, 13, 15.
3. Ibid., 9.
4. Tucker, *Cincinnati during the Civil War*, 5–6; Cincinnati Historical Society, *Queen City*, 52; Taylor, *Frontiers of Freedom*, 1–4, 20; DBA Hispanic Chamber Cincinnati Foundation, *City of Immigrants*, 10.
5. Taylor, *Frontiers of Freedom*, 1–4, 20; DBA Hispanic Chamber Cincinnati Foundation, *City of Immigrants*, 10.
6. Cincinnati Historical Society, *Queen City*, 56–57; DBA Hispanic Chamber Cincinnati Foundation, *City of Immigrants*, 2–7.
7. Soman and Byrne, *Jewish Colonel*, 2–3; DBA Hispanic Chamber Cincinnati Foundation, *City of Immigrants*, 6–15; Klauprecht, *German Chronicle*, 198.

8. DBA Hispanic Chamber Cincinnati Foundation, *City of Immigrants*, 10–11; Fortin, *Fellowship*, 38–40, 78–86.

9. Harrold, "Perspective of a Cincinnati Abolitionist," 173–86; Suess, *Hidden History*, 51–56; Baringer, "Politics of Abolition," 79–98; DBA Hispanic Chamber Cincinnati Foundation, *City of Immigrants*, 12–13.

10. Cooper and Jackson, *Cincinnati's Underground Railroad*, 25, 56, 72, 76, 78–79.

11. Ibid., 86; Hedrick, *Harriet Beecher Stowe*, 67–206.

12. Groen, *History of the German-American Newspapers*, 287–88, 290; Fortin, *Fellowship*, 78–86.

13. Ecelbarger, "Before Cooper Union," 1–17; Pullen, *Map of the Business Portion of Cincinnati*.

14. Greve, *Centennial History*, vol. 1, 748.

Chapter 2. *"Unshrinking Was the First Voice"*

15. Groen, *History of the German-American Newspapers*, 245–46; CVF, April 13, 1861; CDT, April 13, 1861; CDC, April 15, 1861.

16. U.S. Bureau of the Census, *Population of the 100 Largest*; Fortin, *Fellowship*, 73; Tucker, *Cincinnati during the Civil War*, 19.

17. Wimberg, *Off to Battle*, 6–11; CDT, April 18, 1861.

18. CDT, April 15, 1861; CDC, April 15, 1861; Ford and Ford, *History of Cincinnati*, 107.

19. Purvis, *Newport, Kentucky*, 9698; CDG, April 15, 1861; CDT, April 19, 1861.

20. *Literary Club of Cincinnati*, 30–31; Greve, *Centennial History*, vol. 2, 92.

21. CDT, April 17, 1861.

22. CDG, April 16, 1861; CVF, April 16, 1861; Wimberg, *Off to Battle*, 13–17, 19; Tolzmann, *Cincinnati Germans*, 27; Easton, "German Philosophy," 16–19, 26.

23. Reid, *Ohio in the War*, vol. 1, 32; Adams, *Cincinnati's Forgotten General*, 4–6.

24. Wimberg, *Off to Battle*, 16; CDG, CDT, April 23, 1861; Reid, *Ohio in the War*, vol. 1, 32.

25. CDT, April 18, 1861.

26. CDT, April 19, 1861; Wimberg, *Off to Battle*, 25; Tolzmann, *Cincinnati Germans*, 27–29.

27. Wimberg, *Off to Battle*, 25–26, 115

28. Ibid., 25, 28–29, 31; "Lister," Ohio State Archives Series 147, vol. 3–4; CDG, April 21, 1861.

29. Wimberg, *Off to Battle*, 32.

30. Ibid., 3435, 41; OR, 51-I, 1, 339.

31. Ford, *Hamilton County*, 84; OR, 51-I, 1, 339–40.

32. CDT, April 29, 1861; CVF, April 28, 1861.

33. CDT, April 29, 1861.

34. OR, 51-I, 1, 339–40.

35. Wimberg, *Off to Battle*, 46, 72–76; Warner, *Generals in Blue*, 97.

36. Cox, *Military Reminiscences*, vol. 1, 21–22.

37. Wimberg, *Off to Battle*, 49, 53–54.

38. CDT, April 30, May 2, 1861; Fortin, *Fellowship*, 80; Tucker, *Cincinnati during the Civil War*, 19–20; CDC, April 19, 1861.

Chapter 3. Cincinnati Looks Southward

39. Purvis, *Newport, Kentucky*, 102.

40. Webster, *Brief History*, chapter 20; Purvis, *Newport, Kentucky*, 98–100.

41. Purvis, *Newport, Kentucky*, 98–100; Burns, *History of Covington*, 308; Wimberg, *1864*, 37, 118.

42. CDT, April 30, May 2, 1861; Wright, *Kentucky Soldiers*, vol. 1, 14–19.

43. CDC, April 18, 1861; Wimberg, *Off to Battle*, 31–32; 43, 49; W. Smith, *Annual Statement*, 6–7; M. Smith, *Timberclads*, 38–39.

44. Donnelly, *Newport Barracks*, 1–3, 20–31, 46–47; Schottelkotte, "Court Martial," 45–47.

45. Donnelly, *Newport Barracks*, 50–55; Shaler, *Autobiography*, 14.

46. Donnelly, *Newport Barracks*, 51–55; Billings, *Report on Barracks*, 134–38.

47. Wimberg, *Off to Battle*, 54, 58.

48. Ibid., 72–76.

49. Ford and Ford, *Hamilton County*, 84; CDG, September 14, 1861; CDP, October 27, November 2, December 14, 1861.

50. Wimberg, *Off to Battle*, 78, 80, 83–85.

51. Ibid., 62; CDT, May 30, 1861; Tucker, *Cincinnati during the Civil War*, 20.

52. Metz, *Sisters of Charity*, i–4; Wimberg, *Off to Battle*, 87.

53. Wimberg, *Off to Battle*, 102–3; Howe, *Historical Collections*, vol. 1, 772; Wimberg, *1865*, 136.

54. M. Smith, *Timberclads*, 1–2, 11–13, 16–24; Silverstone, *Civil War Navies*, 111; Slagle, *Ironclad Captain*, 112–17.

55. Slagle, *Ironclad Captain*, 115–17; M. Smith, *Civil War Biographies*, 67, 135, 191, 204–5; M. Smith, *Timberclads*, 42–45.

56. Cincinnati Historical Society, *WPA Guide*, 60–61; M. Smith, *Timberclads*, 11–12; White, "Cincinnati Marine Railway," 74, 79–82.

57. White, "Cincinnati Marine Railway," 69–70; Slagle, *Ironclad Captain*, 115–17; M. Smith, *Timberclads*, 60–62, 66–67.

58. M. Smith, *Timberclads*, 63–64, 68–69.

59. Wimberg, *Off to Battle*, 113–14; CDT, July 8, 1861; M. Smith, *Timberclads*, 69; *Williams' Cincinnati Directory* (1863), 31.

60. CEQ, June 21, 1861; CDG, July 6, 1861.

61. CDT, CDG, June 8, 20, 1861.

62. CEQ, July 10, 1861; Ford and Ford, *History of Cincinnati*, 107; CDG, August 9, 31, 1861; Wimberg, *Under Attack*, 8–9, 13; Mendelsohn, "Beyond the Battlefield," 93–97.

63. W. Smith, *Annual Statement*, 5–8.

64. CDT, CDG, July 23, 1861.

Chapter 4. Fortifying the Queen City

65. CDG, August 28, 1861.
66. Howe, *Historical Collections*, vol. 1, 765; Ford and Ford, *History of Cincinnati*, 106; National Archives, RG 77, T12, Civil War Maps File.
67. CDG, September 5, 1861; Wimberg, *Off to Battle*, 142; Ventre and Goodman, *Brief History*, 1–6.
68. Charles Whittlesey Papers, Series 3, Box 2; "Cincinnati City Auditor's Report," 51.
69. CDP, September 30, October 3, 1861; CDG, October 3, 4, 1861; Claims W.2627 (February 12, 1863), Department of the Ohio Records, National Archives; CEQ, October 15, 1861; CEQ, February 11, 1923; Agnello, "Historic Rock Quarries," 1–5; Wimberg, *Off to Battle*, 160.
70. CDG, October 3, 1861; Tenkotte and Claypool, *Encyclopedia of Northern Kentucky*, 192; Terrell, *Indiana in the War*, 464–66.
71. Wimberg, *Off to Battle*, 162, 170.
72. Boynton, *History*; Wimberg, *1863*, 17.
73. Cincinnati Branch U.S. Sanitary Commission, 5; Cincinnati Historical Society, *Queen City*, 50.
74. Baker, *Cyclone in Calico*, 12–13, 36–37, 59, 96–102, 140, 160, 182–84, 188–89, 206, 220; Holland, *Our Army Nurses*, 25, 34.
75. CDG, April 10, 1862; CDC, February 26, 1862; Burns, *History of Covington*, 284; Wimberg, *Under Attack*, 26–32; Wimberg, *1863*, 179.
76. M. Smith, *Joseph Brown*, 55–102, 279, 282; Wimberg, *Under Attack*, 66; Wimberg, *1863*, 1.
77. CEQ, July 12–13, 1862; CDG, July 14–21, 1862.
78. Harding, "Cincinnati Riots," 229–39.

Chapter 5. "Citizens for Labor, Soldiers for Battle"

79. Johnson and Buel, *Battles and Leaders*, vol. 3, 1–7.
80. Warner, *Generals in Blue*, 575; Terrell, *Indiana in the War*, 464–66.
81. Geaslen, *Our Moment of Glory*, 14.
82. Wallace, *Lew Wallace*, vol. 2, 604–5; Stephens, *Shadow of Shilow*, 127–29; McNitt, *Navaho Expedition*, lxi, 232–37, 239–40.
83. Geaslen, *Our Moment of Glory*, 15; Wallace, *Lew Wallace*, vol. 2, 606–10.
84. Cincinnati Historical Society, *Queen City*, 50; Clark, *Black Brigade*, 3–30.
85. Stephens, *Shadow of Shiloh*, 129; Walden, "General's Tour," 8–9, 16–18; Wallace, *Lew Wallace*, vol. 2, 611–20, 626–27.
86. Stephens, *Shadow of Shiloh*, 129; Walden, "General's Tour," 8–9, 16–18; Wallace, *Lew Wallace*, vol. 2, 611–20, 626–27.
87. Tucker, *Cincinnati during the Civil War*, 33; CDG, September 14, 1862.
88. Walden, "General's Tour," 22–23; Tenkotte and Claypool, *Encyclopedia of Northern Kentucky*, 192–93; Wimberg, *Under Attack*, 112; Wimberg, *1864*, 159.

Chapter 6. Copperheads and Raiders

89. Purvis, *Newport, Kentucky*, 103; Ohio Roster Commission, *Official Roster*, vol. 1, 591–92; Ford and Ford, *History of Hamilton County*, 165; Congressional Medal of Honor Society, "Recipients–Full Archive."
90. Wimberg, *1863*, 40.
91. Warner, *Generals in Blue*, 57–58, 575–76.
92. Wimberg, *1863*, 40–44, 46–49.
93. Becker, "Genesis of a Copperhead," 235–36, 251–52; CEQ, March 22, 1863; Wimberg, *1863*, 52–53, 60.
94. Wimberg, *1863*, 52–53, 60.
95. CDG, April 7, 1863; Society of the Army of the Cumberland, *Twenty-First Reunion*, 278–81; Greve, *Centennial History*, vol. 1, 962, 970.
96. Wimberg, *1863*, 60, 72.
97. CDC, May 6, 1863; Wimberg, *1863*, 72–84, 87, 194.
98. CDC, May 6, 1863; Wimberg, *1863*, 72–84, 87, 194.
99. Cahill and Mowery, *Morgan's Raid*, 43–47, 50.
100. Ibid.; Tucker, *Cincinnati during the Civil War*, 34–35.
101. Mowery, *Morgan's Great Raid*, 81–95.
102. Ibid., 112–22, 147, 161–62; CDG, July 14, 1863.
103. Wimberg, *1863*, 158–63, 168, 176; Mowery, *Morgan's Great Raid*, 163–65.
104. Wimberg, *1863*, 201; Warner, *Generals in Blue*, 157.
105. Warner, *Generals in Blue*, 227–28, 233–35; Terrell, *Indiana in the War*, 464–66; Wimberg, *1864*, 10, 137; *Williams' Cincinnati Directory* (1865), 207; Wimberg, *1865*, 140.

Chapter 7. The Slaughter Has Ended

106. Bissland, *Blood, Tears, & Glory*, 336–38, 341; Wimberg, *1864*, 30.
107. Tucker, *Cincinnati during the Civil War*, 21–22.
108. Wimberg, *1865*, 145, 146; CDG, December 15, 1862; Wimberg, *Under Attack*, 162; CEQ, April 12, 1863; CDC, May 19, 1865; Cincinnati, Ohio, Quartermaster Records, Map 274, Folders 1–39, Post & Reservation File, RG 92, National Archives.
109. Covington, Kentucky, Quartermaster Records, Map 62, Sheets 1–37, Post & Reservation File, RG 92, National Archives; Wimberg, *1865*, 104; CDC, May 3, 1865.
110. Zornow, "Clement L. Vallandigham," 21–37; Wimberg, *1864*, 60–78, 84, 152; CDC, September 26, 1864; CDC, November 10, November 11, 1864; CDT, November 9, 1864.
111. Grandstaff, *History of the Professional Theatre*, 83–129.
112. Cincinnati Historical Society, *Queen City*, 51; Wimberg, *1865*, 52, 54, 56–57.
113. Wimberg, *1865*, 58–61.
114. Abraham Lincoln's Gettysburg Address.

115. Beyer and Keydel, *Deeds of Valor*; Ohio Department of Veterans Services, "Medal of Honor Recipients," http://dvs.ohio.gov/main/veterans-hall-of-fame-honorees-MOH.html; Congressional Medal of Honor Society website; Ohio State Archives Series 147, vol. 20; *History of Wyandot County*, 923–24.

116. Bissland, *Blood, Tears, & Glory*, 480–81; Tucker, *Cincinnati during the Civil War*, 37.

Appendix A. U.S. Navy Steamers Built, Refit or Purchased in Cincinnati

117. ORN, ser. 2, vol. 1, p. 27–246; Silverstone, *Civil War Navies*, 4–146; M. Smith, *Joseph Brown*, 5–106, 280–84; Roberts, *Civil War Ironclads*, 211–13; M. Smith, *Timberclads*, 40–69; M. Smith, *Tinclads*, 341–47; *Dictionary of American Naval Fighting Ships* (DANFS); CDT, June 17, 1861; Wimberg, *1863*, 39, 89–91, 201; CEQ, August 4, 1864; CDT, August 24, October 12, 1864; Wimberg, *1864*, 114, 134; Wooldridge, "Names of Steamboats." The "Index of Union Vessels" in ORN, ser. 2, vol. 1, shows purchase dates based on credit fulfillment. The U.S. government bought steamboats on credit and most often paid for the vessels at a date later than the actual purchase date and from a different city than where the purchase was made. This table presents only actual purchase dates whenever Cincinnati was the city of purchase; otherwise, the credit fulfillment date was used. The build and refit dates are mainly based on Cincinnati newspaper or ORN records that indicated when the vessel was ready for service in Cincinnati, which was typically before the vessel's crews were recruited.

Appendix B. Civil War Fortifications Constructed in Greater Cincinnati

118. OR, vol. 16-I, pt. 2, 664–75; OR, vol. 23-I, pt. 2, 347–48, 607–8; OR, vol. 30-I, pt. 2, 557–64; OR, vol. 39-I, pt. 3, 769–77; CEQ, June 27, 1865; CDT, December 13, 1865; Doug VonStrohe and Jeannine Kreinbrink, National Register of Historic Places Registration Form: Battery Bates and Battery Coombs, Covington, Kentucky (Washington, D.C.: U.S. Department of the Interior, National Park Service, 2017); Geaslen, *Our Moment of Glory*, 22–60; Civil War Field Fortifications, "Trace of Field Fortifications, Traditional Forms," http://lly.org/~rcw/cwf/dictionary/dictionary.html; Lippett, *Treatise on Intrenchments*, 17–24; Walden, "General's Tour," 23–33; Webster, *Brief History*, appendix A; USGS Historical Topographic Map Explorer, https://livingatlas.arcgis.com/topoexplorer/index.html.

Appendix C. Civil War Sites in Greater Cincinnati

119. Cincinnati Historical Society, *WPA Guide*, 156–57; Hill, *History of the Inns*, 20–22; Suess, *Lost Cincinnati*, 107–12.

120. Venner, *Queen City Lady*, 94.

121. CDT, May 13, 1861; CEQ, June 23, 1861; CDG, September 19, 1861; Wimberg, *1863*, 99.
122. Cincinnati Historical Society, *WPA Guide*, 184–85.
123. Wimberg, *Off to Battle*, 162–64, 170; Fortin, *Fellowship*, 81; CDC, August 2, 1865; Phillips, *Map of Cincinnati* (1868).
124. Wimberg, *1864*, 134, 137; CDC, October 13, 1864; Wimberg, *1865*, 52; Pullen, *Map of the Business Portion of Cincinnati* (1863).
125. Wimberg, *Off to Battle*, 175; Cincinnati Historical Society, *WPA Guide*, 189.
126. Wimberg, *1863*, 201, 209; Wimberg, *1865*, 116; CDG, October 28, 1865; CDC, November 30, 1865; Metz, *Sisters of Charity*, 19; Greve, *Centennial History*, 957.
127. Cincinnati Historical Society, *WPA Guide*, 201–2.
128. Freking, "Lost City."
129. Wimberg, *Off to Battle*, 25, 30, 131, 160; CEQ, December 8, 1861; Wimberg, *1863*, 30; Wimberg, *1865*, 94; CDG, September 14, October 4, 1861; CDC, June 3, 1865.
130. Greve, *Centennial History*, vol. 1, 576, 956, 1031; Barkley, *Ambulance*; Wimberg, *Off to Battle*, 26–27, 76, 145; Faust, *Historical Times Illustrated*, 451–52.
131. CEQ, June 25, 1883; Warner, *Generals in Blue*, 297; Barnett, "Crime and No Punishment," 29–33; Cincinnati Museum Center, "Ohio Civil War Monuments Database by County: Hamilton County," http://library.cincymuseum.org/civilwar/ohio-monuments.htm.
132. Folzenlogen and Folzenlogen, *Walking Cincinnati*, 90; Riesenberg, *Assessment*.
133. Tolzmann, *Cincinnati Germans*, 148; Durrell, "Time Stands Still," 60–61.
134. CDG, October 29, 1861; *Williams' Cincinnati Directory* (1863), 210, 285; Phillips, *Map of Cincinnati* (1868).
135. *Williams' Cincinnati Directory* (1861–1863), frontispiece map; National Underground Railroad Freedom Center, www.freedomcenter.org.
136. Ecelbarger, "Before Cooper Union," 1–17; Pullen, *Map of the Business Portion of Cincinnati* (1863).
137. Cincinnati Historical Society, *WPA Guide*, 167; Fladeland, "James G. Birney's Anti-Slavery Activities," 251–65; Harrold, "Perspective of a Cincinnati Abolitionist," 173–86.
138. Clark, *Black Brigade*, 17–18; Cincinnati Historical Society, *WPA Guide*, 195–96.
139. Cincinnati Historical Society, *WPA Guide*, 205; Wimberg, *1863*, 104, 176; CDC, July 11, September 11, 1863.
140. Cooper and Jackson, *Cincinnati's Underground Railroad*, 62–63, 95; Union Baptist Church of Greater Cincinnati, https://www.union-baptist.net/about-us/our-history/.
141. Cincinnati Historical Society, *WPA Guide*, 171; Christ Episcopal Church, https://cincinnaticathedral.com/about-history/; Venable, *Centennial History of Christ Church*, 26–29; Wimberg, *Under Attack*, 42, 177; CDC, February 21, June 30, 1862; Pullen, *Map of the Business Portion of Cincinnati* (1863); Brill, "Cincinnati's 'Poet Warrior'," 188.

142. Wimberg, *Off to Battle*, 88, 124; *Williams' Cincinnati Directory* (1864), 182; CEQ, August 29, 1862; *Williams' Cincinnati Directory* (1863), 31.

143. *Williams' Cincinnati Directory* (1863), 9; CDC, July 21, 1864, January 10, 1865; Wimberg, *1865*, 115.

144. *Williams' Cincinnati Directory* (1863), 31; Wimberg, *1864*, 95.

145. Rose, "Lost City."

146. Hill, *History of the Inns*, 20; CDT, April 16, 18, 1861; Venner, *Queen City Lady*, 122.

147. Cincinnati History Library and Archives, "J.P. Ball, African American Photographer," http://library.cincymuseum.org/ball/jpball.htm; *Williams' Cincinnati Directory* (1863), 57; Cincinnati Historical Society, *WPA Guide*, 159.

148. Cincinnati Historical Society, *WPA Guide*, 174–75; Wimberg, *Off to Battle*, 48; Holliday, "Notes on Samuel N. Pike," 165–83.

149. Cincinnati Historical Society, *WPA Guide*, 172.

150. Ibid., 159; Baringer, "Politics of Abolition," 79–98; *Williams' Cincinnati Directory* (1863), 31; Wimberg, *1863*, 68; Wimberg, *1864*, 135.

151. Cincinnati Historical Society, *WPA Guide*, 199.

152. Wimberg, *1865*, 53; *Williams' Cincinnati Directory* (1865), 22, 450; U.S. Sanitary Commission, *U.S. Sanitary Commission*, 357–60.

153. Cincinnati Historical Society, *WPA Guide*, 183.

154. Cincinnati Museum Center "Ohio Civil War Monuments Database by County: Hamilton County," https://www.cincymuseum.org.

155. Ibid.

156. Brill, "Cincinnati's 'Poet Warrior'," 188–201; CEQ, May 19, 1908.

157. Cincinnati Historical Society, *WPA Guide*, 161, 169.

158. Ibid., 168; *Literary Club of Cincinnati*, 117–37.

159. Brill, "Cincinnati's 'Poet Warrior'," 189.

160. Cincinnati Historical Society, *WPA Guide*, 169; Walters, *Stephen Foster*, 11, 74–75, 93–95; Hodges, "Stephen Foster," 99–100.

161. Cincinnati Historical Society, *WPA Guide*, 165–167; Tucker, "'Old Nick' Longworth," 248–51; Sherman, *Memoirs*, vol. 1, 221.

162. Cincinnati Historical Society, *WPA Guide*, 264–65; Alter, "National Weather Service," 139–40; Leonard, *Greater Cincinnati and Its People*, vol. 2, 460–62; Cincinnati Observatory, https://www.cincinnatiobservatory.org/about/our-history-2/.

163. Cincinnati Historical Society, *WPA Guide*, 263.

164. Tolzmann, *Cincinnati Germans*, 146–47.

165. Cincinnati Historical Society, *WPA Guide*, 210–11; Becker, "Ironmaster," 123–28.

166. Cincinnati Historical Society, *WPA Guide*, 216–17; CVF, September 10, 1862; *Williams' Cincinnati Directory* (1861), 219.

167. Tolzmann, *Cincinnati Germans*, 147.

168. Cincinnati Historical Society, *WPA Guide*, 211–12; Wimberg, *Off to Battle*, 25; Wimberg, *Under Attack*, 68.

169. Bachmeyer, "Hospitals of Cincinnati," 38, 43–44; Cincinnati Historical Society, *WPA Guide*, 213; CDC, March 6, 1863; Wimberg, *1865*, 128; Shotwell, *History of the Schools*, 135–66.

170. National Museum of American History, "A Funeral Procession 1,700 Miles Long—Abraham Lincoln: An Extraordinary Life," https://americanhistory.si.edu/lincoln/funeral-procession.

171. *Williams' Cincinnati Directory* (1859, 1860, 1863); Roberts, *Civil War Ironclads*, 212.

172. Suess, *Hidden History*, 71–75.

173. Ibid., 59–63.

174. Suess, *Hidden History*, 59–63; Wimberg, *Under Attack*, 179; *Williams' Cincinnati Directory* (1863), 31; Pullen, *Map of the Business Portion of Cincinnati* (1863); U.S. Naval Enlistment Rendezvous, Cincinnati, 1861–65.

175. Cincinnati Historical Society, *WPA Guide*, 145–47.

176. Ibid., 151–52; Hill, *History of the Inns*, 23.

177. Wimberg, *Off to Battle*, 113, 135; CDG, November 12, 1862; Wimberg, *Under Attack*, 117; Wimberg, *1864*, 21.

178. Wulsin, *Story of the Fourth Regiment*, 9, 112–14, 137–42; Wimberg, *1864*, 22, 25; CDC, March 29, 1866; Village of Cumminsville Committee, "War of the Rebellion, 1861–1865," in *History of Cumminsville*. The camp occupied T. Kirby's lot on the west bluff overlooking Mill Creek, just west of Cumminsville.

179. Find a Grave, "Wesleyan Cemetery, Cincinnati, Ohio," www.findagrave.com; Cooper and Jackson, *Cincinnati's Underground Railroad*, 98.

180. Wimberg, *1864*, 107; Wimberg, *1865*, 101; Find a Grave, "St. Joseph Cemetery, Cincinnati, Ohio," www.findagrave.com.

181. Find a Grave, "Union Baptist Cemetery, Cincinnati, Ohio," www.findagrave.com; Cooper and Jackson, *Cincinnati's Underground Railroad*, 109.

182. Cincinnati Historical Society, *WPA Guide*, 455.

183. OR, vol. 52-I, pt. 1, 379; CDT, May 18, June 6, 1861; Wimberg, *Under Attack*, 170; Phillips, *Map of Hamilton County 1865*. The map shows the location of the Cincinnati Trotting Park where Camp Harrison was established.

184. Cincinnati Museum Center, "Ohio Civil War Monuments Database by County: Hamilton County," cincymuseum.org.

185. Ibid.

186. Riesenberg, *Assessment*; Jewish Cemeteries of Greater Cincinnati, "David Urbansky," https://www.jcemcin.org/david-urbansky/.

187. CDT, April 30, May 2, 1861; CDP, September 8, 1861; Ford, *Hamilton County*, 84.

188. Cincinnati Historical Society, *WPA Guide*, 369.

189. Ibid., 364–65.

190. Ibid., 365.

191. *Williams' Cincinnati Directory* (1859–1863); CDT, June 17, 1861.

192. Hedrick, *Harriet Beecher Stowe*, 67–206.

193. *Williams' Cincinnati Directory* (1859–1863); Suess, *Hidden History*, 71; Roberts, *Civil War Ironclads*, 61; CDT, June 17, 1861; White, "Cincinnati Marine Railway," 79–82.

194. Remarkable Ohio, "The Lane Seminary Debates," www.remarkableohio.org.

195. *Williams' Cincinnati Directory* (1859–1863); M. Smith, *Joseph Brown*, 282–85; M. Smith, *Timberclads*, 60–61; CDT, June 17, 1861; CDG, July 2, 1863; White, "Cincinnati Marine Railway," 79–82.

196. *Williams' Cincinnati Directory* (1859–1863); CDT, June 17, 1861; M. Smith, *Joseph Brown*, 63–65; Silverstone, 9–10; White, "Cincinnati Marine Railway," 79–82.

197. Cahill and Mowery, *Morgan's Raid*, 58–59.

198. National Park Service, "Samuel and Sally Wilson House," https://www.nps.gov/nr/travel/underground/oh10.htm.

199. Six Acres Bed & Breakfast, http://sixacresbb.com; Cooper and Jackson, *Cincinnati's Underground Railroad*, 72–73.

200. CDT, July 10, 1861; Cahill and Mowery, *Morgan's Raid*, 63.

201. Cahill and Mowery, *Morgan's Raid*, 256.

202. Ibid., 62.

203. Remarkable Ohio, "The Eliza House," www.remarkableohio.org. The actual location of the house was found using the *Map of Hamilton County, Ohio, 1856* and *Atlas of Hamilton County, Ohio, 1869*.

204. Cahill and Mowery, *Morgan's Raid*, 61–62.

205. Ibid., 62.

206. Folzenlogen and Folzenlogen, *Walking Cincinnati*, 20.

207. Cahill and Mowery, *Morgan's Raid*, 52–53.

208. Ibid., 243–44.

209. Cincinnati Historical Society, *WPA Guide*, 499; Hamilton Avenue Road to Freedom, https://hamiltonavenueroadtofreedom.org.

210. Metz, *Sisters of Charity*, 50; Cahill and Mowery, *Morgan's Raid*, 56–57.

211. Cahill and Mowery, *Morgan's Raid*, 60.

212. Ibid.

213. Cincinnati Museum Center, "Ohio Civil War Monuments Database by County: Hamilton County," cincymuseum.org.

214. Cahill and Mowery, *Morgan's Raid*, 66–67.

215. Wimberg, *Off to Battle*, 73, 77; Cahill and Mowery, *Morgan's Raid*, 72; Sloan, *History of Camp Dennison*, 6–15, 21–23, 27–31; Penrod, 27–32.

216. Cahill and Mowery, *Morgan's Raid*, 72; Sloan, *History of Camp Dennison*, 9–10, 30.

217. Cincinnati Museum Center, "Ohio Civil War Monuments Database by County: Hamilton County," cincymuseum.org; Sloan, *History of Camp Dennison*, 35–36, 219–20.

218. Robertson, *Medical and Surgical History*, vol. 6, 910; Middleton, Strobridge & Company, *View of Camp Dennison*, 156, 177; Camp Dennison, Ohio, Enclosure from E 225, Sheets 1–3, RG 92, National Archives; Metz, *Sisters of Charity*, i–5; CEQ, November 8, 1865; *Rebecca E. J. Kugler v. the United States*, U.S. Court of Claims (December 1868).

219. Wimberg, *Off to Battle*, 86–87, 89; Metz, *Sisters of Charity*, 5.

220. Cahill and Mowery, *Morgan's Raid*, 68–69.

221. Ibid., 65–66.

222. Ibid., 69.

223. Ibid., 80.

224. Ibid., 76.

225. Ibid., 76–78.

226. Ibid., 69–70, 76–77.

227. Ibid., 261–62.

228. Ibid., 63–64.

229. Tolzmann, *Roebling Suspension Bridge*, 3.

230. Wells, *Roadside History*, 156–57; Folzenlogen and Folzenlogen, *Walking Cincinnati*, 131.

231. Tenkotte and Claypool, *Encyclopedia of Northern Kentucky*, 193; Cooper and Jackson, *Cincinnati's Underground Railroad*, 110; CEQ, February 7, 1997; Wimberg, *Under Attack*, 178.

232. Map 62, Sheets 35 and 37, Post and Reservation File, RG 92, National Archives.

233. Tolzmann, *Roebling Suspension Bridge*, 4–5.

234. *Bulletin of the Kenton County Historical Society*, November/December 2013, 6–7.

235. Folzenlogen and Folzenlogen, *Walking Cincinnati*, 130.

236. Wells, *Roadside History*, 183–84, 257; CDG, July 9, 1863.

237. Tolzmann, *Roebling Suspension Bridge*, 7.

238. Tenkotte and Claypool, *Encyclopedia of Northern Kentucky*, 653–54; Wimberg, *Under Attack*, 155, 162.

239. *Williams' Cincinnati Directory* (1858–1869); Burns, *History of Covington*, 265–84; CDT, October 27, 1862; Roberts, *Civil War Ironclads*, 60–61.

240. Tolzmann, *Roebling Suspension Bridge*, 11–21, 27; Stern, "Suspension Bridge," 211–25.

241. Stern, "Suspension Bridge," 220; Wallace, *Lew Wallace*, vol. 2, 611–12; CEQ, November 7–9, 1862; Tenkotte and Claypool, *Encyclopedia of Northern Kentucky*, 193; *Covington (KY) Journal*, February 15, 1873.

242. *Williams' Cincinnati Directory* (1858–1869); Roberts, *Civil War Ironclads*, 211–12.

243. Cincinnati Historical Society, *WPA Guide*, 534.

244. Donnelly, *Newport Barracks*, 1–3, 64–65; Tenkotte and Claypool, *Encyclopedia of Northern Kentucky*, 654–55.

245. Map Showing the Defenses of Cincinnati, Newport & Covington (1862), Drawer 132–Sheet 5, RG 77, National Archives; Map 62, Sheets 4, 22–34, Post & Reservation File, RG 92, National Archives; Wimberg, *Under Attack*, 92, 176; Wimberg, *1865*, 153; CDT, December 13, 1865; CDC, August 23, November 24, 1866.

246. Walden, "General's Tour," 26.

247. Ibid., 32; Wimberg, *Under Attack*, 121; CDG, September 13, 1862.

248. Find a Grave, "Highland Cemetery, Fort Mitchell, Kentucky," findagrave.com.

249. "Sketch of the Plan of Camp King, Ky.," Henry Otis Dwight Papers, Ohio History Connection, State Archives Library; Map Showing the Military Defenses of Cincinnati, Covington and Newport (1862), G4084.C4 1877.U5, Library of Congress; Tenkotte and Claypool, *Encyclopedia of Northern Kentucky*, 148, 193. The

camp was pinpointed using topographical maps in conjunction with Dwight's plan of the camp, which shows several known reference features.

250. CDP, November 2, December 14, 1861; CDC, December 14, 1861.
251. Geaslen, *Our Moment of Glory*, 70–72.
252. Brent, *National Register of Historic Places Multiple Property Submission*.
253. Trails-R-Us, Kentucky Monuments, http://www.trailsrus.com/monuments/reg4/covington.html.
254. Find a Grave, "Evergreen Cemetery, Southgate, Kentucky," findagrave.com.
255. Clark, *Black Brigade*, 18; Walden, "General's Tour," 32–33.
256. Clark, *Black Brigade*, 19.

Appendix D. Spring Grove Cemetery and Arboretum

257. Spring Grove Cemetery, *History of Spring Grove*.
258. Ibid.; Spring Grove Cemetery, *Visitor's Map*.
259. Dickson, "Abraham Lincoln at Cincinnati," 62–66; Wimberg, *1865*, 136.
260. Cooper and Jackson, *Cincinnati's Underground Railroad*, 70–73, 116.
261. CDG, March 7, 1862; "Civil War at Spring Grove," 74.
262. "Civil War at Spring Grove," 74–75.
263. Ibid., 75; State of Ohio, *Executive Documents*, 299–300.
264. State of Ohio, *Executive Documents*, 299.
265. Ibid.
266. "Civil War at Spring Grove," 76–77.
267. U.S. Senate, *Executive Documents*, no. 79, 82–83.
268. "Civil War at Spring Grove," 77–79.
269. Nuxhall, *Interesting Facts*, 1.
270. Hamilton County Genealogical Society, "Index of Civil War Veteran Burials," https://hcgsohio.org; Find a Grave, www.findagrave.com. The extraordinary research of genealogists and necrologists that is captured on Find a Grave has allowed other historians to know the important persons of our past who are buried in each cemetery. This website was the source used to gain the counts of Civil War brevet brigadier general or higher rank officers buried across the United States.
271. Barnett, "Forty for the Union," 96–121.
272. Nuxhall, *Interesting Facts*, 1–3; Holmes and Nuxhall, *Historic Spring Grove Cemetery*, 1–2; Spring Grove Cemetery, "Congressional Medal of Honor Recipients," springgrove.org; Find a Grave, "Spring Grove Cemetery," findagrave.com.
273. Goss, *Cincinnati*, vol. 4, 554–58.
274. Find a Grave, "Dwight Hamilton Baldwin," findagrave.com.
275. Preston, "Our Rich History"; CEQ, February 7, 1997.
276. Coachbuilt, "Crane & Breed," http://www.coachbuilt.com/bui/c/crane_breed/crane_breed.htm.
277. Spring Grove Cemetery, "Congressional Medal of Honor Recipients."

278. Suess, *Hidden History*, 60.

279. Ibid., 51–56.

280. Cincinnati Historical Society, *WPA Guide*, 184–85; Greve, *Centennial History*, 753–58.

281. William Dickson Papers; Greve, *Centennial History*, vol. 2, 377–78.

282. Goss, *Cincinnati*, vol. 4, 715–16.

283. Spring Grove Cemetery, "Congressional Medal of Honor Recipients."

284. Sealy Factory Direct Mattress, "Stearns and Foster," http://www.factorydirectmattress.com/stearns-foster-2; Goss, *Cincinnati*, vol. 3, 514–15.

285. Goss, *Cincinnati*, vol. 4, 10–21; Cincinnati Historical Society, *Queen City*, 238; manuscript ledgers of James Norris Gamble, Inventor of Ivory Soap and Son of the Co-founder of the Proctor & Gamble Business (1897–1928), PBA Galleries web site, https://www.pbagalleries.com/view-auctions/catalog/id/393/lot/122128/.

286. Cincinnati Historical Society, *Queen City*, 210; McCarthy, "Greetings from Gibson," 13.

287. Greve, *Centennial History*, vol. 1, 866, 935–36; Allen, "Baseball's Immortal Red Stockings," 191–202.

288. Wells, *Roadside History*, 183–84, 257.

289. Becker, "Ironmaster," 123–28.

290. Greve, *Centennial History*, vol. 2, 210–16.

291. Find a Grave, "John Addison Gurley," findagrave.com.

292. Society of the Army of the Cumberland, *Twenty-First Reunion*, 278–81; Greve, *Centennial History*, vol. 2, 397–99.

293. Wittke, "Friedrich Hassaurek," 1–17.

294. Nelson, *History of Cincinnati*, 860–61; Suess, *Lost Cincinnati*, 61–62.

295. McCaul, *To Retain Command*, 179–84.

296. Suess, *Hidden History*, 64–70.

297. Seidman, "Alexander Bonner 'Moses' Latta," 140–48.

298. Harlan, "Autobiography of Alexander Long," 99–127; Perzel, "Alexander Long," 3–17; Tucker, "Hiram Powers," 28–38; Tucker, "'Old Nick' Longworth," 248–59.

299. Spring Grove Cemetery, "Congressional Medal of Honor Recipients."

300. Thomas W. Cutrer, "Luckett, Philip Noland," Texas State Historical Association, https://tshaonline.org/handbook/online/articles/flu05.

301. Stanley T. Matthews Papers.

302. Greve, *Centennial History*, vol. 2, 525–27.

303. Find a Grave, "Daniel McCook, Sr.," findagrave.com; Barnett, "Crime and No Punishment," 29, 33.

304. Cox, *Memorial of Alexander Hamilton McGuffey*, 5–8.

305. *New York Times*, March 15, 1873.

306. Becker Collection Drawings of the American Civil War Era, "James W. McLaughlin (1834–1923)," https://beckercollection.bc.edu/james-mclaughlin; Greve, *Centennial History*, vol. 1, 699–700.

307. Ellis, *Ceramic Career*.

308. Nelson, *History of Cincinnati*, 849–51.

309. "Robert (1811–1899) Furniture Magnate and son: Richard (1850–1925)," http://wwwcam.tripod.com/sherman/id20.html; Greve, *Centennial History*, vol. 2, 297–99.

310. Nelson, *History of Cincinnati*, 859–60; Suess, *Lost Cincinnati*, 58–60.

311. Greve, *Centennial History*, vol. 2, 10–15; Nuxhall, *Interesting Facts*, 1–3; Cincinnati Historical Society, *WPA Guide*, 457.

312. Goss, *Cincinnati*, vol. 4, 396–400; Suess, *Lost Cincinnati*, 60.

313. St. Andrew's Society of Philadelphia, *Historical Catalogue*, 294–95; Spring Grove Cemetery, "Congressional Medal of Honor Recipients."

314. Mach, "Family Ties," 17–29.

315. Greve, *Centennial History*, vol. 2, 301, 359–61.

316. Goss, *Cincinnati*, vol. 4, 10–21.

317. Ross, "Industrialization and the Changing Images," 20–21.

318. Brent Coleman, "As 'The Greatest Show on Earth' Ends, a Reminder of Cincinnati's Robust Circus Legacy," WCPO, https://www.wcpo.com.

319. *Cincinnati Daily Star*, September 11, 1879; Greve, *Centennial History*, vol. 2, 164–65.

320. Bissland, *Blood, Tears, & Glory*, 327–29, 513–14.

321. Greve, *Centennial History*, vol. 2, 60–62.

322. Goss, *Cincinnati*, vol. 3, 514–515.

323. Linden-Ward, "Greening of Cincinnati," 20–39.

324. Guide to the Strobridge Lithographing Company Advertisements, 1910–1954 and undated, Duke University Library, Durham, North Carolina.

325. Tolzmann, *Cincinnati Germans*, 3–4; Greve, *Centennial History*, vol. 2, 136–38.

326. Greve, *Centennial History*, vol. 2, 177–80.

327. Enss, "Wild Women."

328. Schlachter, "Dr. John Aston Warder," 2–12.

329. Find a Grave, "Col. William B. Way," findagrave.com; Wittenberg, *Battle of Monroe's Crossroads*, 20–21, 221.

330. Cincinnati Art Museum, "Discovering the Story: A City and Its Culture—Charles T. Webber," http://www.discoveringthestory.com/ugrr/background.asp#.

331. Corinna Ludwig, "Rudolph Wurlitzer (1831–1914)," Immigrant Entrepreneurship German American Business Biographies, https://www.immigrantentrepreneurship.org/entry.php?rec=45.

Appendix E. Military Units Composed of Cincinnati or Hamilton County Residents

332. Ohio State Archives Series 147, Vol. 7A; Leonard, *Greater Cincinnati*, vol. 2, 544; Wimberg, *1864*, 100.

BIBLIOGRAPHY

ABBREVIATIONS

CDC	*Cincinnati Daily Commercial*
CDG	*Cincinnati Daily Gazette*
CDP	*Cincinnati Daily Press*
CDT	*Cincinnati Daily Times*
CEQ	*Cincinnati Daily Enquirer*
CVF	*Cincinnati Volksfreund*
OR	*The War of the Rebellion: A Compilation of the Official Records of the Union and Confederate Armies*
ORN	*Official Records of the Union and Confederate Navies in the War of the Rebellion*

MANUSCRIPTS AND ARCHIVES

National Archives II, College Park, Maryland:

RG 77: Dr. 132-5 and Dr. 132-13, Kentucky Fortifications Map File, Maps of Covington and Vicinity Showing Defenses Erected by the Union Army 1861–1863; and Plans of the Individual Forts and Batteries of Cincinnati, Ohio, and Covington and Newport, Kentucky, Built 1862–1864.

RG 92: Records of the Office of the Quartermaster General Post and Reservation Map File, 1820–1905 1.158-r. Ohio: A Map of Camp Dennison, and Ground Plan of Camp Dennison 1861 (2 items); Map of Cincinnati Annotated to Show the Locations of Quartermaster Properties, and Floor and Vertical Plans and Photos of the Individual Properties 1864 (39 items).

RG 77: T-12 and P 100; Pub. 1877, No.4, Kentucky Civil Works Map File—Local Defenses (General Guide to Civil War Maps 1.60), Manuscript Map of the Defenses of Cincinnati, Ohio; 23 Plans of Individual Forts and Batteries of Cincinnati, OH, and Covington and Newport, KY, Accompanying J.H. Simpson's Report of November 12, 1862.

RG 92: Records of the Office of the Quartermaster General Post and Reservation Map File, 1820–1905 1.158-f. Kentucky: Views and Floor Plans of Government Buildings around Covington; and Views of Forts Burbank, Kyle, etc. Composing the Defenses of Covington and Newport, KY, and Cincinnati, OH 1863-65 (60 items).

RG 153: Maps and Plans of Former Military Reservations Within the United States, 1838–1930; Newport Barracks, Kentucky.

Other

Stanley T. Matthews Papers, GA-30, Rutherford B. Hayes Presidential Library & Museums, Fremont.

William Dickson Papers, William L. Clements Library, University of Michigan. Ann Arbor, Michigan.

Wooldridge, Captain F.L. "Names of Steamboats." Wooldridge Collection P-013.

Herman T. Pott National Inland Waterways Library, University of Missouri–St. Louis, 1904–1930.

Ohio History Connection, State Archives Library, Columbus, Ohio:

Henry Otis Dwight Papers.

Archives Series 123: Record of Naval Credits Filed by the Cincinnati Provost Marshal, 1864 Feb 24.

State Archives Series 147, Vol. 3–4

Western Reserve Historical Society, Cleveland, Ohio:

Charles Whittlesey Papers, MS3196 and MS2872.

NEWSPAPERS

Cincinnati Daily Commercial, 1861–1866
Cincinnati Daily Enquirer, 1861–1865, 1883, 1907, 1923, 1997
Cincinnati Daily Gazette, 1861–1865
Cincinnati Daily Press, 1861-1865
Cincinnati Daily Times, 1861–1865
Cincinnati Volksfreund, 1861–1865

OFFICIAL RECORDS AND PUBLICATIONS

Billings, John Shaw. *A Report on Barracks and Hospitals, with Descriptions of Military Posts*. Washington, D.C.: Government Printing Office, 1870.

Brent, Joseph E. *National Register of Historic Places Multiple Property Submission: Civil War Monuments in Kentucky, 1865–1935*. Washington, D.C.: National Park Service, 1997.

Cincinnati Branch U.S. Sanitary Commission. *Report of the Cincinnati Branch U.S. Sanitary Commission from December 1, 1861, to December 1, 1864, Three Years*. Cincinnati: Cincinnati Branch U.S. Sanitary Commission, 1865.

"Cincinnati City Auditor's Report." In *Mayor's Annual Message and Reports of the City Departments of the City of Cincinnati, April 14th, 1862*. Cincinnati: Johnson, Stephens & Morgan, 1861.

Congressional Medal of Honor Society. "Recipients–Full Archive." www.cmohs.org.

Naval History and Heritage Command. *Dictionary of American Naval Fighting Ships*. https://www.history.navy.mil/research/histories/ship-histories/danfs.html.

Robertson, James I., Jr., ed. *The Medical and Surgical History of the Civil War*. 15 vols. Wilmington, NC: Broadfoot Publishing, 1990–1992.

State of Ohio. *Executive Documents: Message and Annual Reports for 1866, Made to the Fifty-Seventh General Assembly of the State of Ohio, Begun and Held in the City of Columbus, January 2, 1867*. Part 1. Columbus, OH: L. D. Myers & Bro., 1867.

Terrell, William H.H. *Indiana in the War of the Rebellion*. Indianapolis: Douglass & Conner Journal Office, 1869.

United States Navy Department. *Official Records of the Union and Confederate Navies in the War of the Rebellion*. 30 vols. Washington, D.C.: Government Printing Office, 1894–1922.

United States Senate. *The Executive Documents Printed by Order of the Senate of the United States for the Second Session of the Forty-Second Congress, 1871–72*, vol. 2. Washington, D.C.: Government Printing Office, 1872.

United States War Department. *Atlas to Accompany the Official Records of the Union and Confederate Armies*. Washington, D.C.: Government Printing Office, 1891–1895.

———. *The War of the Rebellion: A Compilation of the Official Records of the Union and Confederate Armies*. 128 vols. Washington, D.C.: Government Printing Office, 1880–1901.

ROSTERS AND UNIT RECORDS

Adjutant General of Indiana. *Report of the Adjutant General of the State of Indiana, 1861–65*. 8 vols. Indianapolis: W.R. Holloway and A. H. Connor, 1865–69.

Adjutant General of Kansas. *Report of the Adjutant General of the State of Kansas, 1861–65*. 1 vol., 2 pts. Topeka: Kansas State Printing Company, 1896.

Adjutant General of Kentucky. *Report of the Adjutant General of the State of Kentucky 1861–65*. 2 vols. Frankfort, KY: State Journal, 1866.

Adjutant General of Maine. *Annual Report of the Adjutant General of the State of Maine*. 3 vols. Augusta, ME: Stevens & Sayward, 1862, 1863, 1866.

Adjutant General of Massachusetts. *Massachusetts Soldiers, Sailors, and Marines in the Civil War.* 8 vols. Norwood, MA: Norwood Press, 1931–1933.

Adjutant General of Minnesota. *Annual Report of the Adjutant General of the State of Minnesota, for the Year Ending December 1, 1866, and of the Military Forces of the State from 1861 to 1866.* Saint Paul, MN: Pioneer Printing Company, 1866.

Adjutant General of Missouri. *Annual Report of the Adjutant General of Missouri, for the Year Ending December 31, 1865.* Jefferson City, MO: Emory S. Foster, 1866.

Adjutant General of Rhode Island. *Official Register of Rhode Island Officers and Soldiers Who Served in the United States Army and Navy, from 1861–1866.* Providence, RI: Providence Press Company, 1866.

Adjutant General of West Virginia. *Annual Report of the Adjutant General of the State of West Virginia for the Year Ending December 31, 1864.* Wheeling, WV: John Frew, 1865.

———. *Annual Report of the Adjutant General of the State of West Virginia for the Year Ending December 31, 1865.* Wheeling, WV: John Frew, 1866.

Ayling, Augustus D. *Revised Register of the Soldiers and Sailors of New Hampshire in the War of the Rebellion 1861–1866.* Concord, NH: Ira C. Evans, 1895.

Brown, George H. *Record of Service of Michigan Volunteers in the Civil War 1861–1865.* 46 vols. Kalamazoo, MI: Ihling Bros. & Everard, 1903.

Chapman, Chandler P. *Roster of Wisconsin Volunteers, War of the Rebellion, 1861–1865.* 2 vols. Madison, WI: Democrat Printing Company, 1886.

Connecticut General Assembly. *Record of Service of Connecticut Men in the Army and Navy of the United States During the War of the Rebellion.* Hartford, CT: Press of the Case, Lockwood & Brainard Company, 1889.

Fallon, John T. *List of Synonyms of Organizations in the Volunteer Service of the United States during the Years 1861, '62, '63, '64, and '65.* Washington, D.C.: Government Printing Office, 1885.

Family Search. www.familysearch.org.

Missouri Military Records 1861–1866.

Ohio, Hamilton County Records, 1791–1994, Military Records, Veterans Discharge Papers, Books 1–2.

U.S. Naval Enlistment Rendezvous Records, 1855–1891, vols. 21–43.

U.S. Registers of Enlistments in the U.S. Army, 1798–1914.

Ford, Henry A., and Kate B. Ford. *History of Hamilton County, Ohio: With Illustrations and Biographical Sketches.* Cleveland, OH: L.A. Williams & Co., 1881.

General Assembly of Maryland. *History and Roster of Maryland Volunteers, War of 1861–65.* 2 vols. Baltimore, MD: Press of Guggenheimer, Weil & Co., 1898.

Hewett, Janet B. *The Roster of Union Soldiers, 1861–1865.* 33 vols. Wilmington, NC: Broadfoot Publishing Company, 1997–2000.

Historical Data Systems Inc. "American Civil War Research Database." http://civilwardata.com.

Illinois State Archives. Illinois Civil War Muster and Descriptive Rolls. https://www.ilsos.gov/isaveterans/civilmustersrch.jsp.

Johnson, Eric Eugene. *Ohio's Black Soldiers Who Served in the Civil War.* Bellville: Ohio Genealogical Society, 2014.

National Park Service. Soldiers and Sailors Database: The Civil War. www.nps.gov.

New York State Adjutant General Office. *Annual Report of the Adjutant General of the State of New York for the Year ...: Registers of the [unit numbers].* 43 vols. New York: Wynkoop, Hallenbeck, Crawford, 1893–1905.

Office of the Adjutant General of Tennessee. *Report of the Adjutant General of the State of Tennessee of the Military Forces of the State from 1861 to 1866.* Nashville, TN: S.C. Mercer, 1866.

Ohio History Connection, State Archives Library, Columbus, Ohio:

State Archives Series 5: Record of Appointments, Commissions, and Promotions of Officers in the Ohio Volunteer Regiments, 1861–1865.

State Archives Series 79: Ohio War Records, 1861–1865.

State Archives Series 89: Record of Militia Drafted in 1862.

State Archives Series 147: Correspondence to the Governor and Adjutant General, 1861–1866.

State Archives Series 1753: Copies of Muster Rolls and Other Correspondence Related to Veteran Credits, 1861–1868.

State Archives Series 2440: Muster-In and Muster-Out Rolls, 1861–1865.

Ohio Roster Commission. *Official Roster of the Soldiers of the State of Ohio in the War of the Rebellion, 1861–1866.* 12 vols. Akron, OH: Werner Co., 1893.

Orton, Richard H. *Records of California Men in the War of the Rebellion, 1861 to 1867.* Sacramento, CA: J.D. Young, 1890.

Peck, Theodore S. *Revised Roster of Vermont Volunteers and Lists of Vermonters who Served in the Army and Navy of the United States During the War of the Rebellion, 1861–66.* Montpelier, VT: Press of the Watchman Publishing Company, 1892.

Peker, M.A., and Edna Mingus. *Soldiers Who Served in the Oregon Volunteers Civil War Period: Infantry and Cavalry.* Portland, OR: Genealogical Forum of Portland, 1961.

Pennsylvania State Archives. Registers of Pennsylvania Volunteers, 1861–1865. www.phmc.state.pa.us.

Phisterer, Frederick. *New York in the War of the Rebellion 1861–1865.* 5 vols. 3rd ed. Albany, NY: D.R. Lyon Company, 1912.

State of Delaware. Volunteers Service Records, 1861–1864. 16 vols. https://civilwar.delaware.gov/volumes/volunteers.shtml.

Stryker, William S. *Record of Officers and Men of New Jersey in the Civil War.* 2 vols. Trenton, NJ: John L. Murphy, 1876.

Thrift, William H. *Roster and Record of Iowa Soldiers in the War of the Rebellion.* 6 vols. Des Moines, IA: Emory H. English & E.D. Chassell, 1908.

Ward, Steven H. *"Buckeyes All": A Compendium and Bibliography, Ohio in the Civil War.* 5 vols. Dayton, OH: Steven H. Ward, 2004.

MAPS

Harrison, R. H. *Titus' Atlas of Hamilton County, Ohio: From Actual Surveys.* Philadelphia: C.O. Titus, 1869.

Mendenhall, E. *Map of Cincinnati, Covington, and Newport.* Cincinnati, OH: E. Mendenhall, 1867.

Phillips, R.C. *Map of Cincinnati.* Cincinnati, OH: Williams Directory Company, 1868.
———. *Map of Hamilton County, Ohio 1865.* Cincinnati, OH: Ehrgott Ehrbriger & Company, 1865.
Pullen, William. *Map of the Business Portion of Cincinnati.* Cincinnati, OH: Tappan, McKillop & Company, 1863.
Spring Grove Cemetery, *Visitor's Map of Historic Spring Grove Cemetery and Arboretum: A National Historic Landmark.* Cincinnati: Spring Grove Cemetery, 2012.

BOOKS AND REMINISCENCES

Adams, Charles S. *Cincinnati's Forgotten General: Read for the Cincinnati Civil War Round Table, April 16, 1958.* Cincinnati: Cincinnati Civil War Round Table, 1958.
Baker, Nina Brown. *Cyclone in Calico: The Story of Mary Ann Bickerdyke.* Boston: Little, Brown, 1952.
Barkley, Katherine Traver. *The Ambulance: The Story of Emergency Transportation of Sick and Wounded Through the Centuries.* Kiamesha Lake, NY: Load N Go Press, 1990.
Beyer, W.F., and O.F. Keydel, eds. *Deeds of Valor: How America's Civil War Heroes Won the Congressional Medal of Honor.* Stamford, CT: Longmeadow Press, 1994.
Bissland, James. *Blood, Tears, & Glory: How Ohioans Won the War.* Wilmington, OH: Orange Frazer Press, 2007.
Boynton, Charles B. *History of the Great Western Sanitary Fair.* Cincinnati, OH: C.F. Vent & Company, 1864.
Burns, John E. *A History of Covington Through 1865.* Covington, KY: Kenton County Historical Society, 2012.
Cahill, Lora Schmidt, and David L. Mowery. *Morgan's Raid Across Ohio: The Civil War Guidebook of the John Hunt Morgan Heritage Trail.* Columbus: Ohio Historical Society, 2014.
Cincinnati Historical Society. *Cincinnati: The Queen City.* 3rd ed. Cincinnati, OH: Cincinnati Historical Society, 1996.
———. *The WPA Guide to Cincinnati, 1788–1943.* Cincinnati, OH: Cincinnati Historical Society, 1987.
Clark, Peter H. *The Black Brigade of Cincinnati: Being a Report of Its Labors and a Muster Roll of Its Members.* Cincinnati, OH: J.B. Boyd, 1864.
Cooper, Richard, and Dr. Eric R. Jackson. *Cincinnati's Underground Railroad.* Charleston, SC: Arcadia Publishing, 2014.
Cox, Jacob Dolson. *Memorial of Alexander Hamilton McGuffey, Adopted by the Trustees of Cincinnati College.* Cincinnati, OH: Robert Clarke Company, 1896.
———. *Military Reminiscences of the Civil War.* 2 vols. New York: Charles Scribner's Sons, 1900.
DBA Hispanic Chamber Cincinnati Foundation, *Cincinnati: A City of Immigrants, Struggling Toward Acceptance and Equality.* Cincinnati, OH: Hispanics Avanzando Hispanics, 2015.
Donnelly, Joseph L. *Newport Barracks: Kentucky's Forgotten Military Installation.* Covington, KY: Kenton County Historical Society, 1999.

Faust, Patricia, ed. *Historical Times Illustrated Encyclopedia of the Civil War.* New York, Harper & Row, 1986.

Folzenlogen, Darcy, and Robert Folzenlogen. *Walking Cincinnati: Scenic Hikes through the Parks and Neighborhoods of Greater Cincinnati & Northern Kentucky.* 2nd ed. Littleton, CO: Willow Press, 1993.

Ford, Henry A., and Kate B. Ford. *History of Cincinnati, Ohio: With Illustrations and Biographical Sketches.* Cleveland, OH: L.A. Williams & Company, 1881.

Fortin, Roger A. *Fellowship: History of the Cincinnati Irish.* Cincinnati, OH: Cincinnati Book Publishing, 2018.

Geaslen, Chester F. *Our Moment of Glory in the Civil War: When Cincinnati, "The Queen City of the West" and Sixth Largest City Was Defended from the Hills of Northern Kentucky.* Fort Wright, KY: City of Fort Wright, 2007.

Grandstaff, Russell J. *A History of the Professional Theatre in Cincinnati, Ohio, 1861–1886.* Ann Arbor: University of Michigan, 1963.

Greve, Charles Theodore. *Centennial History of Cincinnati and Representative Citizens.* 2 vols. Chicago: Biographical Publishing Company, 1904.

Goss, Charles Frederic. *Cincinnati: The Queen City, 1788–1912.* 4 vols. Chicago: S.J. Clarke Publishing, 1912.

Groen, Henry John. *A History of the German-American Newspapers of Cincinnati Before 1860.* N.p., 1945.

Hannaford, E. *The Story of a Regiment: A History of the Campaigns, and Associations in the Field, of the Sixth Regiment Ohio Volunteer Infantry.* Cincinnati, OH: E. Hannaford, 1868.

Hedrick, Joan D. *Harriet Beecher Stowe: A Life.* New York: Oxford University Press, 1994.

Hill, J. Stacy. *A History of the Inns and Hotels of Cincinnati 1793–1923.* Cincinnati, OH: Webb-Biddle Company, 1922.

The History of Wyandot County, Ohio. Chicago: Leggett, Conaway & Co., 1884.

Holmes, Skip, and Phil Nuxhall. *Historic Spring Grove Cemetery: Presidential Connections.* Cincinnati, OH: Spring Grove Heritage Foundation, 2015.

Howe, Henry. *Historical Collections of Ohio in Two Volumes: An Encyclopedia of the State.* 2 vols. Cincinnati, OH: C.J. Krehbiel & Company, 1907.

Johnson, Robert U., and Clarence C. Buel. *Battles and Leaders of the Civil War.* 4 vols. Secaucus, NJ: Castle, 1887.

Klauprecht, Emil. *German Chronicle in the History of the Ohio Valley and its Capital City, Cincinnati, in Particular.* Bowie, MD: Heritage Books, 1992.

Langstroth, T.A. *The History of Lithography, Mainly in Cincinnati.* N.p., 1958.

Leonard, Lewis Alexander, ed. *Greater Cincinnati and Its People: A History.* 4 vols. New York: Lewis Historical Publishing, 1927.

Lippett, Francis J. *A Treatise on Intrenchments.* New York: D. Van Nostrand, 1866.

The Literary Club of Cincinnati, 1849–1999: One Hundred and Fiftieth Anniversary Volume: "Here Comes One with a Paper." Cincinnati, OH: Literary Club of Cincinnati, 2001.

McCaul, Edward B. Jr. *To Retain Command of the Mississippi: The Civil War Naval Campaign for Memphis.* Knoxville: University of Tennessee Press, 2014.

McNitt, Frank, ed. *Navaho Expedition: Journal of a Military Reconnaissance from Santa Fe, New Mexico, to the Navaho Country Made in 1849.* Norman: University of Oklahoma Press, 1964.

Metz, Judith, ed. *The Sisters of Charity of Cincinnati in the Civil War: The Love of Christ Urges Us.* Cincinnati, OH: Sisters of Charity of Cincinnati, 2012.

Middleton, Strobridge & Company. *View of Camp Dennison: 16 Miles Northeast of Cincinnati, Ohio.* Camp Dennison, OH: Swan & Litchfield, 1865.

Mowery, David L. *Morgan's Great Raid: The Remarkable Expedition from Kentucky to Ohio.* Charleston, SC: The History Press, 2013.

Nelson, S.B. *History of Cincinnati and Hamilton County, Ohio: Their Past and Present, Including...Biographies and Portraits of Pioneers and Representative Citizens, Etc.* Cincinnati, OH: S.B. Nelson, 1894.

Nuxhall, Phil. *Interesting Facts about Spring Grove Cemetery and Arboretum.* Cincinnati, OH: Spring Grove Heritage Foundation, 2013.

———. *Notable Burials in Spring Grove Cemetery & Arboretum.* Cincinnati, OH: Spring Grove Heritage Foundation, 2015.

Penrod, Doris. *Waldschmidt: House and Family 1804.* Cincinnati, OH: Capozzollo Printers, 1997.

Purvis, Thomas L., ed. *Newport, Kentucky: A Bicentennial History.* Newport, KY: Otto Zimmerman & Son Company, 1996.

Reid, Whitelaw. *Ohio in the War: Her Statesmen, Her Generals, and Soldiers.* 2 vols. New York: Moore, Wilstach & Baldwin, 1868.

Riesenberg, Michael. *An Assessment of Cincinnati Area Civil War Resources: Preparing for the 150th Anniversary of the Civil War.* Cincinnati, OH: University of Cincinnati, 2010.

Roberts, William H. *Civil War Ironclads: The U.S. Navy and Industrial Mobilization.* Baltimore, MD: Johns Hopkins University Press, 2002.

Shaler, Nathaniel S. *The Autobiography of Nathaniel Southgate Shaler.* Boston: Houghton Mifflin Company, 1909.

Sherman, William T. *Memoirs of General William T. Sherman.* Vol. 1. New York: D. Appleton & Co., 1889.

Shotwell, John Brough. *A History of the Schools of Cincinnati.* Cincinnati, OH: School Life Company, 1902.

Silverstone, Paul H. *Civil War Navies: 1855–1883.* Annapolis, MD: Naval Institute Press, 2001.

Slagle, Jay. *Ironclad Captain: Seth Ledyard Phelps and the U.S. Navy, 1841–1864.* Kent, OH: Kent State University, 1996.

Sloan, Mary Rahn. *History of Camp Dennison, Ohio.* 3rd ed. Cincinnati, OH: Queen City Printing, 2003.

Smith, Myron J., Jr. *Civil War Biographies from the Western Waters: 965 Confederate and Union Naval and Military Personnel, Contractors, Politicians, Officials, Steamboat Pilots and Others.* Jefferson, NC: McFarland & Company, 2015.

———. *Joseph Brown and His Civil War Ironclads: The USS Chillicothe, Indianola and Tuscumbia.* Jefferson, NC: McFarland & Company, 2017.

————. *The Timberclads in the Civil War: The Lexington, Conestoga, and Tyler on the Western Waters.* Jefferson, NC: McFarland & Company, 2008.

————. *Tinclads in the Civil War: Union Light-Draught Gunboat Operations on Western Waters, 1862–1865.* Jefferson, NC: McFarland & Company, 2010.

Smith, William. *Annual Statement of the Commerce of Cincinnati for the Commercial Year, Ending Aug. 31, 1861.* Cincinnati, OH: Gazette Company Steam Printing, 1861.

Society of the Army of the Cumberland. *Twenty-First Reunion, Toledo, Ohio, 1890.* Cincinnati, OH: Robert Clarke & Company, 1891.

Soman, Jean Powers, and Frank L. Byrne. *A Jewish Colonel in the Civil War: Marcus M. Spiegel of the Ohio Volunteers.* Kent, OH: Kent State University Press, 1985.

Spring Grove Cemetery. *History of Spring Grove.* Cincinnati: Spring Grove Cemetery, n.d.

St. Andrew's Society of Philadelphia. *An Historical Catalogue of the St. Andrew's Society of Philadelphia, with Biographical Sketches of Deceased Members, 1749–1907.* Philadelphia: Press of Loughead & Co., 1907.

Stephens, Gail. *Shadow of Shiloh: Major General Lew Wallace in the Civil War.* Indianapolis: Indiana Historical Society Press, 2010.

Suess, Jeff. *Hidden History of Cincinnati.* Charleston, SC: The History Press, 2016.

————. *Lost Cincinnati.* Charleston, SC: The History Press, 2015.

Taylor, Nikki M. *Frontiers of Freedom: Cincinnati's Black Community, 1802–1868.* Athens: Ohio University Press, 2005.

Tenkotte, Paul A., and James C. Claypool, eds. *The Encyclopedia of Northern Kentucky.* Lexington: University Press of Kentucky, 2009.

Tolzmann, Don Heinrich, ed. *The Cincinnati Germans in the Civil War by Gustav Tafel.* Milford, OH: Little Miami Publishing, 2010.

————. *The Roebling Suspension Bridge: A Guide to Historic Sites, People, and Places.* Cincinnati, OH: Archivarium Press, 2017.

U.S. Bureau of the Census, *Population of the 100 Largest Urban Places: 1860.* Washington, D.C.: U.S. Bureau of the Census, 1998.

U.S. Sanitary Commission, *The U.S. Sanitary Commission in the Valley of the Mississippi, During the War of the Rebellion, 1861–1866.* Cleveland, OH: Fairbanks, Benedict & Co., 1871.

Venable, William Henry. *A Centennial History of Christ Church, Cincinnati, 1817–1917.* Cincinnati, OH: Stewart & Kidd, 1918.

Venner, William Thomas, ed. *Queen City Lady: The 1861 Journal of Amanda Wilson.* Cincinnati, OH: Larrea Books, 1996.

Ventre, John E., and Edward J. Goodman. *A Brief History of the Cincinnati Astronomical Society.* Cincinnati, OH: Cincinnati Astronomical Society, 1985.

Village of Cumminsville Committee. *History of Cumminsville, 1792–1914.* Cincinnati, OH: Raisbeck, 1914.

Wallace, Lew. *Lew Wallace: An Autobiography.* 2 vols. New York: Harper & Brothers, 1906.

Walters, Raymond. *Stephen Foster: Youth's Golden Gleam; A Sketch of His Life and Background in Cincinnati, 1846–1850.* Princeton, NJ: Princeton University Press, 1936.

Warner, Ezra J. *Generals in Blue.* Baton Rouge: Louisiana State University Press, 1992.

Webster, Robert D. *A Brief History of Northern Kentucky.* Lexington: University Press of Kentucky, 2019.

Wells, Diana. *Roadside History: A Guide to Kentucky Historical Markers.* Frankfort: Kentucky Historical Society, 2002.

Williams' Cincinnati Directory. Cincinnati, OH: C.S. Williams/Williams & Company, 1858–1869.

Wimberg, Robert. *Cincinnati and the Civil War: Off to Battle.* Cincinnati: Ohio Book Store, 1992.

———. *Cincinnati and the Civil War: Under Attack!* Cincinnati: Ohio Book Store, 1999.

———. *Cincinnati and the Civil War: 1863.* Cincinnati: Ohio Book Store, 2006.

———. *Cincinnati and the Civil War: 1864.* Cincinnati: Ohio Book Store, 2014.

———. *Cincinnati and the Civil War: 1865 with Index.* Cincinnati: Ohio Book Store, 2015.

Wittenberg, Eric J. *The Battle of Monroe's Crossroads and the Civil War's Final Campaign.* El Dorado Hills, CA: Savas Beatie, 2006.

Wright, Steven L. *Kentucky Soldiers and Their Regiments in the Civil War.* 5 vols. Utica, KY: McDowell Publications, 2009.

Wulsin, Eugene. *The Story of the Fourth Regiment Ohio Veteran Volunteer Cavalry.* Cincinnati, OH: Eleanor N. Adams, 1912.

ARTICLES

Agnello, Tim. "Historic Rock Quarries and Modern Landslides in Price Hill." *Ohio Geology*, no. 2 (2005): 1–5.

Allen, Lee. "Baseball's Immortal Red Stockings." *Bulletin of the Historical and Philosophical Society of Ohio* 19, no. 3 (July 1961): 191–202.

Alter, J. Cecil. "National Weather Service Origins." *Bulletin of the Historical and Philosophical Society of Ohio* 7, no. 3 (July 1949): 138–85.

Bachmeyer, A.C. "The Hospitals of Cincinnati during the Last Century." *University of Cincinnati Medical Bulletin* 1, no. 1 (November 1920).

Baringer, William E. "The Politics of Abolition: Salmon P. Chase in Cincinnati." *Cincinnati Historical Society Bulletin* 29, no. 2 (Summer 1971): 78–99.

Barnett, James. "Crime and No Punishment: The Death of Robert L. McCook." *Cincinnati Historical Society Bulletin* 22, no. 1 (January 1964): 29–37.

———. "Forty for the Union: Civil War Generals Buried in Spring Grove Cemetery." *Cincinnati Historical Society Bulletin* 30, no. 2 (Summer 1972): 90–121.

Becker, Carl M. "The Genesis of a Copperhead." *Bulletin of the Historical and Philosophical Society of Ohio* 19, no. 4 (October 1961): 234–53.

———. "The Ironmaster and the Sculptor." *Cincinnati Historical Society Bulletin* 27, no. 2 (Summer 1969): 123–37.

Brill, Ruth. "Cincinnati's 'Poet Warrior': William Haines Lytle." *Bulletin of the Historical and Philosophical Society of Ohio* 21, no. 3 (July 1963): 188–201.

"The Civil War at Spring Grove." *Queen City Heritage* 53, nos. 1–2 (Spring–Summer 1995): 74–79.

Dickson, William F. "Abraham Lincoln at Cincinnati," *Harper's Magazine*, June 1884, 62–66.

Durrell, Jane. "Time Stands Still on Dayton Street." *Cincinnati Magazine*, June 1972, 60–61.

Easton, Loyd D. "German Philosophy in Nineteenth Century Cincinnati: Stallo, Conway, Nast and Willich." *Bulletin of the Historical and Philosophical Society of Ohio* 20, no. 1 (January 1962): 15–28.

Ecelbarger, Gary. "Before Cooper Union: Abraham Lincoln's 1859 Cincinnati Speech and Its Impact on His Nomination," *Journal of the Abraham Lincoln Association* 30, no. 1 (Winter 2009), 1–17.

Ellis, Anita J. *The Ceramic Career of M. Louise McLaughlin*. Athens: Ohio University Press, 2003.

Enss, Chris. "Wild Women of the West: Agnes Lake Thatcher." *Cow Girl Magazine*, June 2019.

Fladeland, Betty L. "James G. Birney's Anti-Slavery Activities in Cincinnati." *Bulletin of the Historical and Philosophical Society of Ohio* 9, no. 4 (October 1951): 250–65.

Freking, Grant. "Lost City: Underground Railroad Sites." *Cincinnati Magazine*, February 2017.

Harding, Leonard. "The Cincinnati Riots of 1862." *Cincinnati Historical Society Bulletin* 25, no. 4 (October 1967): 228–39.

Harlan, Louis R. "The Autobiography of Alexander Long, 1858." *Bulletin of the Historical and Philosophical Society of Ohio* 19 (April 1961): 98–127.

Harrold, Stanley C., Jr. "The Perspective of a Cincinnati Abolitionist: Gamaliel Bailey on Social Reform in America." *Cincinnati Historical Society Bulletin* 35, no. 3 (Fall 1977): 173–90.

Hodges, Fletcher, Jr. "Stephen Foster: Cincinnatian and American." *Bulletin of the Historical and Philosophical Society of Ohio* 8, no. 2 (April 1950): 82–104.

Holland, Mary Gardner. *Our Army Nurses: Stories from Women in the Civil War*. Roseville, MN: Edinborough Press, 1998.

Holliday, Joseph E. "Notes on Samuel N. Pike and His Opera Houses." *Cincinnati Historical Society Bulletin* 25, no. 3 (July 1967): 164–83.

Lackey, Rodney C. "Notes on Civil War Logistics: Facts & Stories." United States Army Transportation Corps, https://transportation.army.mil/History/PDF/Peninsula%20Campaign/Rodney%20Lackey%20Article_1.pdf.

Linden-Ward, Blanche. "The Greening of Cincinnati: Adolph Strauch's Legacy in Park Design." *Queen City Heritage* 51, no. 1 (Spring 1993): 20–39.

Mach, Thomas S. "Family Ties, Party Realities, and Political Ideology: George Hunt Pendleton and Partisanship in Antebellum Cincinnati." *Ohio Valley History* 3, no. 2 (Summer 2003): 17–30.

McCarthy, Carole. "Greetings from Gibson: 125 Years' Worth." *Cincinnati Magazine*, August 1975.

McDowell, George S. "Harriet Beecher Stowe at Cincinnati." *New England Magazine*, March 1895–August 1895, 65–70.

Mendelsohn, Adam. "Beyond the Battlefield: Reevaluating the Legacy of the Civil War for American Jews." *American Jewish Archives Journal* 64, no. 12 (2012): 82–111.

Perzel, Edward S. "Alexander Long, Salmon P. Chase, and the Election of 1868." *Cincinnati Historical Society Bulletin* 23 (January 1965): 2–18.

Preston, Steve. "Our Rich History: Henry Boyd, Once a Slave, Became a Prominent African American Furniture Maker." *Northern Kentucky Tribune*, February 11, 2019.

Rose, Cedric. "Lost City: The Markets." *Cincinnati Magazine*, February 2017.

Ross, Steven J. "Industrialization and the Changing Images of Progress in Nineteenth–Century Cincinnati." *Queen City Heritage* 43, no. 2 (Summer 1985): 20–21.

Schlachter, Roberta L. "Dr. John Aston Warder." *Queen City Heritage* 47, no. 2 (Summer 1989): 2–12.

Schottelkotte, Jim. "Court Martial at Newport Barracks." *Queen City Heritage* 44, no. 1 (Spring 1986): 45–48.

———. "The Suspension Bridge: They Said It Couldn't Be Built." *Cincinnati Historical Society Bulletin* 23, no. 4 (October 1965): 210–28.

Seidman, Sandra R. "Alexander Bonner 'Moses' Latta: Nineteenth-Century Inventor and Entrepreneur." *Journal of Kentucky Studies* 29 (September 2012): 140–48.

Tucker, Louis Leonard. *Cincinnati During the Civil War.* Columbus: Ohio State University Press, 1962.

———. "Hiram Powers and Cincinnati." *Cincinnati Historical Society Bulletin* 25, no. 1 (January 1967): 28–38.

———. "'Old Nick' Longworth: The Paradoxical Maecenas of Cincinnati." *Cincinnati Historical Society Bulletin* 25, no. 4 (October 1967): 246–59.

Walden, Geoffrey. "The General's Tour—Panic on the Ohio! Confederates March on Cincinnati, September 1862." *Blue and Gray Magazine* 3, no. 5 (April/May 1986): 7–33.

White, Robert J. "The Cincinnati Marine Railway." *Queen City Heritage* 57, no. 2–3 (Summer–Fall 1999): 69–83.

Wittke, Carl. "Friedrich Hassaurek: Cincinnati's Leading Forty-Eighter." *Ohio Historical Quarterly* 68, no. 1 (January 1959): 1–17.

Zornow, William Frank. "Clement L. Vallandigham and the Democratic Party in 1864." *Bulletin of the Historical and Philosophical Society of Ohio* 19, no. 1 (January 1961): 21–37.

INDEX

ABOUT THE AUTHOR

David L. Mowery is a native resident of Cincinnati, Ohio, and a graduate of the University of Cincinnati. American military history piqued his interest at an early age. Since childhood, he has researched and visited over seven hundred battlefields across fifty states and nine countries. In 2001, David joined the all-volunteer Ohio Civil War Trail Commission as its Hamilton County representative, but over the years his role expanded to include the final design and historical validation of the entire length of the John Hunt Morgan Heritage Trail of Ohio. He is the coauthor of *Morgan's Raid Across Ohio: The Civil War Guidebook of the John Hunt Morgan Heritage Trail* (Ohio Historical Society, 2014) and the author of *Morgan's Great Raid: The Remarkable Expedition from Kentucky to Ohio* (History Press, 2013). Since 1995, David has been a member of the Cincinnati Civil War Round Table, for which he has written various papers on Civil War subjects and has led many Civil War tours of the Cincinnati region. He has also served with the Buffington Island Battlefield Preservation Foundation, the grass-roots organization working to preserve Ohio's largest Civil War battlefield.

Visit us at
www.historypress.com